THE PARADOX OF RISK

LEAVING THE MONETARY POLICY COMFORT ZONE

T0338849

THE PARADOX OF RISK

LEAVING THE MONETARY POLICY COMFORT ZONE

ÁNGEL UBIDE

POLICY ANALYSES IN INTERNATIONAL ECONOMICS 108

PETERSON INSTITUTE FOR INTERNATIONAL ECONOMICS

WASHINGTON, DC

SEPTEMBER 2017

Ángel Ubide is a managing director at Goldman Sachs' Private Wealth Management group. He was a senior fellow at the Peterson Institute for International Economics from 2009 to February 2016. Prior to joining Goldman Sachs, he worked for a decade and a half in the hedge fund industry, first at Tudor Investment Corporation (2001–12) and later at D. E. Shaw Group (2012–14). He has also worked at the International Monetary Fund (1996–2001). Ubide is deeply involved in the global economic policy debate. He is a member of the Steering Committee of the Euro50 Group and of the scientific board of Progressive Economy. He was board member of the Reinventing Bretton Woods Committee (2007–12); founding member of the European Central Bank's Shadow Governing Council (2002–12); and member of the Centre for European Policy Studies' macroeconomic policy group (2004–07). He has participated in advisory groups at the Center for Strategic and International Studies and the Atlantic Council of the United States. He has written on international macroeconomics, monetary policy, European policy issues, banking, and exchange rates. He was an economic columnist at *El Pais*, the leading Spanish newspaper, during 2001–15, and has been published or cited in leading global newspapers, including the *Economist, Financial Times, Wall Street Journal, Newsweek, Il Corriere della Sera*, and *Yomiuri Shimbun*. He holds a PhD in economics from the European University Institute in Florence, Italy.

The views expressed here are solely of the author and do not represent the views of Goldman Sachs & Co. LLC.

PETERSON INSTITUTE FOR INTERNATIONAL ECONOMICS

1750 Massachusetts Avenue, NW
Washington, DC 20036-1903
(202) 328-9000   FAX: (202) 328-5432
www.piie.com

Adam S. Posen, *President*
Steven R. Weisman, *Vice President for Publications and Communications*

Cover Design by Peggy Archambault
Cover Photo by ©Shutterstock
Printing by Versa Press, Inc.

Copyright © 2017 by the Peterson Institute for International Economics. All rights reserved. No part of this book may be reproduced or utilized in any form or by any means, electronic or mechanical, including photocopying, recording, or by information storage or retrieval system, without permission from the Institute.

For reprints/permission to photocopy please contact the APS customer service department at Copyright Clearance Center, Inc., 222 Rosewood Drive, Danvers, MA 01923; or email requests to: info@copyright.com

Printed in the United States of America
19 18 17   5 4 3 2 1

Library of Congress Cataloging-in-Publication Data
Names: Ubide, Ángel J., author.
Title: The paradox of risk : leaving the monetary policy comfort zone / Angel Ubide. Description: Washington, DC : Peterson Institute for International Economics, [2017] | Includes bibliographical references. Identifiers: LCCN 2016043450 (print) | LCCN 2017000536 (ebook) | ISBN 9780881327199 | ISBN 9780881327205 (ebook) Subjects: LCSH: Monetary policy. | Interest rates. | Risk. | International finance. Classification: LCC HG230.3 .U25 2017 (print) | LCC HG230.3 (ebook) | DDC 339.5/3—dc23 LC record available at: https://lccn.loc.gov/2016043450

This publication has been subjected to a prepublication peer review intended to ensure analytical quality.
This publication is part of the overall program of the Peterson Institute for International Economics, as endorsed by its Board of Directors, but it does not necessarily reflect the views of individual members of the Board or of the Institute's staff or management. The Peterson Institute for International Economics is a private nonpartisan, nonprofit institution for rigorous, intellectually open, and indepth study and discussion of international economic policy. Its purpose is to identify and analyze important issues to make globalization beneficial and sustainable for the people of the United States and the world, and then to develop and communicate practical new approaches for dealing with them. Its work is funded by a highly diverse group of philanthropic foundations, private corporations, and interested individuals, as well as income on its capital fund. About 35 percent of the Institute's resources in its latest fiscal year were provided by contributors from outside the United States.
A list of all financial supporters is posted at https://piie.com/sites/default/files/supporters.pdf.

Contents

Tables

Figures

Box

Preface

A decade after the financial crisis erupted, the major central banks are still struggling to find a robust framework to achieve their mandated economic goals. GDP growth has been restored but, despite very low interest rates, economic slack is still large, investment is unresponsive, and inflation has not credibly returned to safe sustainable levels. The virulence of the crisis caught central banks by surprise and, in many cases, they were reluctant to add to their tool kits. Even when they became more activist in response, they found much suspicion and political resistance. Opportunistic attacks on their strategies, especially on asset purchases, inhibited their actions and made achieving reflation even more difficult. Doubts about the effectiveness of their recent policies remain, only partly justified. More serious concerns about a need to reevaluate long-held assumptions are rightly rising.

In this book, former Institute Senior Fellow Ángel Ubide reviews whether monetary policy has been successful since the global financial crisis, with a focus on operational effectiveness in markets and for macro goals. He argues that monetary policy has worked, but it could have been better and thus have done better. Ubide proposes a revised monetary policy framework for the major central banks that would in practice be strictly symmetric with respect to inflation and deflation and also would stabilize risk aversion within normal ranges. The high inflation of the 1970s and the subsequent Great Moderation created a bias among economists and central bankers against inflation and risk taking. This bias has rendered central banks, and policymakers in general, inactive or largely impotent against periods of prolonged disinflation and risk aversion.

Despite the professed symmetry of their inflation targets, central bank conservatism often leads them to behave in practice as if their targets are ceilings, accepting below-target inflation as a tolerable outcome. This asymmetric inflation bias has created a paradox of risk—thinking that they are being prudent by avoiding inflationary risks, central bankers are creating a riskier environment by perpetuating low inflation.

This paradox of risk runs counter to widely and strongly held fears about the wrong dangers. The Bank for International Settlements has warned relentlessly against supposed potential financial stability risks arising from low interest rates. Some prominent economists, especially but not solely in Germany, argue that if inflation cannot be raised to the targets, the targets should be lowered as Japanese experts did before them. Politicians often complain that low interest rates erode virtuous savers' incomes and that asset purchases distort financial markets, generating moral hazard. Yet, these criticisms are unsupported by the evidence, as Ubide shows in chapter 4. Their persistence blinds policymakers to the fact that monetary policy has to sustainably raise nominal and real economic growth to achieve price stability—and that price stability is itself only a means to an end.

With this in mind, in chapter 5 Ubide proposes a revised monetary policy framework with four main recommendations: Central banks should engage in a process of opportunistic reflation; should retain large balance sheets and use all tools at their disposal; should use forward guidance in a cyclically adjusted manner, in order to stabilize risk aversion; and should change their communications, avoiding the terms "unconventional" and "exit." As Ubide concludes, if central bankers have not hesitated to trigger recessions to end inflationary threats, then they should be equally resolute in boosting growth and even asset prices to end dangerously low inflation. The paradox of risk can be resolved by restoring symmetry.

The Institute has a long history of undertaking relevant studies on monetary policy. Notable among the books are *Currency Conflict and Trade Policy: A New Strategy for the United States* by C. Fred Bergsten and Joseph E. Gagnon (published in 2017), *International Monetary Cooperation: Lessons from the Plaza Accord after Thirty Years* edited by Bergsten and Russell Green (2016), *Managing the Euro Area Debt Crisis* by William R. Cline (2014), *Flexible Exchange Rates for a Stable World Economy* by Gagnon (2011), and *Inflation Targeting in the World Economy* by Edwin M. Truman (2003). Several other studies on monetary policy have been published as Policy Briefs or Working Papers.

The Peterson Institute for International Economics is a private nonpartisan, nonprofit institution for rigorous, intellectually open, and in-depth study and discussion of international economic policy. Its purpose is to identify and analyze important issues to making globalization beneficial and sustainable for the people of the United States and the world, and then to develop and communicate practical new approaches for dealing with them.

The Institute's work is funded by a highly diverse group of philanthropic foundations, private corporations, public institutions, and interested individuals, as well as by income on its capital fund. About 35 percent of the Institute's resources in our latest fiscal year were provided by contributors from outside the United States. A list of all our financial supporters for the preceding year is posted at http://piie.com/institute/supporters.pdf. The Centre for International Governance Innovation (CIGI) provided funding for this study.

The Executive Committee of the Institute's Board of Directors bears overall responsibility for the Institute's direction, gives general guidance and approval to its research program, and evaluates its performance in pursuit of its mission. The Institute's President is responsible for the identification of topics that are likely to become important over the medium term (one to three years) that should be addressed by Institute scholars. This rolling agenda is set in close consultation with the Institute's research staff, Board of Directors, and other stakeholders.

The President makes the final decision to publish any individual Institute study, following independent internal and external review of the work. Interested readers may access the data and computations underlying the Institute publications for research and replication by searching titles at www.piie.com.

The Institute hopes that its research and other activities will contribute to building a stronger foundation for international economic policy around the world. We invite readers of these publications to let us know how they think we can best accomplish this objective.

ADAM S. POSEN
President
August 2017

PETERSON INSTITUTE FOR INTERNATIONAL ECONOMICS

1750 Massachusetts Avenue, NW, Washington, DC 20036-1903 USA
202.328.9000 Tel   202.328.5432 Fax

Adam S. Posen, *President*

BOARD OF DIRECTORS

*Peter G. Peterson, *Chairman of the Board*
*James W. Owens, *Chairman of the Executive Committee*

Caroline Atkinson
Ajay Banga
* C. Fred Bergsten
Mark T. Bertolini
Ben van Beurden
Nancy Birdsall
Frank Brosens
Ronnie C. Chan
Susan M. Collins
Richard N. Cooper
* Andreas C. Dracopoulos
Barry Eichengreen
* Jessica Einhorn
Peter Fisher
Douglas Flint
* Stephen Freidheim
Jacob A. Frenkel
Evan G. Greenberg
Maurice R. Greenberg
Herbjorn Hansson
Stephen Howe, Jr.
Jay Jacobs
Hugh F. Johnston
Neeti Bhalla Johnson
Michael Klein
Nobuyori Kodaira
Charles D. Lake II
Andrew N. Liveris
Sergio Marchionne
Pip McCrostie
* Hutham S. Olayan
Peter R. Orszag

* Michael A. Peterson
Jonathan Pruzan
Ginni M. Rometty
* Lynn Forester de Rothschild
* Richard E. Salomon
Sheikh Hamad Saud Al-Sayari
* Lawrence H. Summers
Mostafa Terrab
Ronald A. Williams
Min Zhu
* Robert B. Zoellick

HONORARY DIRECTORS

George David
Alan Greenspan
Carla A. Hills
Frank E. Loy
George P. Shultz
Jean-Claude Trichet
Paul A. Volcker
Ernesto Zedillo

* indicates Executive Committee member

Acknowledgments

This book was written during 2015–16, but it is the result of two decades of studying, analyzing, and interpreting monetary policy and central banking. This has taken different forms, all of which have shaped my views about the topic. My research and policy work, first at the International Monetary Fund (IMF), then at the Centre for European Policy Studies (CEPS) and, most importantly, at the Peterson Institute for International Economics (PIIE), where I was a Senior Fellow during 2009–16, provided intellectual depth and rigor. My long career as a risk taker and central bank watcher in hedge funds, for 13 years at Tudor Investment Corporation and two more at D.E. Shaw, forced me to understand the many dimensions of monetary policy and its linkages with markets and politics. The decade I spent as a member of the ECB's Shadow Governing Council—and countless discussions over the years with central bank officials—helped me appreciate the uncertainties that central bankers face when they have to reach decisions in real time, and the difficulties that often arise when having to choose among a range of uncertain options.

Most importantly, this book would have never happened without the help of colleagues, friends, and family, to whom I am deeply grateful.

Adam Posen, the president of PIIE but also a sharp intellectual leader and a good friend, enthusiastically supported this project when I told him I was considering taking a break from the markets. This book would not have happened without him.

Markets are lonely places, and I am heavily indebted to many traveling partners that made the journey through markets safer, more enjoyable, and enriching. My endless discussions with Tom Gallagher and Rob Dugger were key to forming my understanding of the interplay of monetary policy, politics, and markets. Many of these discussions were joined by Greg Ip, Roberto Perli and, after they left the Federal Reserve, Vincent Reinhart and Don Kohn. At a later stage, Yuri Okane, Filippo Altissimo, Alberto Musalem, Karim Basta, Tim Stewart, Krishna Guha, Jason Cummings, and Tom Glaessner have been sounding boards in the art of understanding central banks.

Paul Tudor Jones taught me everything I know about financial markets. The trend is your friend, and always, always, always make sure that the ratio of risk to reward of any decision is favorable. Risk is not to be avoided, it is to be managed properly. This is a key insight for policy making that I hope I have conveyed in the book. Endless hours of discussions at D.E Shaw with Max Stone, Daniel Michelow, Natalia Chefer, Brian Sack, and Larry Summers made me realize that markets are efficient most of the time but that persistent biases create opportunities that can be exploited in a systematic manner. These biases are pervasive in markets, but also in policymaking, and have become an integral part of my approach to understanding monetary policy.

Several people, and three referees, read this manuscript at different stages and provided invaluable comments. Among them, I want to thank especially Marc Noland, Joe Gagnon, Signe Krogstrup, Giovanni de l'Arricia, Dave Stockton, Bill Cline, Ted Truman, Paolo Mauro, Lars Svensson, Tam Bayoumi, José De Gregorio, Pedro da Costa, Olivier Jeanne, Ajai Chopra, and Ramon Guzman. Participants at the PIIE's European breakfasts, monetary policy seminars, and research staff luncheons, and at Euro50 conferences and *Tertulias del Tonic*, were a rich source of endless intellectual stimulation.

Owen Hauck and Junie Joseph provided superb research assistance, including, but not limited to, careful work on the charts and tables in the book.

Steve Weisman, PIIE's vice president for communications and publications, convinced me over the years that, in writing, less beats more and simple beats complicated. His editorial suggestions have helped me not just write more clearly but also understand better my own thoughts. He and his editorial team at PIIE, especially Madona Devasahayam and Susann Luetjen, did their magic in transforming the manuscript into its final form.

Finally, and most importantly, I want to thank my family, for the many weekends of work that it has involved and, especially my wife, for enduring the mountains of paper spread around the house that this book has generated. This book is dedicated to my son, Nico. His endless curiosity and his debating spirit triggered thousands of hours of questions and answers during our rides to and from school, playdates, and soccer practice and games. Trying first to answer the many formulations of the question "what do you do at work," and later intensely debating economics and politics while he was in high school, I was forced to distill the essence of economics, monetary policy, politics, and markets. As he starts college while this book is finally published, I hope these conversations will serve him in his journey to adulthood. I leave it to the reader to judge if they helped me find a way to explain the secrets of monetary policy.

Abbreviations

ABSPP	asset-backed securities purchase program
APF	asset purchase facility
APP	asset purchase program
BIS	Bank for International Settlements
BoC	Bank of Canada
BoE	Bank of England
BoJ	Bank of Japan
CAPMs	capital asset price models
CBPP	covered bond purchase program
CFI	corporate finance instruments
CME	Comprehensive Monetary Easing program
EAPP	expanded asset purchase program
ECB	European Central Bank
Eonia	euro overnight index average
ETF	exchange-traded fund
EZLB	effective zero lower bound
FOMC	Federal Open Market Committee
FRFA	fixed-rate full-allotment
FRO	fixed-rate operation
GSE	government-sponsored enterprises
GSE	government-sponsored enterprise

GSFF	growth-supporting funding facility
IMF	International Monetary Fund
IOER	interest on excess reserves
J-REIT	Japan real estate investment trust
Libor	London interbank offered rate
LSAP	large-scale asset purchase
LTRO	long-term refinancing operation
MEP	maturity extension program
MPC	Monetary Policy Committee
MRO	main refinancing operation
NAIRU	nonaccelerating inflation rate of unemployment
NICE	noninflationary, consistently expansionary
OIS	overnight index swap
OMT	outright monetary transactions
PIIGS	Portugal, Italy, Ireland, Greece, and Spain
QE	quantitative easing
QQE	quantitative and qualitative easing
RBNZ	Reserve Bank of New Zealand
REIT	real estate investment trust
SBLF	stimulating bank lending facility
SFSO	special funds–supplying operations
SMP	Securities Markets Program
SNB	Swiss National Bank
Sonia	sterling overnight index average
TARP	Trouble Asset Relief Program
TLTRO	targeted longer-term refinancing operation
VaR	value at risk

Introduction

All courses of action are risky, so prudence is not in avoiding danger
but in calculating risk and acting decisively.

—Niccolò Macchiavelli

The world crossed a financial Rubicon on March 1, 2016, though few people noticed it. Japan, the most indebted country in the world, with government debt 2.5 times its GDP, was able to borrow money for 10 years at –0.02 percent. Investors were willing to pay for the privilege of lending money to the country with the highest debt-to-GDP ratio ever recorded in modern times outside of war periods.[1]

Japan was not alone. At the peak in mid-2016, more than $10 trillion bonds—more than a third of the world's total—were yielding negative interest rates (figure 1.1). The records piled up. After the United Kingdom voted to exit the European Union, bond yields in the United States and United Kingdom, while still positive, reached all-time lows—lower than during the Great Depression or major wars. For a brief period, the whole yield curve in Switzerland, all the way to the 50-year maturity point, was trading at negative yields. Several major central banks—including the European Central Bank (ECB), Bank of Japan (BoJ), Swiss National Bank (SNB), and Sveriges Riksbank—were charging commercial banks negative interest rates on their cash deposits. It was the world upside down.

It was not supposed to be this way. Before the 2007 financial crisis struck, the overwhelming consensus among economists was that we understood well the dynamics of the economy, that we had been able to domesticate economic fluctuations with economic policies, that we had

---

1. Debt surpassed 200 percent of GDP in the United Kingdom in the early 1800s and also in both the United Kingdom and France after World War I.

Figure 1.1   Market value of bonds with negative yields, 2010–17

market value (trillions of US dollars)

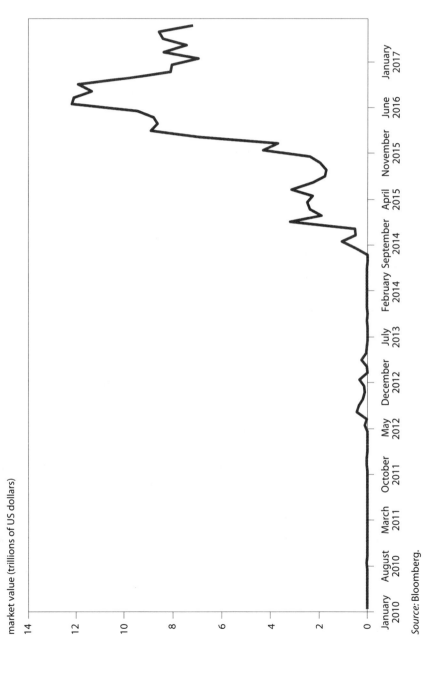

Source: Bloomberg.

tamed the business cycle. We were not humble, and we called the economic period since the mid-1980s "the Great Moderation." We were certain to be able to avoid the policy mistakes that had cost Japan its lost decade of weak growth and very low inflation that followed the burst of its asset bubble in the late 1980s.

We were wrong.

A decade after the financial crisis shook the foundations of the global economy, the world is beginning to climb out of its economic trough. Central banks deployed a massive effort, with the combined balance sheets of the Federal Reserve, ECB, BoJ, Bank of England (BoE), SNB, and People's Bank of China ballooning to more than $18 trillion dollars—equal to more than 20 percent of the world's GDP.

The effort paid off. The feared deflationary spiral did not materialize, the expansion in the United States is already the third longest of the post–World War II period, and some economies are back to near full employment. But, overall, the world struggles to leave what Christine Lagarde, the managing director of the International Monetary Fund (IMF), has christened the "new mediocre." Stock markets and confidence indicators increased after Donald Trump's victory in 2016, celebrating the higher likelihood of fiscal stimulus, and global interest rates increased. Once the smoke cleared, however, little had changed. By mid-2017 interest rates remained very low and still negative in some regions, core inflation was still below target in most developed countries, and global growth expectations had picked up only modestly.

The Paradox of Risk

This book tells the story of how the world got stuck in this environment of low or even negative interest rates through the dialectic of the actions of monetary policy and the reactions of financial markets. It describes how policymakers got trapped in a paradox of risk.

When the crisis erupted and central banks and governments were called to fix it, they hesitated. Their main goal was to minimize the risk they were taking and the possible losses from their actions, rather than maximizing the benefit of their policy decisions. By confusing prudence with avoiding risk, they made the recovery riskier.

How did this paradox of risk happen? The very scary experience of the financial crisis created a sharp increase in risk aversion. Many people had lost their savings and their jobs, many banks and firms had gone under. Fundamental pieces of the financial system that had been taken for granted, such as the availability of liquidity in interbank markets or the ability of firms to issue commercial paper, had temporarily evaporated. It was as if, all of a sudden, water no longer flowed from the taps. Like soldiers returning from the battlefield, households, firms, and financial markets suffered an economic and financial version of posttraumatic stress disorder. Instinctively, people became more risk averse. They looked to the public sector—central banks and governments—for protection, for assurances that everything would turn out all right and that they could go back to their normal lives.

But central bankers and governments were also scared and, to some extent, unprepared. Central bankers had been educated to be conservative, to always aim for lower inflation and less risk. They had earned their credibility fighting the inflation of the 1970s and being vigilant about the risks of financial market exuberance of the 2000s. In Europe they had adopted the additional role of guardians of economic policy rectitude, relentlessly lecturing governments on the need for more fiscal adjustment, structural reforms, and competitiveness gains. Central bankers arrived at the crisis with the conviction that their job was to take the punch bowl away when the party was starting, as the legendary central banker William McChesney Martin quipped. They did not realize that their job now was to spike up the punch to ensure that the party would not end. These mental shackles were often difficult to escape.

The conservative nature of central bankers created a paradox of risk. Faced with a new world of deflationary fears and heightened risk aversion among households, firms, and investors, central bankers had to take risks and provide insurance on the economic outlook, to convince markets that they would do whatever it took to restore growth and inflation. The more insurance central banks provided, the better their policies worked. Yet, concerned about taking too much risk, they often dithered and took only half-measures. Too often, they worried more about when and how to remove the stimulus than about providing the right amount of stimulus, often yielding to political pressures advocating against decisive action.

These political constraints were particularly strong in Europe. For example, the early decision by the ECB to prioritize liquidity provision to banks instead of engaging in large-scale government bond purchases was heavily influenced by strong opposition to asset purchases by German political figures, who cared more about the potential negative impact of asset purchases on fiscal discipline than about supporting the economy with the right amount of stimulus. By the time the ECB finally started buying government bonds, much economic damage had been done.

This widespread hesitation in providing stimulus is largely responsible for the weakness of the global economic recovery. Fed researchers estimate that it accounted for 30 percent of the contraction in GDP in 2009 and an even larger fraction of the slow recovery that followed (Gust et al. 2017).

The recovery saved the world from a second Great Depression, but it was not the recovery that could have been possible had central banks been free of their mental shackles.

The paradox of risk did not apply only to monetary policy. No central bank operates in a vacuum. The consensus narrative of the causes of the crisis was built around the concept that "debt is bad." That notion had two pillars: (1) excessive financial debt led to the financial crisis and (2) excessive fiscal debt led to the euro area crisis and the Greek default. Thus, the consensus argued, debt had to be reduced at all costs. This narrative encouraged private sector deleveraging and fiscal austerity and constituted a strong headwind for monetary policy. After a coordinated, albeit modest and transitory, fiscal expansion in 2009, governments across the globe prematurely declared victory and moved on to fiscal tightening.

The mistaken European strategy of using the threat of sovereign debt defaults as a disciplinary device for the governments of the euro area countries in crisis added to the "debt is bad" narrative, creating an environment in which politicians preferred to cut deficits first and ask questions later, advocating fiscal austerity at all cost to avoid "becoming Greece." Learning from fearful experiences is much faster and creates more persistent effects than other forms of learning (Lo 2017). The fear of default, however irrational, overwhelmed everything.

As it had happened to the central bankers with their anti-inflation worries, this overarching focus on fiscal discipline was based on sound analysis applied to the wrong reality. The mental shackles were at play here as well. Governments and politicians had been educated on a precrisis consensus built on two pillars: (1) fiscal policy should focus on long-term sustainability and leave the management of the business cycle to monetary policy and (2) fiscal contractions were often expansionary, as they lowered interest rates and boosted private sector confidence. This conventional wisdom was correct for a world of small output gaps and positive inflation and interest rates. It was not appropriate for the postcrisis world of very large output gaps, zero interest rates, and very low inflation. In this world, interest rates had little room to decline, and there was no confidence to be gained from austerity. Tightening fiscal policy excessively and prematurely weakened the economy and diminished the effectiveness of monetary policy. Seeking to reduce debt-to-GDP ratios, governments often weakened GDP and increased debt-to-GDP ratios. Like their central banking colleagues, governments and politicians confused prudence with avoiding risks, inadvertently making the environment riskier.

The obstinate focus of the Republican Party on public spending cuts in the United States and the staunch German opposition to a mutualization of euro area fiscal policy that could alleviate deficit reductions in crisis countries are vivid examples of this confusion. It was a textbook case of "motivated reasoning" (Epley and Gilovich 2016), with political goals commanding attention and a selective reading of the evidence guiding reasoning at the expense of accuracy. Retail politics prevailed over economic needs, and fiscal policy became a strong headwind for monetary policy.

This conflict between monetary and fiscal policy is not new. The United States faced the opposite situation in 1981. Two years after Paul A. Volcker, chair of the Federal Reserve in the early years of the Reagan administration, began tightening monetary policy, inflation was proving difficult to tame, because President Reagan was embarking on tax cuts and military spending increases that expanded the fiscal deficit. When Reagan met Volcker for the first time after he became president, he asked him about the rationale for having a Federal Reserve in the first place. Volcker is said to have replied: "We are the only game in town right now fighting inflation. . . . Once the budget gets under control, we'll have a better shot at taking the pressure off of prices" (Mallaby 2016, 263). The political pressure against Volcker's monetary tightening mounted as the recession got deeper. A return to the gold standard was debated.

The lesson was then, and it is now, that it is dangerous for governments to hide behind the central bank and make monetary policy the only game in town. Not surprisingly, governments and politicians ended up disliking the central bank activism they were responsible for.

Of Boring Central Bankers, "NICE" Economies, and the Power of Narratives

Before the crisis there was clear consensus that a "successful central bank should be boring."[2] Yet, since 2007 it has been anything but boring, a reality that is likely to persist for decades.

Central banking was expected to be boring because the economy was enjoying the Great Moderation, the period between the mid-1980s and 2007 that witnessed a dramatic decline in the variability of output and inflation. Back then, with stable inflation, output near potential, and smooth business cycle fluctuations, managing the economy was easy. Simple rules were very good approximations of the process that determined the setting of interest rates, making monetary policy rather predictable. All that central banks had to do was to adjust short-term interest rates in a very gradual manner and wait for the effect to trickle down to the real economy in a predictable way. Back then, cutting rates by 50 basis points was considered "aggressive." Mervyn King, the governor of the BoE, coined an acronym for

---

2. Mervyn King, "Monetary Policy: Theory in Practice," speech, London, January 7, 2000.

this world: the NICE (noninflationary, consistently expansionary) economy.[3]

That NICE economy is ancient history. The brutality and persistence of the crisis; the unexpected linkages across markets, countries, and financial institutions; and the many policy mistakes along the way have created deep scars that will affect the behavior of economic agents for decades. Old paradigms have been replaced with a web of overlapping and competing narratives that affect the behavior of the private sector, governments, and regulators in a persistent, and sometimes perverse, manner. As Nobel Laureate Robert Shiller said, "We have to consider the possibility that sometimes the dominant reason why a recession is severe is related to the prevalence and vividness of certain stories, not the purely economic feedback or multipliers that economists love to model."[4]

This perversity occurs because narratives drive attention, and elevated attention can easily lead to the misleading impression of causality. In his book *Pre-suasion: A Revolutionary Way to Influence and Persuade*, Robert Cialdini, one of the most prominent researchers in the field of psychological influence and persuasion, writes that "what is focal is causal." In experiments in which people were asked to observe conversations between two people that had been carefully scripted so that no one was leading the discussion, observers overwhelmingly concluded that the person whose face was more visible was the leader (Cialdini 2016). People assign causal properties to the narratives that drive the news.

The causal links created by this web of narratives have reduced the effectiveness of monetary policy, in two main ways. First, they have increased risk aversion in a persistent way and across the board. Having missed the crisis and underestimated the severity of its impact, economists, policymakers, and market participants now feel the obligation to consider all possible downside risks. A "not on my watch" narrative has developed. Risk managers must ensure that firms can withstand another shock of the size and persistence of the post-Lehman downturn, however unlikely such a shock may be. Politicians and policymakers must ensure that they are covered against the consensus political narrative of the causes of the crisis: "debt is bad." They thus argue for fiscal discipline and regulatory tightening of the financial sector at all costs, so that another crisis does not happen on their watch. Economists must consider all possible interlinkages and, in case of doubt, always warn about downside risks.

---

3. Mervyn King, speech at the East Midlands Development Agency/Bank of England dinner, Leicester, October 14, 2003.

4. Robert J. Shiller, "Narrative Economics," speech at awards ceremony and presidential address hosted by the American Economic Association, Chicago, January 7, 2017.

The failure to predict the crisis had a persistent impact on the way economic expectations are formed, developing an "it looks wise to be gloomy" narrative. Risk management is an exercise in imagination; what cannot be imagined cannot be insured against. The crisis opened the imagination to negative scenarios that had never been considered before, including the breakup of the euro. As a result, in the postcrisis world it looks wise to be gloomy and imagine ever more pessimistic scenarios. Being optimistic and wrong puts one's job at risk; being gloomy and wrong is considered prudent risk management, even if doing so implies missing a large market rally or a business opportunity. There is a bias toward pessimism, the opposite of the exuberant precrisis period. The tone of the economic debate, casting doubt on the future rate of technological progress or suggesting that secular stagnation has set in, reinforces this sober tone. This pessimistic narrative about the future constrains consumption and investment today and significantly dampens present and future economic growth (Blanchard, Lorenzoni, and L'Huillier 2017).

Second, the causal links have reduced confidence in central banks. The stability of the Great Moderation generated the belief that economic outcomes could be forecast with a high degree of precision. Behavioral economists call people's tendency to think they have more control over events than they really do the "illusion of control." A crisis that was "impossible," according to the available economic models and data, crushed this belief. The fact that most central bank forecasts consistently overestimated the speed of the recovery further eroded the confidence in central banks. A "central banks do not get it" narrative developed that dented the credibility of central banks and raised doubts about the effectiveness of their actions.

The challenging politics of bank rescue programs added to the diminished standing of central banks, creating a "central banks help banks, not citizens" narrative. Putting the central bank balance sheet at risk to save banks from their imprudent behavior is a very difficult political proposition but a necessary action when the banking system is at risk, because the alternative is a major economic collapse.

Contrary to conventional wisdom, the decision to bail out a bank should never be measured by the potential losses for the government or the central bank if the bailout does not work but by the potential losses in terms of forgone GDP if the bailout had not happened. However, the large size of the rescue packages, often wrongly identified as the main culprits of the increases in public debt ratios that occurred during the crisis, created a politically toxic environment that cannot be offset with explanations and data. For example, the Troubled Asset Relief Program (TARP) (the package of bank bailouts the United States deployed) generated a net profit for the US government. But it didn't matter. In the political narrative, using taxpayer money to bail out big banks was fundamentally wrong and generated large losses for taxpayers—and central banks were necessary accomplices in the process.

Just Blame the Central Banks

Behavioral research shows that once a narrative sets in, it is hard to dislodge, especially if the narrative is coherent (Kahneman 2005). This web of narratives has made central banks easy targets for ideological criticism and political instrumentalization. The economy was not NICE anymore. The activism central banks deployed to restore growth was often portrayed as wrong, ineffective, or morally questionable. Politicians needed a culprit; hiding behind the central banks and blaming them for all problems yielded solid political dividends.

Some politicians did not mince their words. The governor of Texas, Rick Perry, accused Fed Chair Ben Bernanke of treasonous behavior: "If this guy prints more money between now and the election, I do not know what you would do to him in Iowa, but we would treat him pretty ugly down in Texas. Printing more money to play politics at this particular time in American history is almost treacherous—or treasonous in my opinion."[5] The US Congress has also been active. The "audit the Fed" movement is seeking to severely constrain the Fed's ability to conduct monetary policy by demanding that its policy actions be audited by the comptroller general of the United States. During the 2016 presidential campaign, Donald Trump openly criticized the low level of interest rates and said that he would not reappoint Janet Yellen as chair. In the euro area, suing the ECB before the German Constitutional Court became a habit among German academics and politicians who fundamentally disliked its attempts to ease monetary policy via asset purchases. All of the attempts failed, but they were responsible in large part for the ECB's delay in adopting quantitative easing (QE). Central bank bashing probably reached its peak in April 2016, when German Finance Minister Wolfgang Schäuble blamed the ECB for the rise of anti-euro sentiment in the German political debate.[6] In what may be the ultimate irony, in a country with a political culture built around the strong independence of the Bundesbank, the government has been trying to intimidate its central bank.

---

5. Chris McGreal, "Rick Perry Attacks Ben Bernanke's 'Treasonous' Federal Reserve Strategy," *Guardian*, August 16, 2011, www.theguardian.com/world/2011/aug/16/rick-perry-ben-bernanke-treasonous (accessed on March 29, 2017).

6. Jeremy Warner, "Europe Doesn't Work for Germany Either, as Schäuble's Faux Pas Demonstrates," *Telegraph*, April 26, 2016, www.telegraph.co.uk/business/2016/04/26/europe-doesnt-work-for-germany-either-as-schubles-faux-pas-demon (accessed on March 29, 2017).

Central banks had been at similar junctures in the past. In September 1979 Fed Chair Arthur Burns delivered a speech entitled "The Anguish of Central Banking," in which he blamed the lack of effective action on inflation on the fact that "the Federal Reserve was itself caught up in the philosophy and political currents that were transforming American life and culture."[7] As Sebastian Mallaby, in his biography of Alan Greenspan, puts it, "Despite the aura of independence that has grown up around central banks, they do not exist in a vacuum. To the contrary, their mandate comes from lawmakers, their legitimacy derives from the climate of expert opinions, and they ultimately depend on the sympathy of voters" (Mallaby 2016, 230). Greenspan was the quintessential political operator; with his shrewd political activity, he managed to keep politicians away from the Fed. Not all central bankers are so politically astute.

Independence and credibility are necessary conditions for the effectiveness of central banks. They have become the object of harsh, repeated, and unfair criticisms—sometimes for doing too much, sometimes for not doing enough. This criticism has diminished the effectiveness of their actions. But when the next recession arrives—and it will likely arrive with interest rates still very low—the world is going to need central bankers to be very active again and at their maximum effectiveness in order to be able to restore growth.

And, then, all those who have opportunistically attacked central banks will lament they did so.

Roadmap of the Book

Against this background, this book has a double objective. First, describe and evaluate the experience with monetary policy in various countries since 2007, extracting best practices and lessons for the future about what worked, what did not, and why. Second, increase the public understanding of how this new multidimensional monetary policy works, in order to help reduce the politicization of monetary policy and the misconceptions about its workings. Some concepts are intellectual zombies that just refuse to die. For example, the argument that increasing the size of the central bank's balance sheet may lead to rampant inflation and currency debasement has survived decades of evidence to the contrary. During the 2016 US presidential election, some candidates used it to argue in favor of a return to the gold standard.

---

7. Arthur Burns, "The Anguish of Central Banking," speech at the Per Jacobsson Lecture, Belgrade, September 30, 1979.

The book tells the story from the perspective of an economist, a risk taker in financial markets, and a consumer of central banking. I have never been a central banker, but my background of academic and policy research, experience in public policy, and long tenure in the hedge fund industry have resulted in a decade and a half of watching central banks, translating the intricacies of monetary policy for markets, and opening the eyes of central bankers to the mysteries of markets. A core tenet of my approach is to explore the interlinkages between politics, policies, and markets, from the principle that everything in life is probabilistic and every decision is about evaluating risk and reward. In the spirit of Isaiah Berlin's famous metaphor, it is the approach of the fox, not the hedgehog.[8] Research shows that foxes are better forecasters than hedgehogs (Gardner and Tetlock 2016). The discipline of financial markets requires the fox's eclectic knowledge of sound economic theory, the inefficiencies and behavioral biases of financial markets, and the incentives of politicians, approaching problems with an open mind that straddles disciplines. This book shares the fruits of my experience.

Chapter 2 provides the intellectual and political background that preceded the crisis and created the context in which the monetary authorities had to act. It describes the building blocks of the precrisis economic debate, the consensus about the workings of monetary policy, the specifics about the euro area that would later condition the ECB's monetary policy response, and the mechanics of expectations formation in financial markets. A few important conclusions emerge. Economists had been educated to worry about high inflation and to assume that economic cycles were stable, that economies always returned to equilibrium, and that monetary policy could not affect potential growth. Central bankers were convinced that zero interest rates and the risk of deflation were the result of the failures and mistakes of the Japanese authorities and would not happen in the West. European politicians, governments, and central bankers were obsessed with internal competitiveness as the key to the success of the euro. And markets had learned to live with the "Greenspan put" (the belief that monetary policy would always come to the rescue of markets), smooth and rather predictable monetary policy, and market regularities that guided their behavior. The crisis smashed all of these paradigms and set in motion a volatile learning process.

Several economic concepts appear recurrently in this book that are key to understanding the story of monetary policy since 2007. They are outlined

---

8. According to Isaiah Berlin, writers and thinkers can be classified into two types: hedgehogs, who know one big thing, and foxes, who know many small things (Berlin 1953). Berlin attributes the concept to the Greek poet Archilochus.

in box 1.1. Building on these concepts, chapter 3 outlines a guiding framework for the analysis of monetary policy in terms of four essential elements:

- the policy goals and the time frame to achieve them,
- the tools to achieve the goals,
- the strategy for using the tools, and
- the communication methods to explain the strategy to the public.

Within this framework, it tells in detail the story of the decisions of the main central banks—the Fed, ECB, BoJ, BoE, and, when relevant, the BoC and SNB—since 2007. It shows that these decisions have affected all four essential elements of the guiding framework. Most central banks have updated or clarified their policy goals and mobilized large-scale asset purchases, liquidity facilities, negative interest rates, and other new tools with the explicit use of forward guidance. And they have sought to elevate the public's understanding of the workings of monetary policy. The monetary policy frameworks of 2017 bear little resemblance to the easy and simple frameworks of 2007. This transformation has been the great experiment in monetary policy.

Did It Work?

Chapter 4 analyzes the impact and effectiveness of monetary policy during this period in terms of whether it affected financial conditions in the desired way; was eased as much as recommended by simple benchmark policy rules; and achieved its objectives in terms of growth and inflation. It also discusses some of the potential costs of monetary policy, including the relationship between money growth and inflation and the impact of monetary policy on financial stability, income inequality, and moral hazard in fiscal policy.

It shows that monetary policy worked—during the crisis and the ensuing recession, monetary policy was effective in restoring market functioning, affecting financial conditions in the desired manner, and boosting growth and inflation—but that it could have done better. In general, central banks delayed action and eased policy less than optimally, struggling at times to maintain price stability and close the output gap.

They were hampered by mistaken, and often contradictory, preconceptions about the potential costs of acting. Some argued that monetary policy would not work and favored structural reforms; others foresaw runaway inflation from zero interest rates and large central bank balance sheets; many feared the distortionary effects of asset purchases. There were worries that QE would lead to fiscal deficits and moral hazard, the

Box 1.1   Some useful concepts

Forward guidance. A strategy in which a central bank provides explicit or implicit guidance about its future policy actions. This guidance can be defined in terms of time or relative to some macroeconomic variables (e.g., stating that interest rates are expected to be on hold for an extended period or until inflation reaches a specific level).

Hysteresis. A process that converts a transitory shock into a permanent one (e.g., when a cyclical increase in unemployment, caused by a recession, becomes a permanent increase in unemployment after people remain unemployed for a very long time and lose the skills and motivation necessary to find jobs). When hysteresis happens, a recession can reduce potential growth. In these cases, a central bank can prevent a deterioration of potential growth by boosting demand.

Knightian uncertainty. Uncertainty that cannot be measured or modeled ex ante because the situation under consideration is unique. Uncertainty is different from risk, which can be measured and modeled ex ante, because there is enough historical data to calculate a probability distribution, and therefore insured against.

Macroprudential policy. Regulatory and supervisory decisions that seek to reduce the macroeconomic financial vulnerability of an economy (e.g., by reducing the maximum loan-to-value ratio allowed in residential mortgages in order to slow the growth of mortgage credit).

Moral hazard. A situation in which economic agents take more risk than they otherwise would because they believe that if something goes wrong someone will come to the rescue to bail them out (e.g., a government running a very large deficit thinking that, if markets punish it and decide to charge a higher interest rate on its debt, the central bank will react and keep interest rates low).

Quantitative easing. A policy in which the central bank purchases assets, public or private, from the market and finances the purchases by issuing money. This process increases the amount of money in circulation; if it lowers interest rates and boosts asset prices, it eases financial conditions.

Reaction function. A quantitative description of the way monetary policy reacts, or is expected to react, to changes in the economic outlook (e.g., how interest rates react to an increase in growth or inflation).

Risk aversion. For economists, risk aversion is a preference parameter in the agent's utility function, invariant over time. Agents are described as *risk neutral* if they are indifferent between options with equal expected payoffs, for example the choice between receiving $100 or a 50 percent chance of receiving $200 and a 50 percent chance of receiving $0. Agents are described as *risk seeking* or *risk averse* if their preferences are not neutral to risk (i.e., if they prefer one of the options described above over the other). However, consumers' risk tolerance can change over time, even if their preferences are unchanged—because, for example, of liquidity or capital restrictions. For ease of language, this book uses the concept of risk aversion to encompass both changes in risk aversion parameters and changes in risk tolerance, though changes in risk tolerance are enough to support most of the conclusions of the book.

debasing of currencies, and competitive devaluations. The evidence shows that none of these fears has materialized and that, if anything, the opposite has been the case—the best example being fiscal policy, which has been too tight, rather than too loose.

Monetary policy when interest rates reached the effective zero lower bound (EZLB)[9] has operated through several channels, including portfolio rebalancing and signaling about the future path of short-term interest rates. Asset purchases have been more effective when they have provided an insurance on the economic outlook, designed in a manner that is both state contingent (that is, explicitly conditional on achieving economic outcomes) and open ended (that is, without a predetermined end date). At the EZLB, with persistent doubts about policy effectiveness and about our collective understanding of the functioning of the economy and markets, the objective of monetary policy must be to restore risk appetite to normal levels and provide markets with an outlook-based framework to appropriately price assets. State-contingent, open-ended polices allow central banks to sell an option on the economic outlook to economic agents and markets, and most central banks have rightly converged toward this model.

Some central banks have been more effective than others. The Fed, after patiently waiting for the output gap to close, has started a gradual tightening cycle, although inflation and inflation expectations are still somewhat below target. In contrast, the ECB is still buying assets in large scale, its deposit rate is still negative, and it is far from achieving its inflation objective. Growth is strong but, given the fragility of inflation expectations and the weakness of wage growth, the ECB would be well advised to design a strategy that allows interest rates to remain as low as needed for as long as needed.

The BoE was also close to declaring mission accomplished, but it was interrupted by the Brexit referendum. The BoE is the only central bank where inflation expectations are well anchored at or above precrisis levels. The BoE's courage in easing policy aggressively during 2009–12 while headline inflation was transitorily very high buttressed its antideflation credibility. The paradox of risk at play. Taking the right amount of risk at the right time pays off.

Finally, the BoJ has shown that, when a central bank is willing to deploy all the necessary ammunition and the government cooperates, it is possible to lift inflation expectations. The BoJ is still far from its 2 percent inflation objective but, if it perseveres, and the Japanese government continues

---

9. As some central banks have cut rates to negative levels, the concept of "zero lower bound" of interest rates has been replaced by "effective zero lower bound."

to cooperate, Japan has a chance of joining the club of countries with 2 percent inflation.

Have We Learned Anything? An Action Plan

Chapter 5 focuses on the future, concluding that central banks must craft a monetary policy framework for all seasons, robust to fight both inflation and deflation. Its key recommendations are that central banks should

- launch a program of opportunistic reflation;
- adopt dual mandates for monetary policy, de facto or de jure;
- be ready to carry large balance sheets and buy all type of assets;
- adopt a strategy of cyclically adjusted forward guidance; and
- improve their communication about monetary policy, including stopping calling it "unconventional."

The experience of the crisis has shown that central banks need to stress the symmetry of their goals and that their inflation targets are too low. Therefore, after this long period of below-target inflation, central banks should first aim for a period of above-target inflation in order to firmly anchor inflation expectations at current targets. Then, they should engage in a program of "opportunistic reflation", which may last more than one business cycle, aiming at higher inflation targets in the 3 to 4 percent range, to soften the implicit lower bound in real interest rates.[10] This lower bound arises because, with inflation at 2 percent, cutting nominal interest rates to zero reduces real interest rates to only –2 percent, and deep recessions require real interest rates well below that. Banks are being asked to raise capital to be able to withstand much bigger shocks than in the past, and monetary policy should do the same by increasing inflation targets. The alternative would be to prepare for more negative nominal interest rates or flatter yield curves. It is a difficult tradeoff, but the potential cost of higher inflation as an insurance against the EZLB is likely smaller than that of very negative interest rates.

The change in goals has to go beyond opportunistic reflation. In a context of very uncertain demographic and productivity trends, and with hysteresis effects at work, the optimal mandate of monetary policy should be to maximize growth and employment subject to price stability. Therefore, central banks should adopt dual mandates, de facto or de jure, for two reasons: first, with inflation increasingly insensitive to growth, this

---

10. This program of opportunistic reflation would be the mirror image of the "opportunistic disinflation" strategy adopted by central banks during the 1980s to gradually lower inflation toward the 2 percent objective (Orphanides and Wilcox 2002).

would ensure that monetary policy always tests the limits of growth and economies don't get stuck in a low-growth trap; second, dual mandates would reinforce the democratic credibility of central banks, easing public concerns about its lack of sensitivity toward employment and growth. This does not imply creating an inflationary bias. It is a reminder that the ultimate objective of monetary policy is maximum growth, and that price stability is just a means to an end.

Central banks should retain large balance sheets. A system of excess reserves enhances the stability of the financial system against liquidity shocks, and the payment of interest on excess reserves (IOER) allows central banks to run monetary policy with large balance sheets. And central banks should be ready to use balance sheet policies at all times, including purchases of all types of private assets and lending against all type of assets (properly discounted). Buying risky assets is an efficient way of reducing elevated risk premia, and avoids creating a shortage of safe assets. The "cost" argument against purchases of riskier assets is misguided—central banks should focus on minimizing the economic cost of recessions, not the potential fiscal costs to their balance sheets—but it is politically relevant. Therefore, central banks should improve their institutional arrangements and increase their ability to withstand losses, to be able to be as effective with balance sheet policies as they would be with interest rates.

Forward guidance should be cyclically adjusted, with varying degrees of explicitness depending on the distance of growth and inflation from their targets and on the level of risk aversion. This cyclical adjustment should be symmetric. When risk aversion is too high, forward guidance should be explicit to foster risk taking, and accompanied by asset purchases to bolster credibility; when risk aversion is too low, forward guidance should be minimized to avoid giving markets one-way bets and incentives for excessive risk taking. In most cases, excessive certainty, and not low interest rates, is the main source of carry trades and disruptive search for yield strategies. When risk aversion is within normal ranges, forward guidance should focus on what the central bank can control, describing its reaction function and potential alternative scenarios, and shy away from near-term guidance and explicit interest rate paths that create confusion. Because asset purchases and forward guidance are intended to affect attitudes toward risk, decisions on macroprudential policies should be delegated to central banks to enhance the coordination and cooperation between monetary policy and macroprudential policies. The better the coordination, the more will monetary policy be able to support growth.

Finally, central banks must communicate better. As Ben Bernanke puts it, monetary policy is "98 percent talk, and 2 percent action" (Bernanke 2015a, 498). Central banks need to diversify and expand their channels of communication to better control the narratives and develop positive messages. They should stop using the concepts of "unconventional" policies and "exit." All policies are conventional, and thus there is no exit. There is easing, and there is tightening, of monetary policy. This would eliminate the stigma associated with balance sheet policies, forward guidance, and negative interest rates that reduces their effectiveness.

The Future Is Not What It Used to Be

Sooner or later, another recession will arrive. If it arrives when global interest rates and inflation are low, the best policy response should include strong forward guidance and a large program of asset purchases combined with a credible and well-designed fiscal expansion. In fact, we have already seen the future. As discussed in chapter 6, the new phase of Abenomics in Japan and the easing package that the BoE adopted after the Brexit referendum in 2016 follow some of the suggestions of this book as regards risk taking, communication, and coordination with fiscal policy.

When inflation and interest rates are low, fiscal policy should be more active and better coordinated with monetary policy, so that monetary policy is not the only game in town. A well-designed and active fiscal policy would increase the neutral interest rate, thus making monetary policy more effective, limit the damage to potential growth, and reduce the impact of recessions on income inequality. The key words are "well designed." Fiscal policy should boost growth, not short-term consumption, leading, yes, to higher interest rates. It requires breaking the mental shackle that active fiscal policy, especially if coordinated with monetary policy, is a bad policy. It is not. It is the right policy response when interest rates are low.

Some have gone further, and argued in favor of helicopter money, a fiscal expansion directly financed by central bank money creation that does not generate new debt (Turner 2015). It was Milton Friedman who first suggested in 1969 (however facetiously) that throwing money from a helicopter would boost growth and inflation (Friedman 1969). In 2002, Ben Bernanke, then a member of the Federal Reserve Board, suggested it as a last resort policy option to combat deflation.[11] Some economists have gone even further, arguing in favor of enabling central banks to force the government to run fiscal deficits to reach the inflation target.[12]

---

11. Ben Bernanke, "Deflation: Making Sure 'It' Doesn't Happen Here," speech before the National Economists Club, Washington, November 21, 2002.

12. Simon Wren-Lewis, "Helicopter Money," Mainly Macro (blog), October 22, 2014, www.mainlymacro.blogspot.com/2014/10/helicopter-money.html (accessed on March 29, 2017).

All this may look right on paper, but the concept of helicopter money carries a stigma, is illegal in several countries, and is a distraction from what really matters, which is to spend money to boost demand.[13] There is no need to go there. In these situations, central banks should demand expansionary fiscal policies, and governments must take responsibility and adopt the right policies. The key is that monetary policy ensures that interest rates do not increase as a result of the fiscal expansion. QE has done precisely that. Helicopters should stay grounded.

Central banking is an exercise in risk management and, to be successful, policymakers, like portfolio managers, must be aware of their behavioral biases (Kahneman 2005). During the crisis, policymakers suffered from the anchoring effect (overweighting the initial pieces of information) when they shifted toward fiscal austerity based mostly on the Greek case. They suffered from the endowment effect (aversion to change by overvaluing what one owns) and loss aversion (holding on to losing positions for too long because of aversion to realizing the loss) when they stuck with the wrong policies for too long (e.g., the ECB's initial opposition to QE, the reluctance by governments to engage in fiscal expansion, central banks' refusal to increase inflation targets). They suffered from overconfidence, by taking the stability of inflation expectations for granted. These biases cannot be eliminated but recognizing them helps reduce their impact.

All strategies entail risks, and central banks must act in a responsible manner. But let's not forget. As Machiavelli told us, irresponsibility is not to take risk. Irresponsibility is to assess a situation and not to take the right amount of risk. Central banks have a symmetric mandate to meet and must do whatever it takes to fulfill it.

13. For example, the Maastricht Treaty prohibits the ECB from engaging in the direct financing of governments, and the Public Finance Act in Japan prohibits the BoJ from directly underwriting Japanese government bonds.

2

The Intellectual and Political Background to the Crisis

If it was meself that was going to Letterfrack, faith, I would not start from here.
—Traditional Irish saying

In *The Structure of Scientific Revolutions*, Thomas Kuhn (1962) argues that scientific progress is rarely slow and gradual, that it happens in fits and starts. A consensus model of thought works for a long time. It shows cracks here and there but is still believed to be the best paradigm. Research is conducted at the margins, extending the central paradigm in several directions. Then, at some point, there is a model crisis. A sudden event shows the deep cracks in the model. The intellectual castle of cards collapses. When it does, people are lost. The paradigm is gone, issuing in what Kuhn calls the "revolution phase."

Competition for a new paradigm starts. Some want to preserve the status quo. Others try new approaches. Confusion ensues for a long time. Success in the revolution phase requires something very difficult to do: mental purging. If the old paradigm does not work, mental structures need to change, the scale of values and preferences needs to be reworked. These mental shackles are difficult to shed.

The intellectual background that preceded the global financial crisis was too rigid and too asymmetric—to a large extent a victim of its own success. It would have been much better to have arrived at the crisis with a different background. But if the background had been different, perhaps the crisis would have never happened.

It All Started in the 1970s: The Anti-Inflation Consensus

The Great Inflation of the 1970s suddenly ended the economic peace dividend of the 1960s. The sudden acceleration of inflation from the 2 percent of the 1960s to the double digits of the late 1970s left a deep mark on the current generation of economists in positions of responsibility, all educated in an environment in which the major challenge was not to reduce unemployment or boost growth but to restrain inflation.

Beating inflation meant that monetary policy became the main policy tool. Economists had discarded Keynes' idea of fiscal demand management—deficit expansion during recessions coupled with austerity during boom times—because of its uncertain response times. Because democratic processes are usually long and slow, by the time fiscal decisions materialize, it is typically too late. Active fiscal policy created more problems than it solved.

The consensus was that monetary policy would manage the business cycle and stabilize unemployment and growth, grounded in the existence of a natural rate of unemployment. This natural rate, and by extension the rate of potential GDP growth, was assumed to be independent from monetary policy. The cornerstone of monetary policy was the relationship between unemployment and inflation. If unemployment increased above the natural rate, inflation was expected to decline, and vice versa. But that relationship entailed a danger: Governments could be tempted to opportunistically boost inflation to reduce unemployment, and it would be self-defeating. During the 1970s, Nobel Laureate Robert Lucas showed that if the public expected the central bank to cut interest rates to boost employment, the relationship between inflation and unemployment broke down: Taking action created inflation with no boost to the real economy, because workers, rationally expecting inflation, demanded higher wages, neutering the expected increase in employment.

From the inflation travails of the 1980s emerged the so-called new classical consensus (also called real business cycle theory), which argued that cyclical policies had no effect on the real economy. In this framework economic cycles are the result of changes in productivity growth. During downturns, lower productivity growth leads to lower wages, and workers offer less labor as a result. Unemployment is the natural reaction to lower wages. These models featured fully flexible prices. As a result, prices always adjusted, and the economy always returned to equilibrium. There was no need for stabilization policy. A depression was just a bigger shock, supposed to happen rarely, that would also self-correct. These models were good laboratory machines, but they were too perfect and unrealistic to be useful for policy analysis.

Against this new classical view emerged the new Keynesian view. New Keynesian models incorporated more realistic frictions, such as price and wage rigidities. Economies in these models may not return to equilibrium after a shock; monetary policy can play a role in stabilizing employment and growth during recessions. Booms are followed by busts; recessions are the necessary medicine to cool overheated economies. These models asserted that the firm anchoring of inflation expectations was critical to ensure the effectiveness of monetary policy and the stability of inflation. The anchoring of inflation expectations had an asymmetric meaning for most economists—anchoring to prevent too high inflation, not too low inflation.

The independence of central banks—their ability to adopt politically difficult decisions to reduce inflation—was critical to achieving the credible anchoring of expectations. Cooperation or coordination between monetary and fiscal policy was considered a dangerous enterprise. Governments could not be trusted because, to be reelected, politicians would be tempted to renege on their commitments in order to generate more growth, even if at the cost of higher inflation.

Over time the methodologies and concepts of both strands merged in the new neoclassical synthesis, which comprised intertemporal optimization, rational expectations, and price and wage rigidities. In these models monetary policy can affect output in the short run but not the long run; money is neutral. Inflation has negative welfare effects. Price stability—defined as zero inflation, plus some small buffer to take into account measurement errors—is therefore a key policy objective.

With the development of inflation targeting as a policy framework, some consensus emerged that an inflation target of 2 percent, or a bit lower, was optimal. But context mattered. Inflation was above 2 percent almost everywhere, and inflation targeting was developed mostly as a disinflationary framework, to help countries reduce inflation toward price stability. The consensus on 2 percent inflation was not unanimous. For example, during Federal Open Market Committee (FOMC) discussions about the right inflation objective, Alan Greenspan liked to describe price stability in qualitative terms, as a situation in which "expected changes in the general price level do not effectively alter business or household decisions" (Mallaby 2016, 489).

Monetary policy in the new neoclassical synthesis was typically modeled as a policy rule, in which short-term interest rates were a function of the output gap (the difference between current and potential output) and the inflation gap (the difference between actual or forecast inflation and the inflation objective). A key result of these models was the "divine coincidence"—the fact that stabilizing inflation at the target implied closing the output gap and stabilizing output at potential (Blanchard and Galí 2005). Therefore, a single price-stability mandate for monetary policy was enough to achieve potential growth. This result was a very important driver of monetary policy decisions during the crisis.

Two important elements were largely absent in the new neoclassical synthesis: an active role for fiscal policy and a dynamic role for the financial sector. In this consensus the role of governments was to meet their long-run budget constraint: to ensure balanced budgets and stable debt ratios. There was no role for discretionary fiscal policy to smooth the business cycle. Smoothing was accomplished by so-called automatic stabilizers—the automatic reaction of government spending and tax revenues to the business cycle. During good times, revenues increase (because tax receipts are a function of economic activity) and spending declines (because expenditures such as unemployment benefits decline), automatically reducing the fiscal deficit. During bad times, the opposite happens, and deficits expand. Discretionary fiscal policy should therefore be neutral or, if anything, contractionary, to unleash "expansionary fiscal contractions."

This view of fiscal policy, based on the German ordoliberal tradition and the early work of Alberto Alesina and Roberto Perotti (1997), argues that fiscal contractions, even during downturns, are expansionary because they improve the sustainability of public finances and, as a result, improve private sector confidence and reduce long-term interest rates. The strong consensus around this idea, built over many decades of deficit reduction, was at the heart of the austerity drive that took place after 2010 and left monetary policy as the only game in town. When, in early 2009, the managing director of the IMF, Dominique Strauss-Kahn, gave an interview to the *Financial Times* in which he advocated a large, coordinated fiscal expansion, the surprise could be felt across the globe. The IMF, the guardian of the essences of the expansionary fiscal contraction doctrine, had changed its view. Unfortunately, the International Monetary Fund (IMF) would remain a lone voice in its support for active fiscal policy.

The financial sector also played a secondary role in these macroeconomic models. It was just a veil, a black box that appeared in the models, not a relevant source of fluctuations or an amplification mechanism. Sadly, this secondary role was largely a consequence of segmentation in economic research, not lack of knowledge. Corporate finance and banking models allowed for nonlinearities, runs, crises, or contagion, with excessive risk taking the result of limited liability, asymmetric information, and leverage. However, most of these developments remained on the periphery of macroeconomics, because they introduced complications that interfered with the elegance and precision of standard macroeconomic models (see Caballero 2010). In those standard macromodels, banks were just intermediaries that ensured the smooth transmission of monetary policy actions. They included just one interest rate and assumed that the spread between the short-term policy interest rate and the interest rate charged by banks to the private sector was constant.

One of the rare exceptions was research by Ben Bernanke and Mark Gertler (1995) on the "financial accelerator." It is revealing that their paper was entitled "Inside the Black Box: The Credit Channel of Monetary Policy

Transmission." Bernanke and Gertler tried to incorporate some of the results from the banking and finance literature into macroeconomics. One of the most important ones was the balance sheet channel of monetary policy, whereby changes in interest rates affect the balance sheet of both borrowers and lenders, via, for example, changes in interest rate expenses and asset price values. But this line of research was intended more to assess empirically its existence than to incorporate it in macroeconomic models; the channel was not considered a major potential source of shocks or of amplification of their effect. This lack of attention to the potential amplification effect from financial markets gave a false sense of comfort to policymakers early in the crisis.

In hindsight, another element of consensus was critical in determining the initially tepid policy reactions to the crisis. Inherited from the new classical school, the economics profession had converged toward the use of dynamic stochastic general equilibrium (DSGE) models as the workhorse model for economic analysis and simulations. These models had some attractive features, such as microfoundations (relationships based on the optimizing behavior of economic agents) and elegant mathematical properties that permitted the analysis of the impact of economic shocks on the economy. However, a side effect of these properties made these models unfit for what was coming: To function properly, they usually required that the economy return to equilibrium after a shock, regardless of the size of the shock. There was no hysteresis. This belief was a major determinant of the timid initial response when the crisis hit.

The inflation of the 1970s had created a school of economic thought that focused on beating inflation. In its models, the central bank's only worry was to lower inflation; for a generation of economists, the only experience was beating inflation down. Central banks had to be independent and never coordinate their actions with fiscal policy. Fiscal policy was a bad instrument to use during recessions, financial markets were not considered critical elements for understanding macroeconomic fluctuations, and the models used for policy analysis had a natural tendency to return to equilibrium after a shock. Monetary policy could do nothing to improve potential growth. These mental shackles were critical in designing the response to the crisis and delaying the adoption of the right policies.

Deflation and Zero Interest Rates? That's Such a Japanese Thing

Before the crisis the intellectual consensus on the risk of deflation and hitting the zero lower bound of interest rates, and how to deal with it, was based largely on the Japanese experience with QE. The theoretical research devoted to it was scarce. Paul Krugman (1998a) was one of the first to warn of the potential consequences of falling into a liquidity trap as a result of zero interest rates (for other early research on this issue, see Reifschneider and Williams 2000; Benhabib, Schmitt-Grohé, and Uribe 2001; and Eggertson and Woodford 2003). Bernanke showed how central bankers looked at the deflation risk from a distance.[1]

Studies of the BoJ experience suggested that its QE did not have a major impact beyond signaling that interest rates would remain at zero for a long time, for two reasons. First, the BoJ's asset purchases focused on short-term government bonds, which were very close substitutes for bank reserves and thus served solely to increase the quantity of money rather than reduce term premia (chapters 3 and 4 discuss the different channels of operation of asset purchases). Second, the BoJ leadership had not been very enthusiastic about the QE program, putting more emphasis on the moral hazard it created for fiscal consolidation and the need for structural reforms to lift potential growth. Presenting QE as temporary dampened its effect (see, e.g., Ugai 2007; Krugman 1998a, 2000; and Eggertsson and Woodford 2003).

After the 2000–01 recession, inflation in the United States and Europe declined to a bit below 2 percent. Its drop spurred more research and debate on how to deal with the risk of deflation. Alan Greenspan warned about the risk of "corrosive deflation." Ben Bernanke, Vincent Reinhart, and Brian Sack (2004) provided a guide on dealing with the risk of zero interest rates. The conclusion was that it would be better to avoid zero interest rates but that, if interest rates would fall that low, monetary policy would still have the tools to stimulate the economy.

The sentiment within the economics profession was that zero interest rates were mostly an intellectual curiosity that would materialize only following a policy mistake, as the Japanese situation was assessed to have been (see Bernanke 2000 and Ito and Mishkin 2006). In hindsight a key reason behind this assessment was the "curse of the Great Moderation": Because most economic research was based on the post–World War II period, when shocks were "small" and nonpersistent, all of the conclusions in the literature were limited to a specific subset of possible macroeconomic paths. This curse of the Great Moderation explains why, based on the economic projections performed with models estimated with data available through 2007, the crisis was deemed essentially "impossible" (what actually happened in 2008 was outside the probability distribution of possible paths generated by most models) and why the economics and central banking profession

---

1. Ben Bernanke, "Deflation: Making Sure 'It' Doesn't Happen Here," speech before the National Economists Club, Washington, November 21, 2002.

had to improvise as events unfolded.[2] It also explains why markets, lacking a model and a set of credible outlooks on which to base risk management, overshot to the downside while preparing for the worst possible scenario. Macroeconomic expectations became unanchored, compounded by the incentive structure of analysts and pundits, who looked wiser the gloomier they were and the more catastrophic the scenarios they could imagine. It had become clear that risk management failures had been a failure of imagination—of imagining a Lehman Brothers type of scenario. There was thus a premium on considering the implausible.

The policy prescription that arose from the precrisis literature was that, facing a scenario in which interest rates may have to be cut to zero, policy should be eased aggressively precisely to avoid getting to zero; interest rates should then be kept low for longer than a standard policy rule would suggest, in order to build enough cushion and avoid a relapse (see, e.g., Reinhart 2004). The underlying assumption was that monetary policy at zero interest rates, including QE, would be less efficient than standard interest rate policies and that its impact would be largely unknown (and, based on the Japanese experience, possibly very small). It was therefore better to avoid having to try it. This conclusion was the opposite of the suggestions to "keep the powder dry"—namely, delay cutting rates to avoid reaching zero—that would become part of the debate as the crisis unfolded and unduly delay the necessary easing.

The precrisis consensus had also abandoned the view that money growth was the main determinant of inflation. With the notable exception of the ECB, most central banks had stopped monitoring monetary aggregates as part of their evaluation of the inflation outlook—and even the ECB had downgraded its emphasis on money. Back in 1998 the ECB had adopted a two-pillar strategy to assess the inflation outlook. The first pillar focused on money developments; the second on economic developments. After a difficult period in the early 2000s—when the ECB had to devote a large amount of research to explain that the acceleration in money growth was not inflationary but the result of portfolio rebalancing that introduced instability in money demand—the ECB decided to change its strategy and downgrade the monetary pillar. It remains part of its formal framework of analysis but only as a second pillar to complement the economic analysis.

However, old ideas have lasting power. When, in 2007, the moment came to expand central bank balance sheets by large amounts, monetarism suddenly reappeared, even in the United States (see, e.g., the caution

---

2. See Simon Potter, "The Failure to Forecast the Great Recession," Liberty Street Economics (blog), November 25, 2011, libertystreeteconomics.newyorkfed.org/2011/11/the-failure-to-forecast-the-great-recession.html (accessed on March 28, 2017).

expressed in Bullard 2010), and worries about high inflation became a central part of the debate, with some apocalyptic warnings.[3]

Ironically, skepticism about QE came from both sides—from people who thought it might not work (based on the Japanese experience) and from people who thought it may work too well and generate rampant inflation (based on the monetarist view). This two-sided skepticism was central to explaining central bank actions during the crisis, as discussed below.

The European Obsession with Competitiveness and Reforms

Economic views in Europe had some idiosyncratic nuances. The consensus thinking had two additional anti-inflation characteristics. The first was a heightened sensitivity toward inflation, especially in Germany. The legacy of the hyperinflation of the early 1920s—when the value of the deutsche mark plummeted from 4.2 per dollar to 4.2 trillion per dollar—had left deep scars, reinforced by the view that, in the eyes of many Germans, the political upheaval created by the hyperinflation opened the door to Hitler's rise to power. The process of construction of the euro added to the sensitivity toward inflation.

Adopting the euro meant that Germany had to surrender monetary policy to the ECB, a new institution that lacked the strong anti-inflation credentials of the Bundesbank. The added fear that countries like Italy could take advantage of this new central bank to impose a higher inflation regime generated a strongly asymmetric view of inflation in the euro area. The ECB was created with the most independent statute in the world. Its independence was enshrined in the Maastricht Treaty and could be changed only by a unanimous decision of all countries, thereby giving veto power to Germany. But the treaty also explicitly forbade countries from engaging in monetary financing of government deficits. Later on this fear of fiscal dominance, of a situation in which governments could force central banks to finance their debts, became an additional political impediment to the adoption of a program of purchases of government bonds. The heightened sensitivity toward inflation materialized in the ECB's adoption of an asymmetric definition of price stability: below 2 percent. It was later revised to "close to, but below, 2 percent," but the asymmetry remained in the ambiguity and would become an important reason why the ECB tolerated a larger decline in inflation than other central banks.

---

3. See Cliff Asness et al., "Open Letter to Ben Bernanke," Real Time Economics (blog), *Wall Street Journal*, November 15, 2010, blogs.wsj.com/economics/2010/11/15/open-letter-to-ben-bernanke (accessed on March 28, 2017).

The second anti-inflationary element was rooted in the imperfect institutional framework of the euro area. Because the euro area was a monetary union with a common currency and monetary policy but national fiscal policies, which were constrained by the Stability and Growth Pact, an integral part of the intellectual consensus among euro area policymakers was the need to achieve internal convergence. A key element of this process of convergence was convergence in competitiveness indicators. Because euro area countries could not devalue within the monetary union, convergence was expected to be achieved through gains in productivity, containment of costs, and moderation of salary increases.

Convergence was expected to increase the synchronicity of the business cycles of the different euro area countries, reducing asymmetries and making the euro area a more perfect monetary union. However, the combination of German unification in the 1990s and the worldwide reduction in interest rates of the 2000s (amplified in the euro area by the common monetary policy, which generated a significant reduction in interest rates in euro area periphery countries) threw a curve ball to this objective of internal convergence. The process of German unification disrupted the synchronicity of the German economic cycle with the rest of the euro area. While the countries that would later join the euro languished economically in the 1990s, Germany experienced a postunification boom. Its housing market appreciated significantly and, because of the decision to convert the East German currency at parity with the deutsche mark, its cost structure appreciated significantly. In sum, Germany experienced a significant competitiveness loss when it joined the euro in 1998. As a result, its growth weakened in the 2000s while the rest of the euro area was booming. In fact, at the time Germany was called the sick man of Europe.

To address this competitiveness loss, Germany embarked on a process of competitive disinflation via wage moderation. At the same time, some euro area countries, such as Spain, Ireland, and Greece, experienced very strong growth and significantly higher inflation than Germany, as a result of the triple positive shock of low interest rates, strong capital inflows, and an initially weak exchange rate (the euro was launched at an exchange rate of 1.17 but rapidly depreciated to 0.87 to the dollar, forcing intervention by the ECB to arrest the decline). This inflation divergence raised alarms at the ECB, which worried that these widening inflation differentials posed a threat to internal convergence and therefore the stability of the monetary union. At Eurogroup meetings (the regular meetings of European finance ministers), Jean-Claude Trichet, the president of the ECB, used to display a set of charts and tables with measures of competitiveness (such as the evolution of wages, unit labor costs, or real effective exchange rates) of each of the euro area countries, highlighting the dangerous divergence that was taking place (Papaconstantinou 2016). This need to recover competitiveness via competitive disinflation and wage moderation became one of the main driving forces of economic thinking in the euro area once the crisis erupted. It added to the anti-inflation bias of the ECB's policy framework and higher tolerance for low inflation.

The sequence of events that led to the euro area crisis amplified this anti-inflation bias of European policymaking. The euro area was a club that was supposed to be built on trust, but trust was very weak. Rules (such as the complex web of rules of the Stability and Growth Pact) were pervasive because trust was thin. And there was a moral characterization of policies: Saving was good, borrowing was bad, "excessive" deficits were subject to sanctions. The fact that the euro area crisis started with an episode of misreporting of growth and fiscal data in Greece set the tone for the subsequent policy response. Very quickly the consensus narrative of the euro area crisis became a crisis of excessive public debt and deficits, compounded by the need to discipline untrustworthy governments. The worst fears of the German public—that the euro area would become a transfer union in which German savings went to bail out irresponsible Southern governments—were at risk of materializing. The concept of a transfer union was a loaded term in German politics, as it referred to the cost of unification (the transfers West Germany made to East Germany). This process was not to happen in the euro area. There could not be mutualization of the cost of solving the euro area crisis.

Sharp discipline was needed for the countries that had committed excesses, and monetary policy would quickly become the means to impose it. The ECB became part of the Troika (the group, composed of the IMF, the European governments, and the ECB, that managed the rescue packages for Cyprus, Greece, Ireland, Portugal, and Spain). During the early stages of the euro crisis, avoiding moral hazard and forcing reforms on countries became more important for the ECB than the achievement of price stability, and financial conditions were kept too tight. The subsequent collapse of inflation expectations, which put price stability at serious risk, was the result of this strategy. Ironically, the most independent central bank became the most politically driven central bank.

The Diabolical Politics of Rescue Programs

In his book on the financial crisis, *Stress Test*, former US Treasury Secretary Timothy Geithner (2014, 9) writes, "Uncertainty is at the heart of all financial crises. They do not end without governments assuming risks that private investors won't, taking catastrophe off the table." He is right. Over and over in history, financial crisis have been crises of confidence—about the ability of a country to repay its debt, about the ability of banks to meet withdrawals at the window. Lack of confidence morphs into panics and, before one knows it, the situation is out of control.

The solution, as Geithner argues, is simple: When the private sector panics, the public sector must step in and take the risk that the private sector does not want to take. The public sector must sell insurance on the future, calm the panickers and ensure that everything will be okay. The public sector is well placed to perform this role because, if the crisis is of confidence about the domestic banking sector, the government and the central bank have potentially unlimited amounts of money to deploy. They can credibly say that everything will be okay.

Of course, providing this assurance is easier said than done. Managing and solving a systemic banking crisis requires a complex set of decisions—about which banks are insolvent (and therefore need to be closed), which banks are solvent but illiquid (and therefore need to be rescued), and which banks may be insolvent but too big to unwind in an orderly fashion (and therefore need to be rescued as well). Nonperforming assets on the banks' balance sheets need to be dealt with, preferably by taking losses as early and credibly as possible, so that investors can have a good sense of the true value of the bank and recapitalization can proceed. A banking crisis generates losses; its management is essentially the process of deciding how to allocate them.

Doing so is a political minefield, because of two main objections to rescuing a bank. The first is that doing so is morally wrong. According to this view, the sinners must pay, period. The second objection is that bailing out banks creates moral hazard. If banks do not suffer the consequences of their mistakes, they will engage in the same behavior in the future. Because bailouts often implied expanding the fiscal deficit and issuing debt to finance them, very quickly the narrative became "privatizing profits, socializing losses."

These concerns are valid. But a decision to bail out a bank should not be based only on these concerns. If the bank in trouble is small and the economy is healthy, its failure will likely have little impact on the rest of the economy, and the moral view can prevail. But if the whole financial system is in trouble, the guiding principle must change. The question to ask is: What is the course of action that minimizes the cost in term of forgone GDP, in terms of welfare for citizens? If the problem is systemic enough, if it has metastasized through the economy, bailouts are likely to be a better solution for all citizens than allowing banks to fail on moral grounds. The objective must always be to protect the innocent, even if sometimes the troublemakers have to be rescued.

Politicians dislike bank rescues, because they are difficult to explain to voters. They therefore dither and load the burden on central banks. In the United States, the Fed had to find creative ways to lend to investment banks in trouble while the Congress sat idly by. When the Fed could not justify lending to Lehman for lack of collateral, it had to let it fail. But immediately afterward, it arranged the rescue of the insurer AIG, the collapse of which threatened to bring down the US financial system. After much dithering, and a dramatic first negative vote on September 29, 2008, that sent global equity markets down a cliff, on October 3, 2008, Congress finally approved the request to fund the Troubled Asset Relief Program (TARP). Tellingly, opponents of the TARP noted the lack of public support for bailing out banks and the potentially large size of the program.

In the end, TARP was a success. Although it ended up being used for something slightly different than originally planned—the original plan was to use the money to buy toxic assets, but Treasury secretary Henry Paulson soon changed the strategy, redirecting it toward bank recapitalization—it was a major contributor to arresting the loss of confidence in the US banking sector (as it was a credible backstop to the recapitalization of banks). It generated a small profit (about $15 billion) for the US taxpayer. One of the best-kept secrets of banking crises is that bank bailouts typically make money. If properly designed, governments buy at fire sale prices and sell at higher prices, after confidence has been restored.

In the euro area, the diabolical politics of rescue programs applied mostly to relationships across countries. As the ECB adopted its policy of unlimited provision of liquidity to all banks at its regular weekly auctions, this liquidity started to redistribute itself across euro area countries based on the characteristics of each country's banking system as well as market pressures. Banks in weak countries had to increase their reliance on ECB liquidity. Because the total amount of liquidity that a central bank creates cannot leave the system (unless it is converted into foreign currency), heavy borrowing from the ECB by some banks in debtor countries had its mirror image in large deposits at the ECB by some banks in creditor countries. To a large extent, this liquidity distribution mapped the relative economic performance of countries, especially of their external sectors. The result was large deposits by banks in Germany and large borrowing by banks in the periphery countries under stress. These flows were intermediated by the Target 2 system (the interbank payment system of the euro area). They became very large as the ECB pumped liquidity into the system (figure 2.1).

Germany's creditor balance accelerated rapidly. Very quickly these Target 2 flows became the source of political conflict. German politicians and academics started to point to these flows as a backdoor bailout of the ECB to the periphery countries that created a large potential liability

Figure 2.1 Target 2 balances in selected European countries, 1999–2016

billions of euros

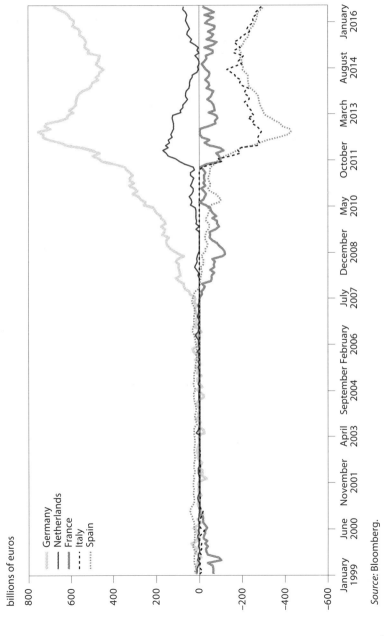

Source: Bloomberg.

for Germany if one of those countries were to default. This criticism was mostly theoretical and largely unfounded. The large creditor position of Germany in Target 2 largely reflected its current account surplus versus the rest of the euro area countries; Germany was at risk of losing money only if a country were to leave the euro and default on those loans. Moreover, these large inflows drastically reduced German interest rates, boosting German growth. But these facts did not matter. The ECB had become too juicy a target for German politicians; the campaign was very effective in initiating a negative narrative in Germany against the policies of the ECB that has only increased over time.

The ECB's decision to be part of the Troika in the rescue programs of the crisis countries added to the political dimension—and room for criticism—of monetary policy in the euro area. The Troika used the ECB's monopoly over liquidity provision to exert leverage over problem countries. Ratings downgrades implied that the debt of these countries was at risk of not being eligible as collateral for the ECB's open market operations unless the troubled countries agreed to a rescue program. The ECB justified its actions as prudent risk management: It could not continue to accept as collateral assets at serious risk of default. From the point of view of the affected countries, however, its decision was tantamount to blackmail, as the risk of being cut off from the ECB's liquidity contributed to the risk of default. The fact that banks from core countries, especially Germany, unloaded a large part of their holdings of periphery bonds before the Troika's decision to restructure Greece's debt added to the controversy. The result was heightened political criticism of the ECB and its policies—in Germany because the ECB was doing too much to help the crisis countries, in the crisis countries because it was not doing enough.

Lean versus Clean—or How the Deep Origin of the Crisis Lies in a Bathtub

An important element of the precrisis consensus dates back to a bathtub in Washington, DC during late 1996. The effect of Alan Greenspan's famous "irrational exuberance" speech, concocted during one of his morning baths, was the opposite of what he had intended. Greenspan wanted to warn markets that equity valuations were becoming frothy, hoping to slow their appreciation. In his address at the annual gala of the American Enterprise Institute, he wondered: "How do we know when irrational exuberance has unduly escalated asset values?" Markets ignored his warning; after a brief blip, they continued to roar forward.

The Dow reached 6,000 in mid-October 1996. Greenspan gave his speech in early December; by January 1997 the Dow was at 7,000. Rate increases did little to slow the stock market, cementing Greenspan's view that monetary policy was not the instrument for dealing with potential financial market excesses.

In fact, according to his thinking, it could be counterproductive. Interest rates are too coarse an instrument to affect financial markets; unless the central bank is ready to act aggressively and trigger a recession, small moves in interest rates intended to slow asset prices run the risk of failing and negatively affecting the credibility of the central bank. Additionally, at times of rapid technological change, it is difficult to tell whether markets are properly valuing assets. Central banks have no advantage over markets in distinguishing true technological progress from asset bubbles. They can make mistakes and create unnecessary recessions, stifling innovation along the way. With these concerns in mind, most central banks decided that rather than leaning against financial markets, it was better to be ready to clean up after the fact. Monetary policy should focus on price stability; regulatory and supervisory policies should deal with financial stability risks.

The "clean" view was validated, to some extent, by the aftermath of the burst of the Nasdaq bubble in 2000. The stock market suffered severe losses, but the economic impact was small. In fact, the recession of 2001 is one of the shortest and mildest in postwar US history. To a large extent, irrational exuberance had been harmless.

This assessment was not shared elsewhere. From a quiet town in Switzerland, the "lean" view was gathering support. Economists at the Bank for International Settlements (BIS), in Basel, were worried that rapid credit growth was becoming a major economic risk. Household debt was increasing briskly, and annual housing price appreciation was approaching double digits in several countries. Global interest rates were low, the result of a combination of low inflation that was keeping short-term interest rates low and a steady increase in savings in emerging markets, as they accumulated foreign exchange reserves to better manage their currencies. Ben Bernanke called this phenomenon the "global savings glut." These excess savings were being invested mostly in developed countries' government bonds, reducing long-term interest rates, creating what Greenspan called the "conundrum" of low long-term interest rates: The Fed and other central banks were gradually raising rates in an attempt to tighten monetary conditions, but long-term rates refused to respond. The result was a growing concern about global imbalances, with the US current account deficit ballooning to a peak of 6 percent of GDP in 2006 while the current accounts of China and commodity-producing countries increased steadily and their holdings of foreign exchange reserves reached record highs. Worries about a US dollar crisis became widespread. In the "lean" view, the Fed's focus on low inflation and disregard for financial stability were partly responsible; monetary policy should lean against the wind of financial risks and tighten policy beyond what would be necessary to achieve price stability. Prevention was better than the cure.

In 2005 Raghuram Rajan, at the time chief economist of the IMF, gave what perhaps was the most articulated version of the "lean" view, in a speech at the annual conference of the Federal Reserve Bank of Kansas City in Jackson Hole, Wyoming. His main point was that a combination of technology, deregulation, and low interest rates could be creating a situation in which, although the number and diversity of financial market participants able to absorb risks had increased, the financial risks that were being created were increasing as well. Combined with a higher correlation of behaviors induced by competition, these factors could increase the probability of a catastrophic meltdown. Rajan worried that low interest rates could be creating perverse incentives among financial market participants and that central banks should therefore balance these costs against the benefits of avoiding deflation. However, he stopped short of advising a material tightening of monetary policy. He had an intuition but not a practical strategy for how monetary policy should respond to it.[4]

During this time, financial markets were developing at breakneck speed. The strong demand for risk-free assets generated by the rapid accumulation of foreign exchange reserves in emerging markets and the widespread development of private pension schemes met the dearth of issuance of government bonds, as fiscal deficits across the world were declining. How times have changed. Only a decade ago central banks were debating how to run monetary policy without a deep and liquid market for government bonds (see, e.g., Wheelock 2002). The relative scarcity of government bonds, of public risk-free assets, led to the development of private risk-free assets. Government bonds are considered risk free because of the taxing capacity of the government and the backstop role played by the central bank. To create private risk-free assets, financial engineering was needed. One could create assets divided into tranches; tranches with the highest priority were considered risk free, tranches at the bottom of the priority scale were considered risky. Thus were created credit derivatives, initially promoted in the US mortgage market to facilitate the securitization of mortgages guaranteed by Fannie Mae and Freddie Mac (and in some European countries to facilitate the liquidity management of mortgages issued by their savings banks). Increasingly complex and sophisticated credit derivatives were soon available for all types of assets.

---

4. During the question and answer session at the conference, he was heavily criticized—even called a Luddite—for what some people in the audience interpreted as a critique of financial innovation.

The "clean" view saw this rapid development of derivatives as a positive development, because it contributed to financial market deepening, the diversification of risks, and market monitoring. The "lean" camp was less sanguine, worrying about rapid credit growth, greater complexity and opacity, and a deterioration in credit quality.

When the financial crisis erupted, the "lean" view felt vindicated. Never mind that the main event that the "lean" view had forecast—a collapse of the dollar as a result of the growing global imbalance and the large US current account deficit—never happened. Never mind that in its 2007 annual report, the BIS worried about the low saving rate in the United States and the high investment rate in China as the main sources of risks, only to then wonder in its 2008 report "how could problems with subprime mortgages, being such a small sector of global financial markets, provoke such a dislocation?" (BIS 2008, 3). The "lean" view just connected the dots and concluded that low interest rates and easy monetary policy were dangerous and created financial risks and that financial development and derivatives were sources of instability.

This narrative would become an integral part of the crisis policy framework: It is fine to cut rates, but always be mindful of potential financial stability risks. It created a schizophrenic environment. The main channel of transmission of many of the monetary policies implemented during the crisis was to encourage the private sector to take more risk, but policymakers were constantly cautioning against the risks of higher inflation and financial risk taking and engaged in a widespread process of financial sector regulatory tightening to limit the risky activities of financial market participants. It was like pushing and pulling at the same time. No wonder the public was confused.

Bayesian Inference Meets Politicians in a Rush—and Austerity Is Born

When your only tool is a hammer, everything looks like a nail. People's attitudes toward an issue depends on their preconceptions; no one starts with a clean slate. The British statistician Thomas Bayes conceptualized the way people form beliefs. The concept he developed—Bayesian inference—implies that how one reacts to new evidence depends not just on what the evidence shows, but on how much one believed the initial hypothesis to begin with. If people believe that all the balls in an urn are red and they draw a red ball, their belief in their theory increases, although the red ball that was drawn may actually be the only red ball in the urn. People have a set of "prior beliefs." After an event occurs, they update their degree of belief in different theories, generating "posterior probabilities." The priors describe the beliefs before the event occurs, the posteriors describe the beliefs after the event occurs. They then become the new priors.

Now imagine one's economic priors are based on the German ordoliberalism doctrine. Under this doctrine the role of the state is just to provide a framework for markets to operate. A combination of effective regulation and budgetary discipline generates a framework of order and stability in which the private sector can thrive. State intervention is permitted to make markets possible but not to offset their undesirable consequences. Crises happen because of policy failures generated by excessive government action or large fiscal deficits. Discipline is paramount. Discipline bolsters confidence for the private sector to invest, create jobs, and boost growth. When a crisis occurs, fiscal discipline is key to restoring confidence. Fiscal support for the economy only precludes the necessary adjustment from happening, delaying resolution of the problems. Fiscal discipline, combined with structural reforms to enhance the operations of the private sector, solves the crisis.

These ordoliberal priors are the source of the European policy framework, which comprises an independent central bank, rules to ensure fiscal discipline, and an obsessive focus on structural reforms. When European policymakers discovered the large fraud in the Greek public deficits, they saw a fiscal crisis in an uncompetitive economy creating a financial crisis and putting the euro area at risk. At that point Bayesian inference kicked in: The degree of belief in the ordoliberal priors increased, as this new evidence confirmed that fiscal profligacy and lack of competitiveness created crises. The politics of austerity were thus born: A package of fiscal adjustment and reforms was needed to solve the crisis. Never mind the depth of the recession or the lack of an exchange rate to cushion its impact via depreciation. Fiscal adjustment and structural reforms, the ordoliberal package, would boost confidence and restore growth.

The impact of the Greek events on the mindset of policymakers across the globe cannot be stressed enough. Not becoming Greece became the rallying cry of politicians across the political spectrum. Deficits and debt were bad, period. For conservative governments keen on reducing the size of government, it was political manna from heaven. In the United Kingdom, the Conservative government presented a very aggressive program of fiscal consolidation, with the tacit approval of the BoE. In the United States, the Tea Party faction of the Republican Party saw the opportunity to advance its small government program, unleashing a sharp fiscal tightening that greatly complicated efforts by the Federal Reserve to boost growth and inflation. The brief period of Keynesianism that followed the G-20-coordinated fiscal stimulus of 2009 died with the discovery of the Greek fiscal fraud. Research by Carmen Reinhart and Kenneth Rogoff

(2009) suggesting that debt ratios above 90 percent of GDP were a recipe for a fiscal crisis provided the mental anchor for the fiscal adjustment movement. Never mind that Reinhart and Rogoff's research was shown to have errors and that the evidence only partly supported their conclusions. The damage was done. It made little economic sense to engage in fiscal adjustment in the middle of a severe economic contraction, with the euro area entering a deep existential crisis. But the priors were very strong, and the evidence was confirming them. Growth was not going to be enough to reduce debt levels. Fiscal austerity, spending cuts, and tax increases were needed.

Politicians were in a hurry to find a narrative to navigate the crisis, and the fiscal adjustment strategy provided it. It could be explained in simple terms that the general public could understand—the government should behave like a prudent household and not spend more than it earns—even if the economics of this analogy were wrong. Simple trumped accurate. The message was clear: To restore confidence, adjustment was needed. The political reputational risk of any government that failed to follow this strategy was very high. The power of peer pressure among policymakers and politicians is enormous.

Alberto Alesina, one of the fathers of the research on expansionary fiscal contractions, was invited to give a presentation to the Ecofin meeting in Madrid in April 2010. His conclusion was clear: Fiscal adjustment was needed, the more "credible" the better. "Credible" was code for a large and frontloaded adjustment. The composition of the adjustment was critical: His research showed that permanent spending cuts, especially in government payrolls and social safety nets, were more credible and effective than tax hikes. These conclusions gave academic credentials to the political strategy, completing the process of Bayesian updating for policymakers. Austerity was going to deliver growth. This language was adopted by the Ecofin, the ECB, the UK Treasury, and eventually the G20 at its June 2010 meeting in Toronto, which called for "countries to put in place credible, properly phased and growth-friendly plans to deliver fiscal sustainability" (see the in-depth discussion in Blyth 2013). "Growth-friendly fiscal adjustment" became the political version of the expansionary fiscal contraction doctrine. Little attention was paid to the fact that most of the case studies supporting the expansionary fiscal contraction thesis had featured large exchange rate depreciations, which are a form of expansionary monetary policy. Despite the weakness of the global economy, and the existential crisis in the euro area, a program of global fiscal adjustment was put in place that lasted until 2014. Bayesian inference made monetary policy the only game in town.

Markets and the Crisis: In Search of Analogues

While policymakers were dealing with their demons of preventing inflation, avoiding risk taking, and consolidating the public finances, markets were trying to figure out how to navigate uncharted waters. The 2007 crisis was a systemic banking crisis that risked toppling the global financial system and triggering a Great Depression. Monetary policy had become unpredictable, public debt levels were rising rapidly. The euro area crisis had the potential to unravel the euro, with consequences that no one could imagine. Because there was no roadmap for the effects of the bankruptcy of a major investment bank, no collective memory in markets of the dynamics of the Great Depression, and no precedent for the unpacking of a monetary union of the size and complexity of the euro area, markets were at a loss. Knightian uncertainty took over and amplified the impact of the shocks that were hitting global markets. Scenarios of potential losses in global banking sectors flowered everywhere, with ever larger numbers but very little confidence in the scenarios. Measures of the size of the needed rescue packages for euro area countries grew by the day. At the same time, Congress did not want to authorize enough money to buy nonperforming assets and clean up the balance sheets of US banks. Euro area policymakers were building new institutions as the problems arose. The firehouse was being built as the fire was raging, and the sense of despair in markets was growing.

Markets lacked direction. They had no framework to think about the future, making the pricing of financial assets and the transmission of the monetary policy actions difficult. Markets were used to the Greenspan put, the belief that central banks, especially the Fed, would always be able to come to the rescue. But reality crashed in. Markets realized that, this time, they had to take matters into their own hands.

Markets like analogues. They find comfort in exploring similar situations from the past as a guide for the future. They prefer case studies that can narrow the specifics of a problem to a situation already lived in the past to econometric regressions that average over long periods of time and different scenarios. If they cannot find analogues, they create them.

Ray Dalio, manager of Bridgewater, one of the largest hedge funds, compiled a sequence of news events and market prices from the period of the Great Depression and conducted exercises in which he was fed news and market prices from that period and traded against them. He wanted to experience the Great Depression, the reaction of markets and news to the events of that era, to be able to better understand the Great Recession.

Other hedge funds went even farther. In a castle on the outskirts of Paris, a group of traders, academics, and former policymakers gathered in 2011 to play a war game of the euro area crisis. The range of actors involved—

the IMF, the ECB, debtor and creditor countries, domestic banks, and inves- tors—was too large and complex for mathematical models. The interactions among them were impossible to predict and, more importantly, lacked a good historical precedent. A war game was created to generate analogues, profiles of market action and reaction that could serve as a guide for future events.

At research houses around the world, analysts were busy compiling tables ranking the euro area countries by degrees of vulnerability. Markets were scrambling for information after a decade of paying no attention to the macroeconomic details of individual euro area countries (they were all now part of the euro, so national differences were supposed to matter little; sectoral differences inside the euro area were supposed to be more relevant). Markets were scrambling for information, and these tables had a profound anchoring effect. The countries rated most vulnerable became the targets of financial markets. These tables were the new anchor, the new framework of reference that guided investor behavior. Based on public and external deficits and debt ratios, the ranking was soon clear: Greece, Ireland, Portugal, Spain, and Italy. The PIIGS (Portugal, Italy, Ireland, Greece, and Spain) were born.

They were the countries that could be at risk of needing a bailout, the next domino to fail. Fairly or unfairly, these countries became the center of attention. When euro area policymakers started to discuss the possi- bility of debt restructuring as a condition for bailouts, traders started to price the bonds of these countries as credit, not bonds. The prices of these bonds became a function of expected default probabilities, not expected nominal GDP growth. Rating agencies responded to the menace of debt restructurings by downgrading the bonds of these countries. With the ECB firmly opposed to QE, bond yields among the PIIGS skyrocketed, sharply tightening financial conditions in these countries and, as a result, in the euro area.

I Wouldn't Start from Here

Policymakers arrived at the crisis worrying about inflation, debt, defi- cits, moral hazard, and excessive financial risks. Markets quickly shifted to worry about recession, deflation, and defaults. Despite the rapid and unprecedented expansion of central bank balance sheets, financial markets never expected inflation much above 2 percent, let alone runaway infla- tion. Despite the overall increase in fiscal deficits and public debt, markets priced meaningful probabilities of default only in countries that were explicitly threatened by the Troika with debt restructuring as a condition for rescue packages. In the biggest irony for the deficit worriers, when the

United States lost its AAA rating, bond yields declined, not increased, as bond markets worried about the potential implications for growth, not the potential probability of default.

When Congress threatened not to extend the debt ceiling, bond yields also declined: Only the yield of very short-term bills, which could be directly affected by a suspension in debt service, rose. Politicians, policymakers, and pundits were arguing over the inflationary, financial stability, and moral hazard potential of their actions while markets were looking in the opposite direction, worried about not enough growth and not enough inflation.

Politicians and policymakers were worried about taking too much risk. In doing so, they did not take enough, and made the recovery riskier and more fragile. This is the paradox of risk.

3

The Great Experiment in Monetary Policy: Central Bank Actions since 2007

Do or do not. There is no try.

—Yoda

On the morning of August 9, 2007, three investment funds managed by BNP Paribas temporarily suspended redemptions, blaming a "complete evaporation of liquidity in certain segments of the United States securitization market."[1] The interest rate banks charged one another in interbank markets spiked, and bank funding markets panicked.

The next day the ECB decided to inject €95 billion into the system—at the time the largest-ever liquidity injection, greater than the €69 billion injected after the 9/11 terrorist attacks. It also made the unprecedented pledge to fully meet all funding requests of all financial institutions. This pledge had a validity of one day.

Little did the ECB know that, with that decision, it started the great experiment in monetary policy that the world has been witnessing since 2007. A liquidity injection of €95 billion looked enormous then; some commentators, and even colleagues at other central banks, criticized the ECB for panicking and exaggerating. Compared with the dozens of trillions of dollars central banks have since injected into financial markets, €95 billion now looks like a rounding error. The pledge for one day of unlimited liquidity provisions soon became permanent: Except for a few brief intervals, the ECB has continued to provide unlimited liquidity to European banks until today.

---

1. Anuj Gangahar, "BNP Paribas Investment Funds Hit by Volatility," *Financial Times*, August 9, 2007, www.ft.com/content/9a4cabc4-464d-11dc-a3be-0000779fd2ac#axzz4DdH1S4r2 (accessed on March 29, 2017).

Conventional versus Unconventional Monetary Policy

The period since 2007 can be described as the great experiment in monetary policy. In normal times, when interest rates are above zero and financial intermediation operates via well-functioning arbitrage, what is now called "conventional" operation of monetary policy involved managing the short-term nominal interest rate. Because inflation expectations do not immediately react one to one to changes in interest rates, by moving the nominal interest rate central banks also control the real interest rate. Via arbitrage in financial markets, these interest rate changes would be expected to be transmitted along the yield curve and into private interest rates. This process would achieve a constellation of real interest rates that would, in principle, deliver the central bank's growth and inflation forecast via its impact on credit, asset prices, and the exchange rate. All that was needed was to change the short-term policy interest rate. Monetary policy was easy before 2007.

The crisis shattered this operational framework of monetary policy, in several ways. First, short-term interest rates reached zero, depriving the central bank of its main instrument. Second, the transmission of short-term interest rate changes along the yield curve and into private rates was disrupted. Some markets just ceased to operate. Others, critical as providers of collateral for lending operations, changed their nature and became informationally sensitive. This was particularly acute in the market for asset-backed securities (ABS). Before the crisis, investors in ABS thought that there was no need to evaluate the quality of the ABS's individual components. Ratings on the ABS were enough to make investment decisions; ABS were thus informationally insensitive. All of a sudden, these assets became suspect, and the quality of their components had to be evaluated one by one. They had become informationally sensitive, and their role as collateral severely damaged. Third, Knightian uncertainty increased sharply. The lack of understanding of why the crisis was so deep and wide ranging, and the absence of a credible model on which to base economic forecasts, generated extreme risk aversion. Fourth, mistrust about the solvency of banking intermediaries became widespread, introducing counterparty risk as a main element of asset pricing. Suddenly assets had to be valued based not just on the discounted stream of future earnings but also on the soundness of the bank that intermediated them. The combination of these changes created a vicious circle of declining asset prices and forced liquidations that had to be arrested.[2]

The policy response had to address all four failures of the system. It had to find an alternative instrument to the short-term interest rate; fix the transmission mechanism of interest rates, mostly via liquidity injec-

---

2. See Ubide (2008) for a detailed discussion of the dynamics of a credit crisis.

tions, and create markets in some assets; restore confidence in the future by providing insurance and minimizing the occurrence of bad equilibria; and restore the solvency of the banking system to eliminate counterparty risk.[3]

To address these failures, at some stage most major central banks introduced what were initially called "unconventional" measures. The term "unconventional" arose because there was a strong conviction that the crisis would be temporary and that monetary policy would soon return to its "conventional" mode of just changing the short-term interest rate. That assumption was unrealistically optimistic; a decade later most of the unconventional measures are still in place.

The Fed, the ECB, and the BoE were at the center of the crisis. They acted to address the four failures of the system. The BoJ already had many of these policies in place, having been at the zero bound for a long time; it kept its policy framework mostly unchanged until mid-2013, when it launched quantitative and qualitative easing (QQE). Other central banks had to act along some of these dimensions. Denmark had a brief period of negative interest rates to contain large capital inflows resulting from fears of a euro breakup. The Swiss National Bank cut rates to negative levels and shifted to an exchange rate floor supported by heavy interventions in the foreign exchange market. The Bank of Canada (BoC) was a pioneer in forward guidance.

Multiple attempts to declare mission accomplished failed. In the end all G-10 central banks that hiked rates after 2010 had to reverse course and ease policy. Some of them are still doing so.

This chapter describes the main monetary policy decisions and the commonalities and differences across them. Appendix A shows the chronology and nature of the measures undertaken by the main central banks, distinguishing between actions affecting quantities, interest rates, and guidance.

How to Do Monetary Policy? Goals, Tools, Strategies, and Communication

Conceptually, the policy framework of a central bank has four main components:

- the policy goals and the time frame to achieve them (e.g., an inflation rate of 2 percent over two years)
- the tools to achieve the goals (e.g., short-term interest rates, asset purchases, foreign exchange intervention)

---

3. Restoring the solvency of the banking system was mostly a government policy. It is not discussed here.

- the strategy for using the tools (e.g., a policy rule linking the short-term interest rate to the outlook for inflation)
- the communication methods to explain the strategy to the public (e.g., statements describing the decisions, minutes explaining the decisions, forecasts documenting the central bank view of the economic outlook).

Changes in monetary policy since 2007 have affected all four components. Most central banks have updated or clarified their policy goals. They have used new tools, such as large-scale asset purchases, liquidity facilities, and negative interest rates. They have revamped or improved strategies, with a very strong emphasis on forward guidance. And they have expanded communication, in order to improve the public's understanding of the workings of monetary policy.

Policy Goals: Is Clarifying Price Stability Enough?

All major central banks except the ECB clarified or changed their policy goals since 2007 in the direction of strengthening the symmetry of their objectives and improving their ability to overcome deflation. At its most basic level, inflation depends on two main factors: the amount of slack in the economy (the more slack, the stronger the disinflationary pressures and vice versa) and inflation expectations. Over the last decades, the effect of slack on inflation has diminished (in technical terms, the Phillips curve has flattened), and the role of expectations increased.

A strongly held view among economists is that strong anchoring of inflation expectations at the target level is the key instrument in the fight against deflation: If everyone believes that inflation will be positive in the future, people will behave today in a way that ensures that inflation will remain positive (e.g., by demanding wage increases proportional to the target inflation level). If expectations about future inflation were to become unhinged, that would change people's behavior today. For example, if people believe that prices will decline in the future, they will postpone their purchases, which will suppress demand and lower prices today, generating deflation. A condition for a strong anchoring of inflation expectations around the target is that the target be well defined and clearly communicated. Clarifying and strengthening the resolve to avoid deflation is therefore an important step in ensuring price stability.

The Fed entered the crisis without a numerical definition of price stability that could help anchor inflation expectations. Under Alan Greenspan it had been very reluctant to specify an inflation objective, mostly to avoid losing flexibility in monetary policy. Greenspan was a believer in risk management in monetary policy; he believed that a careful assessment of costs and benefits was necessary before policy changes. An explicit inflation objective could interfere with this risk management approach. He preferred to define price stability as a level of inflation that does not affect the behavior of economic agents. Speeches and testimonies implied that the Fed interpreted price stability as an inflation level of about 2 percent, but uncertainty remained.

Ben Bernanke had a different view of monetary policy. During his academic career, he was a strong advocate of inflation targeting and believed that a clear and transparent inflation objective was important at all times, particularly when there was a risk of deflation. During his chairmanship he pushed the Fed to clarify its objectives and policy strategy.

Doing so was not easy. Because of its dual mandate from Congress, which specifies both maximum employment and price stability as policy objectives, the Fed could not adopt a numerical inflation target as its exclusive goal. But it also could not adopt an employment target, as the maximum level of employment that can be sustained over the longer run is determined primarily by factors—such as demographics, labor market institutions, and technology—that the central bank does not control. There was also no agreement on the numerical target, with some members favoring 2 percent and others favoring 1.5 percent or even lower.

In the end Bernanke prevailed: In January 2012 the FOMC agreed to a statement that defines price stability as an annual change of inflation (measured by the personal consumption expenditures [PCE] deflator) of 2 percent over the long run (Federal Reserve Board 2012). The employment side of the mandate is described as an objective that will evolve over time and be updated quarterly with the publication of the *Summary of Economic Projections*. The FOMC further added that it would take a balanced approach in mitigating deviations of inflation and employment from its objectives, taking into account the magnitude of the deviations and the potentially different time horizons over which employment and inflation are projected to return to levels judged consistent with its mandate.[4] The FOMC committed to reaffirming and updating these principles every January. In January 2016 it specified that the 2 percent inflation objective is symmetric and that the FOMC would be concerned "if inflation were running persistently above or below this objective" (Federal Reserve Board 2016a). Over this period the Fed thus adopted a numerical inflation objective, described a balanced approach to meet its dual mandate, and specified the symmetry of its inflation objective.

The BoJ had long been clarifying the meaning of price stability. In March 2006 it introduced its "understanding of medium- to long-term

---

4. In technical terms, the FOMC decided that the lambda (the ratio of the speed of closing of the output gap and of the inflation gap) would be time varying.

price stability," which defined an approximate range of 0–2 percent, with a median level of 1 percent. In December 2009 it changed this definition by stating that "the understanding fell in a positive range of 2 percent or lower" and that "the BoJ did not tolerate" an annual inflation rate equal to or below zero percent.[5] This understanding was defined as the aggregation of the views of the BoJ board members and therefore subject to change. In February 2012 the BoJ decided to introduce the "price-stability goal in the medium to long term," defined as inflation in a positive range of 2 percent or lower, and set a goal at 1 percent "for the time being." This goal became the inflation objective the BoJ aimed to achieve, no longer just an "understanding." On April 4, 2013, the BoJ further revised its definition of price stability, declaring that it would aim to achieve a target of 2 percent annual inflation at the earliest possible time, with a time horizon of about two years. It took almost a decade for the BoJ to finally adopt a 2 percent inflation objective, similar to the rest of the developed world.[6]

Part of the reason for this very slow progress toward a 2 percent target was plausibility. When inflation was running below zero, the BoJ did not want to set an inflation target that could be seen as unrealistic. There was also a gradualism motive. After many years of zero or negative inflation, the BoJ was concerned about the behavior of households and economic agents if the inflation objective changed too abruptly. This gradualism also reflected the lack of desire to do what it took to achieve the target, as shown below.

The BoE adopted an inflation-targeting regime in 1997. Its mandate is described in its remit, which the Treasury must update at least once a year but can modify at any time. The remit defines the objective of price stability as an annual inflation target of 2 percent. This target applies at all times. The BoE's remit incorporated an implicit dual mandate as it gave the BoE the mandate to support the economic policies of the government subject to price stability. This gave the BoE a degree of constrained discretion in the speed at which to return inflation to the target (Bean 1998). The remit was revamped in March 2013 with the objective of providing additional political backing to the BoE's discretion and boosting the economic recovery (Osborne 2013). It clarified that, faced with a large negative shock to growth,

---

5. This more aggressive antideflation stance was accompanied, however, by an explicit warning against the possible accumulation of financial imbalances.

6. Bank of Japan, "The Introduction of a New Framework for the Conduct of Monetary Policy," March 9, 2006, www.boj.or.jp/en/announcements/release_2006/k060309b.htm; "Clarification of the 'Understanding of Medium- to Long-Term Price Stability,'" December 18, 2009, www.boj.or.jp/en/announcements/release_2009/un0912c.pdf; "The Price Stability Goal in the Medium to Long Term," February 14, 2012, www.boj.or.jp/en/announcements/release_2012/k120214b.pdf; and "Introduction of the 'Quantitative and Qualitative Monetary Easing,'" April 4, 2013, www.boj.or.jp/en/announcements/release_2013/k130404a.pdf.

the BoE should provide more information about the tradeoffs inherent in setting monetary policy to meet the 2 percent inflation target. De facto the Treasury told the BoE that it could prioritize growth in the short run and delay the return to the inflation target in order to avoid undue output volatility and a deeper economic contraction. The Treasury suggested the use of intermediate thresholds and explicit forward guidance and asked the BoE to provide an assessment in its August 2013 *Inflation Report* (BoE 2013). The BoE announced that interest rates would remain unchanged until the unemployment rate fell below a new policy threshold of 7 percent, with two explicit additional conditions that, if broken, would invalidate the threshold[7]: Annual inflation would be forecast to be 2.5 percent or below 18–24 months out, and inflation expectations would remain well anchored. There was also an implicit financial stability condition: The newly created Financial Policy Committee (FPC) agreed to alert the Monetary Policy Committee (MPC) of potential threats to financial stability arising from the monetary policy stance. Although the thresholds "expired" after they were met, the spirit of the new remit persisted, at the margin softening the infla-tion-targeting regime and providing more flexibility to the BoE to return to the inflation target after a large shock. This change in the remit moved the BoE de facto closer to the Fed's dual mandate.

The ECB is the only major central bank that did not explicitly update its mandate during the crisis. It defines price stability as a year-on-year increase in the harmonized index of consumer prices (HICP) of less than 2 percent.[8] Because the definition contains the word *increase*, it explicitly rules out negative inflation. The ECB's governing council further clarified the mandate as aiming to maintain inflation rates below, but close to, 2 percent over the medium term. The lack of a precise point target opens the door to divergent interpretations by different ECB board members, with some interpreting the definition as a symmetric inflation target of just below 2 percent and others interpreting it as a more hawkish 1–1.5 percent. This ambiguity results from divergent political interests across euro area countries. It arguably increased the threshold for the ECB to undertake QE and dented the effectiveness of its efforts to restore price stability. As argued above, if it is not clear what the objective is, markets and economic agents have a harder time internalizing it in their daily lives. I have proposed that the ECB move closer to best practices, changing its definition of price stability to a symmetric 2 percent, in order to support its efforts to restore inflation back to that level (Ubide 2014).

---

7. The BoE called these conditions "knock-outs."

8. See European Central Bank, "The Definition of Price Stability," www.ecb.europa.eu/ mopo/strategy/pricestab/html/index.en.html (accessed on March 29, 2017).

All of the changes undertaken during this period move in the direction of a more precise definition of price stability (numerical and symmetric) and a balanced approach to achieving price stability and sustainable growth, whether de jure (as in the Fed's dual mandate) or de facto (as in the BoE's flexible inflation-targeting regime). Chapter 5 highlights the importance of doing so.

Policy Tools

When the Unconventional Is Conventional

When central banks reached the zero lower bound of interest rates and started buying assets, monetary policy measures were described as "unconventional." This name was more aspirational than accurate, because it revealed the hope that short-term interest rates would soon return to positive territory and asset purchases would be a very temporary phenomenon. The term was not accurate, as purchases and sales of assets have always been an integral part of monetary policy.

Central banks operate at all times by changing the monetary base (currency and bank reserves) to affect some interest rate.[9,10] There is therefore nothing unconventional about changes to central banks' balance sheets. They can affect interest rates in two ways: by buying from and selling bonds to the public or by borrowing from and lending money to the public. The difference between these two options is a time dimension: Buying and selling make the impact more "permanent," whereas lending and borrowing make the impact more "transitory" (the two types of actions can be made equivalent by choosing the appropriate time horizons and techniques).

When short-term interest rates are positive, monetary policy operates via changes in the short-term interest rate, which shifts the term structure of real interest rates. These changes in real interest rates affect the economy via two main channels: asset prices and credit conditions. The asset price channel is well understood: Changes in real interest rates shift asset prices and affect investment and consumption decisions. The credit channel assumes that changes in real interest rates affect some financial frictions, such as adverse selection (the fact that people who are more willing to borrow are typically lower-quality borrowers), that influence borrowing and lending decisions. This adverse selection effect is more pervasive during downturns,

9. Central banks often operate mostly via the threat of intervention to change the monetary base. For example, the Fed's intervention in the fed funds market was minimal, because the market adjusted to the Fed's target, allowing the Fed to intervene only to smooth deviations from the target.

10. Central banks with surplus liquidity can also directly change the interest rate they pay on central bank reserves.

as "good" borrowers become more risk averse and borrow less while "bad" borrowers gamble for resurrection. Banks are cognizant of this worsening of the pool of borrowers during downturns and become more reluctant to lend, exacerbating the slowdown. By easing financial conditions and raising asset price levels, central banks can improve the solvency of borrowers and reduce these frictions, softening the tightening of lending standards.[11] When interest rates are positive, monetary policy can thus affect both asset valuations and attitudes toward risk.

When short-term interest rates reach zero, monetary policy has to operate via direct changes in longer-term interest rates. This adds an extra dimension, because real long-term interest rates are a combination of average expected short-term rates, the term premium, and expected inflation. "Unconventional policies" (both asset purchases and forward guidance) operate by affecting some or all of these elements. Changes to the policy reaction function, via either explicit forward guidance or the signaling effect of asset purchases, affect expected short-term rates. The scarcity and duration effect of asset purchases is the biggest determinant of term premia, although forward guidance can contribute, via its impact on reducing term premia at the front end of the yield curve.[12] The overall message that monetary policy offers, including asset purchases, guidance, and commitment to achieve the monetary policy goals, affects inflation expectations. Conventional policies are thus just a special case of unconventional policies, with one exception: When arbitrage and market functioning are disrupted, asset purchases and lending facilities are deployed to fix the disruption regardless of the level of short-term interest rates.

Conceptual Debate on Asset Purchases

Although there was nothing unconventional about them, asset purchases were a big novelty when they were introduced. For some investors and analysts, they brought to mind the fears of monetary financing and hyper-inflation that had wrought havoc in some economies in the past. The lack of practical experience with large asset purchases added to the angst, as there was no template, or empirical evidence, that could serve as a guide. Learning by doing became the only possible strategy.

Conceptually, asset purchases have two effects: a quantity effect (whereby the central bank expands its balance sheet by creating money) and

---

11. See the seminal paper by Bernanke and Gertler (1995) and the analysis by Ciccarelli, Maddaloni, and Peydró (2010) on the impact of the bank lending channel in the euro area.

12. A growing body of literature argues that conventional monetary policy also affects term premia via its impact on risk taking (see, for example, Gilchrist, López-Salido, and Zakrajsek 2013).

a maturity extension effect (whereby the central bank buys longer-maturity assets with this newly created money). In principle, asset purchases should not affect asset prices beyond the assets being purchased, because the price of an asset should depend only on its own risk-adjusted expected returns. However, the existence of frictions, related mostly to imperfect information and segmentation, implies that there are a few additional channels through which asset purchases may have an impact beyond an asset's price:[13]

1. **Signaling channel.** Because it takes time to implement a program of asset purchases, such a program credibly commits the central bank not to change the direction of policy at a minimum during the time it takes to implement the purchases. Purchases (or long-term loans) can thus be both a complement to forward guidance and a substitute for it. For example, the length of the ECB's long-term refinancing operations (LTROs) at a fixed rate was considered a subtle way to signal that rates were on hold during that period.

2. **Scarcity/portfolio-rebalancing channel.** Central bank asset purchases reduce the supply of a particular asset and investors react to this scarcity by bidding up the price of the asset.[14] This scarcity channel doesn't exist in standard models of asset pricing (where assets are priced based on their expected payoffs in different states of the world) and typically requires some segmentation, as in, for example, preferred-habitat models, where some agents (e.g., pension funds, insurance companies, and sovereign wealth funds) are constrained in the assets they can hold (see Modigliani and Sutch 1966; Bernanke, Reinhart, and Sack 2004; and Vayanos and Vila 2009). If the price is bid high enough, unconstrained investors may shift to other assets and rebalance their portfolios. The central bank typically buys relatively safe assets, such as bonds, with the intention of forcing private investors to shift toward riskier assets.[15] In principle, bond purchases would affect only the risk-free component of asset prices, whereas lending programs would affect the term premium of all assets that can be posted as collateral for the loans.[16]

---

13. There is an additional channel through which asset purchases may affect the economic outlook, namely the exchange rate. But this is not specific to asset purchases, it is just a reflection of changes in relative interest rates.

14. Tobin and Brainard (1962) and Tobin (1969) developed the portfolio balance theory.

15. An alternative way of thinking about this channel is that the central bank buys assets that carry some risk and replaces them with riskless cash, in order to remove risk from the system and entice investors to spend some of this cash in riskier assets, such as equities. From this standpoint, the most effective way to engage in QE would be to buy the riskiest assets.

16. Portfolio rebalancing can also happen via the issuance of central bank reserves (see Christensen and Krogstrup 2016).

3. **Duration channel.** By making large purchases of long-maturity bonds, the central bank makes investors' portfolios safer, by reducing exposure in the market as a whole to interest rate risk.[17] Everything else equal, it increases the price of risky assets.

4. **Liquidity premium channel.** By actively encouraging trading in assets, the central bank can reduce the liquidity premium during times of stress.

5. **Insurance channel.** By credibly and transparently communicating that it is ready to ease policy as much as needed to achieve its objectives, the central bank can reduce the overall level of risk of the economy and limit the tails in the scenarios economic agents use for risk management. Doing so improves the demand outlook, boosting asset prices, softening lending standards, and lifting inflation expectations and reducing real rates.[18] At times of elevated uncertainty, the insurance channel of monetary policy is the most powerful, because it avoids multiple equilibria. When no one wants to take risk, the central bank has to compensate and take more risk.

6. **Bank lending channel.** By buying assets from nonbanks, the central bank increases the amount of reserves available to banks, at the margin increasing banks' incentives to lend.

7. **Bank capital relief channel.** By increasing the price and reducing the risk of the assets banks hold on their balance sheets, central bank purchases free capital on banks' balance sheets, which they can use to support lending. This channel may be especially relevant when one class of assets dominates balance sheets or banks face funding constraints because of weak capitalization.

An additional point of debate on the impact of asset purchases is whether they operate via stock or flow effects. The stock theory argues that asset purchases operate via adjustments to the price of the asset once the new supply/demand balance is known (i.e., when the announcement of new asset purchases is made, markets reevaluate the new supply/demand equilibrium and fix the price accordingly; all of the impact occurs upon announcement). The flow theory argues that asset purchases operate by injecting money into the system with each purchase, money that is then channeled into another asset (i.e., the announcement has no impact; each purchase has an impact). The economic theory and empirical evidence side mostly

---

17. Duration is a measure of the sensitivity of the price of a bond to changes in interest rates.

18. This channel is prominent in models such as that of Kocherlakota (2016) in which, when short-term interest rates are zero, current economic outcomes are highly sensitive to beliefs about the long-run level of activity.

with the stock theory, although the flow could have some impact at the micro level and carry information about the total final stock of purchases.[19] Most critics of asset purchases focus on the flow theory, arguing that the money simply inflates stock prices, bypassing the real economy, and that when asset purchases end, stock prices fall to the pre–asset purchase level.

Central Bank Actions During the Crisis

The combination of a financial crisis, soaring commodity prices, and high headline inflation made the initial reaction of the central banks very complex. The tradeoff between potentially lower future growth and high current inflation created a dilemma that different central banks approached in different ways. The memory of 1998, when the Fed cut rates 75 basis points in response to the crisis in emerging markets and the failure of hedge fund LTCM, only to realize that the US economy had been barely affected, was in the minds of many economists and central bankers.[20] There was therefore initial hesitancy to react aggressively. In fact, some observers thought that the initial liquidity injection by the ECB (a "mere" €95 billion) was excessive (the Fed had injected "only" $24 billion). Once the extent of the crisis became clear, however, central banks responded with a wide arsenal of tools, including interest rate cuts, liquidity provision, and asset purchases.

Interest rate cuts started hesitantly but accelerated once the magnitude of the problem was well understood. The ECB was the exception among the main central banks, initially focusing more on the inflationary potential of commodity prices than on the disinflationary potential of the recession risk. As discussed in chapter 2, the anti-inflation focus was sharper and more asymmetric among European policymakers. This narrow anti-inflationary mindset led the ECB to raise rates in 2008, just a couple of months before Lehman failed, to then having to reverse the rate increase quickly. It repeated the same mistake in 2011 (figure 3.1).

---

19. At the FOMC Press Conference April 25, 2012, Chair Bernanke responded to a question by stating: "There's some disagreement, I think, about exactly how balance sheet actions by the Federal Reserve affect Treasury yields and other asset prices. The view that we have generally taken at the Fed, for which I think the evidence is pretty good, is that it's the quantity of securities held by the Fed at a given time, rather than the new purchases, the flow of new purchases, which is the primary determinant of interest rates" (Ben S. Bernanke, "Transcript of Chairman Bernanke's Press Conference," Federal Reserve Board, April 25, 2012, www.federalreserve.gov/mediacenter/files/FOMCpresconf20121212.pdf [accessed on March 28, 2017]).

20. At the September 18, 2007, FOMC meeting, David Stockton, the Federal Reserve Board's research director, stated: "Part of our mistake in 1998 was a failure to appreciate just how strong the US economy was when we entered that period" (transcript). Michael Mussa, the former chief economist of the IMF, said that in 25 years of forecasting the US economy, his biggest forecasting mistake occurred at the end of 1998, when, in the face of financial market turbulence from Russia and the blow-up of LTCM, he reduced his 1999 GDP growth forecast to 1.8 percent (the actual figure turned out to be 4.2 percent) (Mussa 2007).

Figure 3.1 Policy interest rates in selected countries, 1999–2017

percent

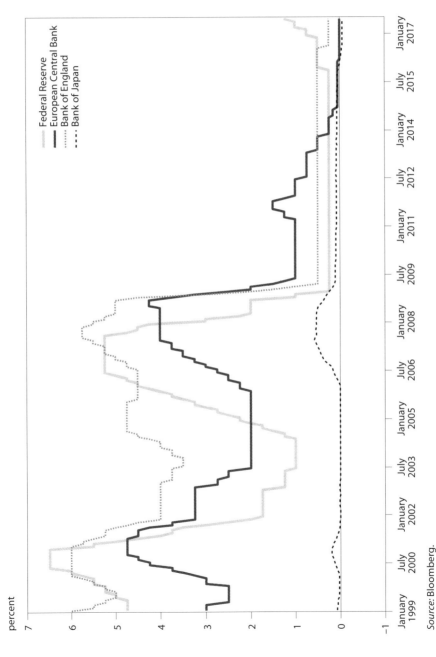

Source: Bloomberg.

This crisis differed from previous recessions in that it created systemic worries about the soundness of the global banking sector. It violated one of the assumptions of standard macroeconomic models—namely, that there is only one interest rate in the economy and that the transmission of central banks' interest rates to the rest of the economy happens smoothly. Central bank interest rates and private interest rates started to diverge significantly, as market participants started to charge large risk premia to lend to banks in the unsecured interbank market. The spread between the London interbank offered rate (Libor) and the short-term policy rate widened sharply (figure 3.2). It became a symbol of the crisis, with market participants reacting instinctively with panic every time they saw it increase.

The increase in Libor–OIS spreads more than offset the central bank rate cuts and led to a sharp tightening of financial conditions. Central banks had to establish a wide range of liquidity facilities to normalize funding markets and reduce these spreads. These facilities involved two main actions: (1) the provision of liquidity to an extended range of counterparts against a wider range of collateral and a longer time horizon (e.g., the Fed's Term Auction Facility and Primary Dealer Credit Facility or the ECB's LTROs); and (2) the provision of credit directly to borrowers and investors in credit markets (e.g., the Fed's Commercial Paper Funding Facility).[21]

Despite their novelty, there was nothing really unconventional in these actions—they simply extended the traditional lender of last resort function of the central bank to other institutions and markets. Central banks were established precisely to ensure well-functioning markets; they were applying Bagehot's classic dictum to lend freely against sound collateral to solvent institutions. Where markets were not willing to lend, the central bank replaced them, lending at longer maturities and against a wider range of collateral. These liquidity facilities were combined with cuts to the standard marginal lending facilities and actions to reduce the stigma associated with the use of such facilities.[22]

Asset purchase programs revealed a very clear learning-by-doing pattern, with incremental levels of central bank risk taking. Sizes rose as conviction about the programs increased. Initially, purchases were in fixed quantities for short periods of time; later they became open ended and contingent on economic outcomes. Worries about potential losses featured

---

21. The Fed website provides a detailed summary of all its facilities. See Federal Reserve Board, "Crisis Response," www.federalreserve.gov/monetarypolicy/bst_crisisresponse.htm (accessed on March 29, 2017).

22. For example, the Fed cut its discount window rate on August 17, 2007, reducing the spread with fed funds from 100 to 50 basis points, and tried to convince all banks to use it so that markets would not view the cut as a negative action.

Figure 3.2   Spread between Libor and three-month policy rates in the United States, United Kingdom, euro area, and Japan, 2002–16

percentage points

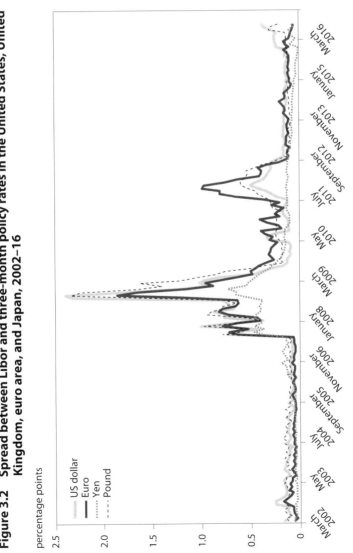

Libor = London interbank offered rate

Source: Bloomberg.

strongly initially but faded later on. At the beginning, central banks focused on their ability to exit the programs and reduce their balance sheets; later they stressed their ability to conduct monetary policy with large balance sheets. Very quickly the unconventional became conventional.

Some central banks focused more on public debt, others on private assets. The differences depended on the legal constraints (e.g., the Fed cannot buy corporate bonds or equities), the specific needs of each economy, and in some cases dogmatic beliefs, such as the staunch opposition of the ECB while Jean-Claude Trichet was president to buying government bonds for monetary policy purposes. The Fed and the BoE actively added monetary accommodation with aggressive purchases; the ECB passively accommodated liquidity needs with LTROs. Some central banks focused mostly on shorter-term assets, to reduce potential losses; others focused on longer-term assets, to increase the effectiveness of policy. To avoid reducing the collateral available as a result of the government bond purchase programs, most central banks made the bonds purchased through securities lending programs available to market participants.

Most central banks used asset purchases once they had exhausted the room to cut interest rates. The ECB, however, adopted a sharp separation principle, using interest rates to address risks to price stability and lending facilities and asset purchases to stabilize the transmission mechanism of monetary policy. Under this framework it moved rates and asset purchases in opposite directions twice during the crisis, increasing interest rates once in 2008 and twice in 2011 to address potential upside inflation risks while using liquidity facilities and asset purchases to stabilize markets. In both cases the rate increases were promptly reversed, suggesting that the concept behind the separation principle, while perhaps sound in theory, is very difficult to apply in practice. After all, financial instability almost always has a significant negative impact on growth and inflation.

The rest of this chapter describes the responses of each central bank in detail. Tables A.1–A.5 in appendix A show the chronology of actions by each institution.

Fed's Different Asset Purchase Programs

With the US housing market at the epicenter of the crisis, the Fed was the first central bank to ease policy, cutting interest rates by 50 basis points at its September 2007 meeting. The move surprised markets, at the time priced for a cut of less than 25 basis points. Many observers thought that the action was a way to do "one and done," a larger than expected cut to shore up expectations.

When the growth outlook started to worsen, the Fed did not hesitate. It had had a deflation training episode in 2003, when interest rates fell to 1 percent and worries of deflation, however small, appeared. The conclusion from that episode was clear: When at risk of hitting the EZLB, cut rates faster and more aggressively than usual, in order to boost the economy and avoid reaching it. "Keeping the powder dry" was a recipe for failure. In the event the Fed cut rates by 500 basis points in two stages, from 5.25 percent to 2 percent between September 2007 and April 2008 and from 2 percent to 0.25 percent between October 2008 and December 2008.

Once interest rate cuts had been exhausted, the Fed initiated a series of different programs of large-scale asset purchases (LSAPs) in late 2008.[23] The Fed had the advantage of being led by Ben Bernanke, who had been a leading scholar of monetary policy and had advised Japan on how to overcome deflation. There was no learning curve for him. The title of his 2002 speech said it all: "Deflation: Making Sure 'It' Doesn't Happen Here."[24] All he had to do was apply his own recommendations.

Despite Bernanke's predisposition to buy assets, however, the Fed behaved in a very incremental manner. Concerns about interfering with credit allocation and uncertainty about the impact of the purchases kept the packages small at the beginning. In November 2008 the FOMC announced a program to purchase $600 billion in agency mortgage-backed securities and agency debt (QE1). In March 2009 it expanded this purchase program substantially, announcing that it would purchase up to $1.75 trillion of assets, this time also including $300 billion of longer-term Treasury debt, to be completed in early 2010.

In August 2010 the FOMC decided to start replacing maturing mortgage-backed securities with US Treasuries, in order to stop the passive tightening generated by the decline in the size of the Fed's balance sheet. The August 27 Jackson Hole speech by Bernanke, and the statement of the September 21 FOMC meeting, set the stage for the next round of QE in November 2010, when the FOMC announced the purchase of an additional $600 billion of longer-term Treasury securities over a period ending in mid-2011 (QE2).[25] In September 2011 the FOMC introduced a variation of its earlier purchase programs, known as the maturity extension program

---

23. The Fed also adopted several liquidity facilities to ease pressures in funding markets, such as the Term Auction Facility, the Primary Dealer Credit Facility, and the Term Securities Lending Facility (see table A.1 in appendix A).

24. Ben S. Bernanke, "Deflation: Making Sure 'It' Doesn't Happen Here," speech before the National Economists Club, Washington, November 21, 2002.

25. Ben S. Bernanke, "The Economic Outlook and Monetary Policy," speech at the Federal Reserve Bank of Kansas City's Annual Economic Symposium, Jackson Hole, WY, August 27, 2010; FOMC (Federal Open Market Committee), Federal Reserve Board, press release, September 21, 2010, www.federalreserve.gov/newsevents/press/monetary/20100921a.htm (accessed on March 31, 2017).

(MEP), under which the Fed would purchase $400 billion of long-term Treasury securities and sell an equivalent amount of shorter-term Treasury securities over the period ending in June 2012, subsequently extended through the end of 2012. By reducing the average maturity of the securities held by the public, the MEP attempted to put downward pressure on longer-term interest rates without increasing the Fed's balance sheet.

These limited packages were not successful: Growth remained weak and inflation expectations low. The persistent euro crisis was affecting risk attitudes, and fiscal policy was being tightened significantly. Monetary policy was the only game in town.

In September 2012 the FOMC changed its strategy. It launched a new LSAP program, this time open ended and defined by a monthly amount of purchases rather than a total amount. It announced the purchases of $40 billion a month of agency mortgage-backed securities, which was increased to $85 billion a month, including Treasury purchases, in December 2012. This program was threshold based: Purchases would continue until the outlook for the labor market improved "substantially." The insurance channel of monetary policy was finally at play. The Fed reassured markets that it would not stop until the economy looked right, whatever it took.

This new strategy was eventually successful. The Fed started tapering its asset purchases in December 2013, when the unemployment rate reached 7 percent. It ended its asset purchases in October 2014.

The Fed had spent six years buying assets, in an almost uninterrupted manner, spending $3.5 trillion. In December 2015, eight years after the first rate cut, it hiked interest rates for the first time, declaring mission accomplished, though perhaps prematurely. It would be another year before it raised rates again.

Different Phases of ECB Policies

The ECB lagged significantly behind in the rate-cutting cycle. Conviction that the financial crisis was just a US-centered crisis that would have only minor spillover effects on the euro area and heightened attention to high headline inflation (driven mostly by commodity prices) put the ECB in a different mindset, worried more about upside inflation risks than downside growth risks. Confident that the liquidity facilities put in place to shore up the banking sector were enough to contain the financial turmoil, the first ECB move was a surprise increase in interest rates in July 2008, from 4.0 to 4.25 percent, responding to perceived upside risks to inflation from commodity prices. Two months later Lehman Brothers failed, and the world experienced one of the deepest economic contractions ever. The ECB reversed the rate increase in September 2008, cutting rates to 1 percent in a few steps.

This mistake was repeated in 2011. While the euro area crisis was still in full force, the ECB hiked rates 50 basis points in 2011 (in April and July), to contain perceived upside inflation risks. A mild recovery in GDP growth, the belief that most of the decline in growth in the euro area had been permanent, combined with stubbornly high headline inflation (still driven by commodity prices and, this time, increases in the value added tax [VAT]), as well as still robust wage growth in some countries (such as Spain) created the conditions for some at the ECB to see the need to tighten policy, despite important downside risks lingering from the euro crisis. It reversed these rate increases in October 2011, at the first meeting with Mario Draghi as president of the ECB. It then gradually moved interest rates into negative territory. Twice during the crisis the ECB miscalculated the severity of the situation. Its excessive focus on upside inflation risks surely contributed to the later decline in inflation expectations.

The first phase of ECB asset purchases started in mid-2007. It focused on easing financial conditions for banks while minimizing support for government bonds, in order to put maximum pressure on governments of the countries under stress to adopt the needed fiscal and structural measures. In August 2007 the ECB started to provide unlimited liquidity to banks[26] (in "fixed-rate full allotment" tender procedures), reducing the minimum reserve requirement from 2 percent to 1 percent in late 2011. It also lengthened the maturity of its supply of liquidity. From the precrisis one-week maturity for the main refinancing operations (MROs) and three months for LTROs, the ECB extended the maturity of LTROs to six months (April 2008), then to one year (June 2009), three years (December 2011), and ultimately four years (September 2014). No other central bank has ever extended loans to banks of such long maturity. Despite its initial hesitancy, and probably because of it, the ECB ended up taking on a lot of risk.

Asset purchases focused initially on private assets. Unlike the Fed, which is authorized to buy only government bonds and mortgages, the ECB faced no restrictions. But it restricted itself to not buying government bonds. There was no impediment in the Maastricht Treaty to buying government bonds in the secondary market, but politics prevailed. In May 2009 the ECB announced a program of purchases of €60 billion of covered bonds (the primary source of market funding for European banks) over 12 months. It launched a second covered bond purchase program in November 2011 (€40 billion over 12 months). It also eased collateral requirements by expanding the list of eligible assets and lowering the minimum acceptable rating (driven largely by the steady ratings downgrades of euro area sovereigns).

---

26. Limited only by the banks' quantity of adequate collateral.

In May 2010, as the euro area crisis deepened and sovereign spreads skyrocketed, the ECB launched the Securities Markets Program (SMP) to buy sovereign bonds of euro area countries in distress. It made the point that these purchases had no impact on its monetary policy stance, that they were sterilized via liquidity-absorbing operations. SMP purchases were concentrated in May–June 2010 and August–November 2011. They reached a maximum of €220 billion. Initially, they were limited to Greece, Portugal, and Ireland. In August 2011 they were extended to Spain and Italy.

In September 2012 the SMP was replaced by the Outright Monetary Transactions program (OMT). It authorized potentially unlimited purchases of short-term government bonds (up to three years) of euro area countries, under the strict conditionality associated with a program with the European Stability Mechanism (ESM). The OMT program was launched to back up the famous "whatever it takes" speech by President Draghi (July 26, 2012), in order to reduce mounting expectations of a breakup of the euro and contain the sharp increase in sovereign spreads that was severely tightening financial conditions. These are the key words from that speech: "Within our mandate, the ECB is ready to do whatever it takes to preserve the euro. And believe me, it will be enough."[27]

Why did Draghi have to make such a commitment? During 2007–11, under the leadership of Jean-Claude Trichet, the ECB had put very strong emphasis on disciplining governments, at times tolerating a sharp tightening in financial conditions and losing sight of its price-stability mandate. At times monetary policy became an instrument for unelected officials—central bankers—to impose conditionality over democratically elected governments, focused mostly on forcing governments to implement structural reforms, including through the threat of leaving the euro. The ECB allowed markets to think that the sovereign debt of euro area countries was, de facto, foreign exchange–denominated debt, which created fertile ground for speculative attacks. As a result, doubts about the future of the euro skyrocketed. Draghi's "whatever it takes" speech is another example of the insurance channel of monetary policy. He assured the world that the ECB would preserve the integrity of the euro and fulfill its mandate. The speech marked a turning point. Spreads declined after the SMP was launched, and the program has never been activated.

The appointment of Mario Draghi at the helm of the ECB opened a new phase and orientation of ECB policies, though it took a while to implement the shift. During 2012–14 the ECB tolerated a significant reduction of its balance sheet, from €3 trillion to about €2 trillion, as the LTROs were repaid. With the Fed moving in the opposite direction and expanding its

---

27. Mario Draghi, speech at the Global Investment Conference, London, July 26, 2012.

balance sheet significantly, this reduction kept the euro strong and financial conditions too tight for the euro area.

In mid-2014, as downside risks to price stability from this tight policy stance mounted, the ECB finally understood the urgent need to shift gears. Its new strategy marked the transition from providing a passive supply of liquidity (endogenously meeting the needs of banks via liquidity facilities) to actively easing policy (via asset purchases intended to reduce long-term rates and risk premia). President Draghi outlined the new approach in a series of speeches.[28] The ECB contemplated a three-pronged strategy: It would address an unwanted tightening in financial conditions (from contagion from the Fed's exit strategy or an appreciation of the euro) with rate cuts and/or forward guidance, an impairment of the transmission mechanism of policy with LTROs and private asset purchases, and a worsening of the medium-term inflation outlook with a broad asset purchases program.

With this in mind, the ECB cut interest rates a few times in the second half of 2014, reducing the MRO rate to 0.05 percent and the deposit rate to –0.2 percent. In June 2014 the ECB introduced a longer-term refinancing program, the targeted longer-term refinancing operation (TLTRO), which aimed to provide incentives for banks to channel liquidity to nonfinancial corporations. TLTRO funds of up to four-year maturities were made available in four auctions (September and December 2014, March 2015, and June 2016), subject to specific conditions related, in the initial phase, to the outstanding stock of credit to nonfinancial firms and subsequently to the creation of additional net lending of the same type.

Both cases excluded credit to households for home purchases. The TLTROs offered funds until the end of 2018, at a rate initially fixed at 10 basis points over the MRO rate prevailing when the TLTRO was stipulated (this spread over the MRO rate was eliminated in January 2015). These TLTROs were unsuccessful, as banks were flush with liquidity. Before they were introduced, the ECB had relied on the banking sector to borrow from the ECB to bid up asset prices. That strategy was no longer effective. It was time for the ECB to buy the assets directly.

At the Jackson Hole conference in August 2014, Draghi delivered a strong hint that asset purchases were the next step. In September the ECB added two programs of private asset purchases, the asset-backed securi-

---

28. See Mario Draghi, "A Consistent Strategy for a Sustained Recovery," lecture at Sciences Po, Paris, March 25, 2014; "Monetary Policy Communication in Turbulent Times," speech at the conference "De Nederlandsche Bank 200 Years: Central Banking in the Next Two Decades," Amsterdam, April 24, 2014; and "Unemployment in the Euro Area," speech at the Annual Central Bank Symposium, Jackson Hole, WY, August 22, 2014.

ties purchase program (ABSPP) and the third covered bond purchase program (CBPP3).[29] It completed the transition in January 22, 2015, when it introduced the expanded asset purchase program (EAPP), a program of secondary market purchases of baskets of euro area government bonds weighted by the ECB's capital key.[30] Purchases would total about €60 billion a month, with residual maturities of 2–30 years; they were initially intended to last until end-September 2016 (for a minimum amount of about €1.1 trillion) or later if needed to ensure the achievement of price stability.[31] The ECB expanded this program several times. In December 2016 it extended it through at least December 2017. It increased the size of its monthly purchases to €80 billion between March 2016 and March 2017 and subsequently reduced it back to €60 billion between April and December 2017. It also expanded the range of assets to include corporate bonds. In March 2016 the ECB cut the deposit rate to a low of –0.4 percent.

Despite the existential crisis of Europe's economy, the ECB started a program of large-scale asset purchases six years later than the Fed. It took the ECB six years to convincingly reassure markets that it was serious about its price-stability objective. This very long delay had a significant negative effect on inflation expectations, which became dangerously low, to the point of casting doubt on the credibility of the price-stability objective (as discussed in the next chapter). Even when it finally capitulated to buy government bonds, the ECB could not help focusing on moral hazard as a main concern. The decision to buy bonds based on the capital key (rather than on market weights, which would have been more effective), and with minimal sharing of risks among national central banks, displayed a desire to minimize the political costs rather than maximize economic effectiveness.

The ECB's easing program is unlikely to end before late 2018, completing at least 11 years of continued easing of policy. The ECB initially worried too much about taking risks, focusing too sharply on avoiding moral hazard and limiting the growth of its balance sheet. It will end up growing a very large balance sheet. It did not want to buy government bonds; it will end up owning a large amount of them for a very long time. Not taking enough

---

29. The ABSPP was also intended to foster the development of the asset-backed securities market in Europe, to help reduce the dominance of banks in the financing of the economy.

30. The EAPP aimed at purchasing euro-denominated investment-grade securities issued by euro area governments and agencies and European institutions.

31. The ECB introduced two restrictions on the program: a limit of 25 percent per issue (raised to 33 percent in September 2015) and 33 percent per issuer and the exclusion of bonds with yields below the deposit rate. The second restriction was lifted in December 2016, to facilitate the extension of the program. Differently from other monetary policy operations, in which the risk was shared across ECB members, it agreed that, for the EAPP, each national central bank would bear the bulk of the risk of its own purchases (see Ubide 2015a).

risk at the right time may force a central bank to take a lot of risk—it is the paradox of risk.

Bank of Japan's Qualitative Change in Strategy

The BoJ was a pioneer in QE, launching its first program in 2001.[32] It entered the crisis with an asset purchases program (the Rinban program) in place. This program focused on short-term government bonds. It was launched to supply currency to the economy subject to the banknote principle (i.e., the outstanding volume of banknotes in circulation would limit the outstanding amount of the BoJ's holdings of Japanese government bonds).

Like the ECB, the BoJ focused on avoiding moral hazard and limiting losses—hence the restriction in the Rinban program to short-term bonds and the self-imposed banknote rule. The result was a very limited easing of monetary policy and little progress in overcoming deflation. The BoJ was concerned about the high level of public debt and wanted to force the government to undertake fiscal consolidation. Its governor, Masaaki Shirakawa, believed that the problems facing the Japanese economy were structural and that there was little monetary policy could do. The BoJ was trying to overcome the deflationary risks, but with little conviction. As a result, inflation remained stuck around zero. The pattern is clear: Little insurance, little gain.

Some of the self-imposed limits were lifted with the launching of the Comprehensive Monetary Easing (CME) program in 2012. It included a new asset purchases program of short-term government securities, commercial paper, corporate bonds, exchange-traded funds (ETFs), and Japanese real estate investment trusts (J-REITs), in addition to a fixed-rate funds-supplying operation against pooled collateral. The program was not subject to the banknote principle.

The strategy changed drastically with the election of Shinzō Abe and the launching of Abenomics. The Abenomics quiver held three arrows: monetary easing, fiscal easing, and structural reforms. In early 2013 Abe appointed Haruhiko Kuroda as governor of the BoJ. In April 2013 Kuroda replaced the CME program with a program of quantitative and qualitative easing (QQE).

QQE represented a sharp change from the past. The BoJ changed its main operating target for money market operations from the uncollateralized overnight call rate (interest rate) to the monetary base (quan-

---

32. The first QE program lasted until 2006. It targeted the volume of excess reserves, based on the concept that pushing excess reserves onto the banks would increase lending. It failed, because the banks' demand for reserves increased in parallel with the increase in the supply of reserves.

tity) and targeted an increase in the monetary base at an annual pace of about ¥60–¥70 trillion, with the objective of doubling its size in two years. Doubling the size of the monetary base was the core of the new "2-2-2" strategy, which sought to achieve 2 percent inflation in two years.

To achieve this increase in the monetary base, the BoJ targeted purchases of Japanese government bonds at a pace of about ¥50 trillion a year, with maturities of up to 40 years. These purchases would more than double the average remaining maturity of the BoJ bond purchases, extending it from about three years to about seven years, matching the average maturity of the bonds issued. The BoJ also increased its purchases of ETFs, J-REITs, commercial paper, and corporate bonds to complement its government bond purchases. In October 2014 the BoJ surprised markets and expanded QQE by accelerating the purchase of government bonds to ¥80 trillion a year, increasing the average maturity to 7–10 years and tripling the purchases of ETFs and REITs. In December 2015 it extended the average maturity of government bonds to 7–12 years, marginally increasing ETF purchases to include the new JPX-Nikkei Index 400 and increasing the upper limit on J-REITs from 5 to 10 percent of the total amount issued. In January 2016 the BoJ cut its main interest rates to –0.1 percent, renaming its strategy "quantitative and qualitative monetary easing with a negative interest rate."[33]

This strategy changed yet again in late 2016, to a yield curve management strategy (discussed in chapter 6). By the end of 2017, the BoJ will have been buying bonds uninterruptedly for 16 years, and its balance sheet will have reached almost 100 percent of GDP. It was very hesitant at the beginning, and ended up having to be very aggressive. The less risk the central bank took initially, the more it had to take later on. It is the paradox of risk.

Bank of England's "Boring" Quantitative Easing Program

Compared with the Fed, ECB, and BoJ, the BoE's QE program was "boring," focusing solely on the purchases of government bonds, mostly from nonbanks.[34] Mervyn King, the governor of the BoE, had an old-fashioned view of QE, based mostly on the transmission of policy via an increase in money. The first purchases of government bonds were calibrated to achieve an increase in money that would lead to an increase in nominal GDP growth of 5 percent, the calculated output gap at the time (Monetary Policy Committee 2009).

---

33. Bank of Japan, Introduction of "Quantitative and Qualitative Monetary Easing with a Negative Interest Rate," January 29, 2016, www.boj.or.jp/en/announcements/release_2016/k160129a.pdf.

34. The BoE bought small portions of commercial paper and corporate bonds in 2009, but with the purpose of restoring liquidity in dysfunctional markets, not as part of QE.

After cutting rates to what the BoE considered it to be its effective zero lower bound (0.5 percent), in March 2009 the BoE launched a program of purchases of government bonds, initially amounting to £75 billion over three months and expanded in various steps to £200 billion by November 2009. The BoE expanded the purchases by £75 billion in October 2011, £50 billion in February 2012, and £50 billion in July 2012, bringing total asset purchases to £375 billion.

The BoE conducted these large purchases despite very high headline inflation. The combination of high oil prices, the depreciation of the currency, and increases in indirect taxes pushed headline inflation in the United Kingdom to 5 percent in late 2011. The BoE considered this inflation spike transitory and continued with its asset purchases. There was some wisdom in this strategy: Although they were very persistent, the three elements driving headline inflation were known to be transitory. Indeed, headline inflation declined toward 2 percent in 2013.

There was another argument for the BoE's reluctance to react to higher inflation: It had an implicit deal with the government in which the government would tighten fiscal policy to reduce the deficit while the BoE would keep interest rates low. In this case monetary policy was the only game in town by design, not by default, as in the case of the Fed. This tolerance of transitorily high inflation compares positively with the ECB's intolerance. Inflation expectations remained well anchored in the United Kingdom while they declined in the euro area (as discussed in the next chapter). Actions matter for credibility.

On July 13, 2012, as discussions of the marginal effectiveness of government-bonds-only QE increased,[35] the BoE and the British government launched the Funding for Lending Scheme (FLS), to offset the increase in funding costs of UK banks resulting from the crisis in the euro area. Banks could borrow up to 5 percent of their stock of loans plus any net expansion of their lending to the end of 2013 in a program that amounted to about £80 billion. The cost was 0.25 percent a year for banks that maintained their stock of lending, with a graduated increased schedule for banks that reduced their stock of lending. The BoE extended the FLS several times.

Unlike the Fed, the BoE never raised rates. The conditions were in place, with the output gap closing and inflation approaching the target, when the Brexit referendum forced a new easing of monetary policy in 2016, which is discussed in chapter 6.

---

35. Adam Posen, among others, argued forcefully for an extension of the QE program to private assets. Reuters, "BoE's Posen: BoE should buy more private-sector debt," February 2, 2012, www.reuters.com/article/britain-boe-posen-tuc-idUSL9E7MT01420120202.

Swiss National Bank's Exchange Rate Floor

The Swiss National Bank (SNB) faced a dilemma. Because markets viewed Switzerland as a safe haven, it became a recipient of capital inflows. The result was a relentless appreciation of its exchange rate since 2007 that created disinflationary pressures and significant downside risks to growth, putting price stability at risk. Interest rates were already very low and soon reached zero.

One reason markets considered Switzerland a safe haven was its sound fiscal situation. But the country's very low level of public debt became a problem for monetary policy: Once interest rates reached zero, the SNB found itself unable to engage in QE in the required size, as there were just not enough government bonds to buy. It could have bought private assets, for example equities, but doing so would have made the central bank the majority owner of the Swiss stock market, creating potential governance problems. The government could have undertaken a fiscal expansion, but it was constrained by the Swiss fiscal rules. The SNB thus had only one option to ease policy: purchasing foreign assets by intervening in the foreign exchange market.

The SNB started intervening in March–December 2009 in order to put a floor on the euro–Swiss franc exchange rate (lower means a stronger Swiss franc) and slow its appreciation. The intervention was accompanied by a rate cut and purchases of private sector bonds. It failed. The euro crisis was unraveling, but the SNB was allowing the Swiss monetary base to contract (as foreign exchange swaps the SNB had launched to provide foreign banks with Swiss franc liquidity during 2008–09 were rolling off), thus tightening financial conditions. As a result, the euro–Swiss franc exchange rate appreciated sharply.

After a new round of interventions during January–June 2010, the SNB launched operations to mop up liquidity. It was intervening and adding liquidity to weaken the currency but then quickly reacting to mop up liquidity because of inflationary fears. It was pulling and pushing at the same time. Not surprisingly, the Swiss franc continued to appreciate, reaching an all-time high (on a trade-weighted basis) in August 2011.

The SNB shifted to a more aggressive strategy, injecting liquidity and selling foreign exchange swaps (selling Swiss francs in the spot market with a commitment to repurchase them later) and engaging in verbal intervention, declaring the exchange rate "massively overvalued" and a downside risk to price stability. This policy package was stronger but still too timid; it had only transitory success.

Finally, in September 2011, the SNB set a floor for EURCHF (the exchange rate of the Swiss franc vs. the euro) at 1.20. It accompanied this measure with forceful and unambiguous communication—the minimum exchange rate would be enforced with the "utmost determination"—and unlimited foreign currency market interventions.

Intervention was heavy in 2012 and again in 2014, leading the SNB to accumulate more than CHF 500 billion of foreign exchange reserves (figure 3.3). After a period of stability where EURCHF traded above the floor and the SNB did not have to intervene to support the floor, this strategy was threatened by the ECB's decision in late 2014 to ease monetary policy aggressively. The SNB was initially reluctant to cut rates to more negative levels to match the ECB actions, probably because of worries about the impact on its financial system, but in the end it had to capitulate. It discontinued the minimum exchange rate on January 15, 2015, on the grounds that divergences between monetary policies in major currency areas had increased and were expected to become even larger.[36] Faced with potentially huge foreign exchange intervention needs (which could have reached CHF 100 billion a month),[37] the SNB abandoned the foreign exchange floor and increased the interest rate differential versus the euro area, lowering the interest rate on sight deposit account balances to –0.75 percent and the target range for the three-month Libor to between –1.25 percent and –0.25 percent.[38] EURCHF plummeted from €1.20 to a low of €0.86 the day the floor was removed, gradually bouncing back above €1. It has remained in the €1–€1.10 range since then.

The main reason why the SNB decided to end the minimum exchange rate regime was the size of actual and potential losses from the accumulation of reserves. The rapid appreciation of the Swiss franc after the floor was abandoned led to losses in the first half of 2015 of CHF50 billion—more than 7 percent of GDP.[39] These losses carried political weight in Switzerland, because the SNB's profits are an important component of the financing of the Swiss cantons. The SNB had to balance political and economic risks. In the end it chose to prioritize the minimization of political risks. It repeated a pattern seen across central banks. They all started with small operations, worrying about the exit and potential losses. They

36. Thomas Jordan, "Introductory Remarks," speech at Swiss National Bank press conference, January 15, 2015.

37. Alice Baghdjian, "Swiss National Bank Says Stands Ready to Intervene in FX Market," Reuters, January 26, 2015.

38. In 2015, during the Greek crisis, the SNB intervened sporadically to prevent the Swiss franc from appreciating with respect to the euro (Joshua Franklin and Paul Arnold, "UPDATE 1: SNB Head Confirms Weekend Intervention to Weaken Franc," Reuters, June 29, 2015).

39. George Dorgan, "Weekly SNB Intervention Update: Sight Deposits and Speculative Position," SNBCHF.com, February 8, 2016.

Figure 3.3   Intervention in foreign exchange market by Swiss National Bank, 2007–16

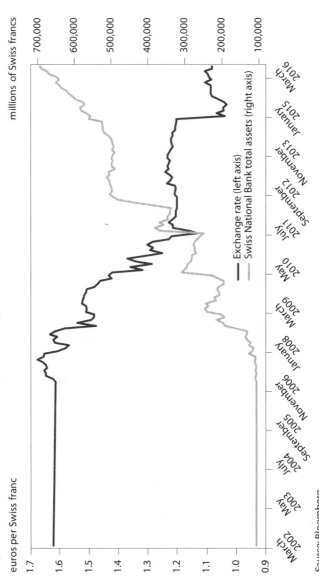

euros per Swiss franc

millions of Swiss francs

— Exchange rate (left axis)
— Swiss National Bank total assets (right axis)

Source: Bloomberg.

all ended up doing much more than they ever expected. Not wanting to take much risk, they ended up having to take much more risk.

Leaving the Comfort Zone of Monetary Policy

Several threads run across the actions of all the central banks as they started to expand their balance sheets that showcase the tensions in the deployment of their strategies. They were supposed to be fighting disinflation, but they were too keen on reassuring the public and markets that they would be ready to exit and contain inflation effectively. Examples include the "small" size of the Fed's initial packages and its combination with a discussion of exit strategies, which dampened the easing impact of the packages[40]; the ECB's insistence on the self-absorbing nature of LTROs as an explanation of why they represented a better policy than QE; or the BoE's decisions on QE on a three-month horizon basis. As they collected more information about the impact of these new policies, central banks became bolder in applying them. Most of them adopted some form of open-ended QE.

Central banks were supposed to be the lenders or buyers of last resort. They do not need capital to operate, but there was concern that eventual loses could potentially affect their independence. Examples include the Fed's debate on the cost-benefit of QE (see Carpenter et al. 2013); the BoE's decision to obtain an explicit indemnity from the Treasury for its QE program; the ECB's request for a commitment from the governments to be recapitalized if any losses were to arise from its SMP; the BoJ's long-standing reluctance to buy Japanese government bonds with maturities of more than two years for fear of heavy losses if interest rates rose sharply; and the tremendous pressure on the SNB because of the accounting losses derived from its intervention to defend the EURCHF peg.

Central banks wanted to change financial conditions, but they worried about interfering with credit allocation, which explains why they shied away from private asset purchases once the acute phase of the crisis was over. The BoJ's ETF and REIT purchases were designed not to interfere with market pricing. In the case of the ECB, the political constraints, coming especially from Germany, conditioned its strategy. The persistent debate about the legality of purchases of government bonds under the Maastricht Treaty (which led to legal challenges before the German Constitutional Court and the European Court of Justice) led the ECB to rely for too long on the provision of liquidity to banks as an indirect way to ease financial conditions.

These contradictions reflected legitimate concerns, as central banks had to take risks and leave their comfort zone. More experimentation was

---

40. Ben S. Bernanke, statement before the Committee on Financial Services, US House of Representatives, February 10, 2010.

yet to come. Some central banks would decide to pay banks interest to hold excess reserves, others would decide to pay people to borrow by charging negative interest rates on reserves. The main central banks agreed to lend—and thus to take risk—in foreign exchange.

Paying Interest on Reserves: Breaking the Link between Money and Inflation

As central banks started to expand their balance sheets, they became unable to control their short-term reference interest rates. The size of their balance sheets (and therefore the amount of excess reserves in the banking system) rose rapidly, driven by policies aiming to restore market functioning and reduce risk premia. Short-term interest rates fell below the intended policy rates, at times by large amounts (e.g., the effective fed funds rate was more than 50 basis points below the policy rate in late 2008). In addition, central banks had to ensure that, when the moment came, they would be able to raise interest rates even if they needed to keep much larger balance sheets.

These two concerns led to the adoption of systems of payment of interest on excess reserves (IOER), which New Zealand, Norway, and Sweden had successfully implemented. The objective was to create a floor for short-term interest rates and to sever the link between the provision of liquidity (driven by the size of the balance sheet and the level of excess reserves) and the short-term interest rate. The Fed, BoE, and BoJ all introduced changes along these lines. The ECB did not need to change its framework, as it already had a corridor system compatible with excess reserves, but it allowed the bottom of the corridor to become the policy reference rate.

Before the crisis US banks operated with minimum excess reserves, trading in the fed funds market to smooth transitory reserve needs. The Fed set monetary policy by directing the NY Fed desk to operate in the market to balance the supply and demand of fed funds at a level compatible with the fed funds target rate.

When excess reserves skyrocketed as a result of asset purchases (which rose from a marginal amount to about 15 percent of GDP), this strategy became unworkable, as the excess reserves pushed the fed funds rate near zero. The Fed therefore adopted an IOER system in October 2008, with the objective of setting a floor for short-term rates.[41] This floor would be achieved via the arbitrage banks can perform by borrowing in the fed funds market and holding the proceeds in reserves at the Fed, a process that earns

---

41. The academic foundation for the IOER dates to the early 2000s, when Fed interest rates reached a low of 1 percent (see Goodfriend 2002).

the banks the spread between the fed funds rate and the IOER and eventually leads to the convergence of the two rates.

Two factors distorted the system. First, some participants in the fed funds market (mostly government-sponsored enterprises) cannot earn interest on their excess reserves and thus lend large amounts in the fed funds market. Second, the Federal Deposit Insurance Corporation (FDIC) charges banks a fee proportional to the size of their balance sheets. As a result, fed funds have been trading about 10–15 basis points below the IOER rate.[42]

The ECB has always operated a corridor system, with the ceiling and the floor formed by the interest rates on the marginal lending facility and the deposit facility, with the MRO rate in the middle. Before the crisis this corridor was symmetric, with a spread of 100 basis points from the MRO in each direction. In normal times the main short-term interest rate, the euro overnight index average (Eonia), fluctuated near the middle of the corridor and close to the MRO. When the ECB changed its liquidity provision to fixed-rate full allotment, it created excess liquidity, and the Eonia rate dropped toward the bottom of the corridor, the deposit facility rate. The ECB continued to use the MRO rate as the policy rate, but it shifted to the deposit rate as the interest rate that defined the monetary policy stance. After the shift to full allotment in October 2008, the ECB initially narrowed the corridor to 50 basis points in order to minimize the deviation of Eonia from the MRO, but shortly thereafter (in January 2009) it widened the corridor to 100 basis points, in order to further ease monetary policy. As it cut rates toward zero, the ECB initially hesitated to set the deposit rate in negative territory. It ultimately capitulated, setting the rate at a low of –0.4 percent. As a result, Eonia rates have been in negative territory since mid-2014.

Since 2006 the BoE has been operating a system of "reserves averaging," in which banks are allowed to set voluntary reserves targets. If a bank's average reserves balance is within a specified range around that target, the balance is remunerated at the Bank rate (the BoE policy rate). If market rates deviate from the Bank rate, banks have an incentive to arbitrage away these deviations.

With QE the BoE faced a problem similar to the Fed's. It shifted to a floor system in which it remunerates all reserves at the Bank rate (Winters 2012). This floor system has been effective. Short-term market interest rates (Sonia) have been trading very close to the Bank rate, albeit a bit below the floor, likely because nonbank participants in the money market do not have access to a BoE reserve account.

---

42. Gagnon and Sack (2014) argue that this regime is inefficient and confusing. According to them, a better solution would be to adopt the reverse repo rate as the operational target, set at the level of the IOER.

The BoJ also introduced a system of payment of interest on excess reserves in order to keep short-term money market rates positive. The Complementary Deposit Facility pays interest on excess reserves at the target overnight call rate minus a spread. In October 2010 the BoJ set the interest on excess reserves in this facility at 0.1 percent (BoJ 2017). It changed the rate when it cut rates to negative levels, as discussed below.

With these changes, central banks severed the link between money and inflation. Inflation is no longer a monetary phenomenon in a strict sense—different levels of money growth can deliver the same level of inflation. Inflation has become a monetary policy phenomenon. Central banks can set interest rates independent of the level of monetary aggregates, giving them more flexibility, for example, to address transitory liquidity shortages, real or expected. In June 2016, for example, as the British referendum on the European Union approached, the BoE announced that it would provide extra liquidity to the system to ensure that banks were properly funded. In this way it contributed to financial stability without affecting short-term rates.

Negative Interest Rates: Is the World Upside Down?

Paying someone to lend him money sounds counterintuitive, yet it is happening. Several central banks have cut interest rates to negative territory, changing the meaning of the zero lower bound (figure 3.4). Banks have to pay interest to keep their reserves at the central bank. The Danmarks Nationalbank, the Sveriges Riksbank, and the BoJ have adopted a tiered system that applies negative rates to only a small portion of the reserves, thereby minimizing the impact on banks' profitability. The Riksbank and the SNB cut their main policy rate to lows of –0.5 and –0.75 percent, respectively. The Danmarks Nationalbank and the ECB have kept their policy rate at zero but cut the deposit rate to lows of –0.75 and –0.4 percent, respectively. The BoJ cut the deposit rate to –0.1 percent, which then became its policy rate as well. In some cases these negative short-term interest rates have extended along the yield curve, at times in an extraordinary manner. Swiss 30-year rates reached –0.01 percent in the aftermath of the Brexit referendum, for example (figure 3.5).

The motivation to cut rates to negative levels has been largely to deter capital inflows and contain currency appreciation, directly or indirectly. Denmark and Switzerland saw their currencies appreciate massively as the risk of a euro breakup increased. The ECB signaled that negative rates were the preferred tool to contain excessive currency appreciation; the Riksbank shadowed the ECB to contain the appreciation of the krona versus the euro. The BoJ's surprise cut to negative rates was intended to lower the risk of a sharp appreciation of the yen.

Figure 3.4   Negative central bank policy rates in selected economies, 2008–16

policy rate (percent)

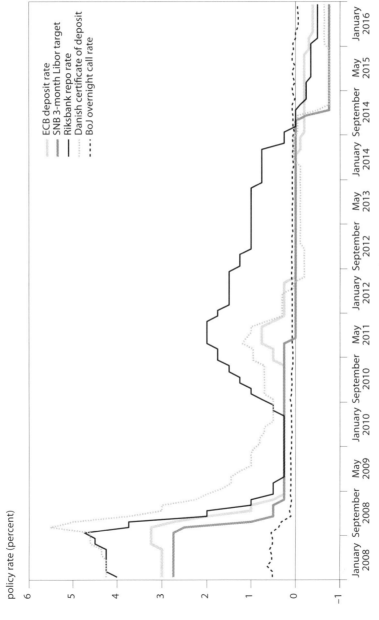

ECB = European Central Bank; SNB = Swiss National Bank; BoJ = Bank of Japan
Source: Bloomberg.

Figure 3.5   Government yield curves in selected countries, as of September 2, 2016

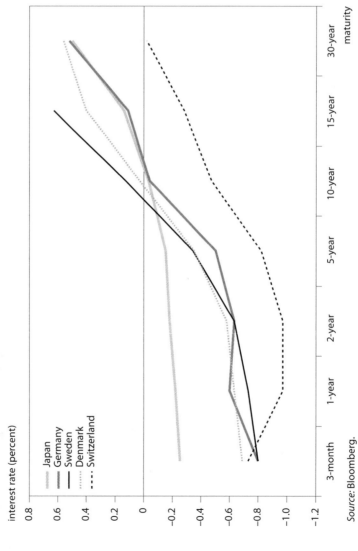

Source: Bloomberg.

From a macro standpoint, there is nothing special about negative nominal interest rates. What matters for consumption and investment decisions is real, not nominal, interest rates, and negative nominal rates do not preclude arbitrage to generate the yield curve. Negative nominal interest rates are useful to lower real interest rates when inflation is very low.

However, negative rates introduce some complications. By imposing a cost on holders of cash, especially banks, which are forced to hold cash reserves, they could induce banks to take money away from the central bank and store it in warehouses. Doing so would not be easy. Banks would face storage, transportation, and logistical costs associated with creating a system that would give them ready access to cash at all times, which is much more cumbersome than managing transactions electronically. They would also face insurance costs, as removing the cash from the central bank system introduces risk and uncertainty, and regulatory capital costs, as the supervisor could add a capital charge to compensate for the uncertainty of the new organizational structure of the bank.

Negative interest rates could create problems for financial institutions and products that offer a guaranteed positive nominal return (implicit or explicit) and restrict their asset mix. For example, US money market funds implicitly promise not to "break the buck" (not yield less than the principal invested). Pension funds and insurance companies have to match liabilities with long-duration risk-free assets to meet solvency regulations (such as the European Union's Solvency II directive). Negative interest rates also reduce the interest rate margin of banks, potentially reducing their profitability, especially in countries where loans are indexed to the policy or short-term interest rates. The evolution of private lending and deposit rates in Switzerland suggests that the main impact has been on mortgage rates (figure 3.6).

Banks have so far refrained from charging explicitly negative interest rates to retail customers, but a few banks in Switzerland and Germany have started charging corporate customers negative rates, and many banks are trying to recoup their costs via higher fees (e.g., on ATM transactions). And higher lending, if the negative rates contribute to stronger economic activity, may boost profits.[43] No one knows what the true bottom in interest rates is; it will be found via trial and error. It seems that –0.75 percent, the rate charged by the SNB and the Danmarks Nationalbank, is not generating cash outflows from the system. Harriet Jackson (2015) argues that cash outflow could start at about –200 basis points.

---

43. Zero or negative interest rates reflect the underlying macro fundamentals, not the whim of central bankers. They should be a signal for banks and financial institutions to revisit their business models to make them compatible with this reality.

Figure 3.6 Selected interest rates in Switzerland, 2009–16

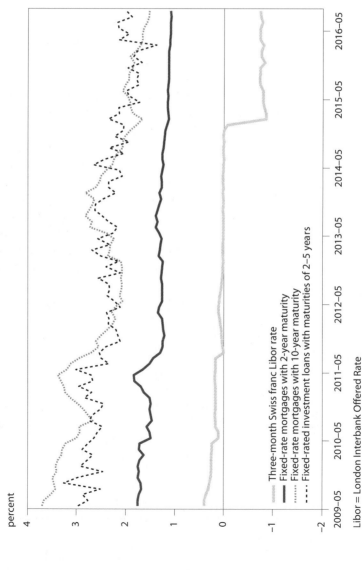

percent

Three-month Swiss franc Libor rate
Fixed-rate mortgages with 2-year maturity
Fixed-rate mortgages with 10-year maturity
Fixed-rated investment loans with maturities of 2–5 years

Libor = London Interbank Offered Rate
Source: Swiss National Bank.

These mixed assessments of negative rates made the BoE, Fed, and BoJ very reluctant to adopt them. The BoE looked into negative rates in 2013. It concluded that there were no technical obstacles but worried about cash outflows and the negative impact on bank profitability, although that effect could be attenuated with a tiered system.[44] A tiered system would require changes in the way the BoE operates, however, as it does not contemplate a division between required and excess reserves. In the case of the Fed, in addition to the concern about money market funds discussed above, there has been a desire to preserve the integrity of the fed funds market, where liquidity could disappear if rates became negative. The experience of Japan in 2005, when the BoJ had to give markets a year of advance notice of the first interest rate hike so that money markets could be rebuilt, is a cautionary tale. There are also logistical issues. For example, Treasury bills cannot be auctioned at a premium, although that rule could be changed.

Fed officials expressed varied views about negative rates. At the December 2015 meeting, Minneapolis Fed president Narayana Kocherlakota presented an optimal path for interest rates in his submission for the "dot plot" that included negative interest rates in 2016. In January 2016 New York Federal Reserve president Bill Dudley suggested that negative interest rates could be used if needed.[45] The Fed's 2016 stress testing exercise included a "severely adverse scenario" in which short-term interest rates decline to –0.5 percent as part of a policy easing package. The Fed explicitly stated that it assumed that the adjustment to negative rates "proceeds with no additional financial market disruptions" (Federal Reserve Board 2016b). This view changed during the course of 2016. The negative market reaction to the BoJ's shift to negative rates led Fed officials to strongly argue that negative rates were not likely in the United States.

The BoJ provides a very interesting experiment on the impact of negative rates. For a long time it had argued that preserving positive interest rates was a critical element in the success of QQE. It was concerned that if it were to cut the 0.1 percent that it paid on bank reserves, banks would not be willing to sell their government bonds to the BoJ. Banks' holdings of excess reserves are huge. In early 2016 the BoJ's balance sheet was almost 80 percent of GDP and projected to grow by 16 percentage points a year. In addition, Japanese government bonds are held mostly by Japanese institutions. If negative rates led to fears of large losses by increasing their reserves,

44. Charles Bean, "Note on Negative Interest Rates for Treasury Committee," letter from Treasury Select Committee, Bank of England, May 16, 2013.

45. Richard Leong, "Negative Interest Rates a Potential Policy Tool–Fed's Dudley," Reuters, January 15, 2016, www.reuters.com/article/usa-fed-dudley-negativerates-idUSL2N14Z186 (accessed on March 28, 2017).

banks could refuse to sell their bonds to the BoJ. If they refused, the BoJ would miss its QE targets, and its policy framework would lose credibility. The arguments against negative rates were thus solid.

However, the BoJ decided to surprise markets in January 2016 by cutting the deposit rate to –0.1 percent. To try to minimize the impact on banks' profitability, it adopted a three-tier system, in which banks' current accounts at the BoJ (the cash banks need to operate) would be compensated at 0.1 percent, required reserves (the additional reserves the BoJ requires banks to hold as a precaution) would be compensated at 0 percent, and excess reserves (the reserves the BoJ generates with its purchases of assets) would be charged a rate of 0.1 percent.[46,47]

The introduction of a tiered system creates a dual interest rate system, with lower rates along the yield curve to contain upward pressures on exchange rates and higher rates to minimize the damage on banks' profitability. The tiering is flexible, as the BoJ has discretion to reassign part of the reserves in the lowest tranche to the middle tranche, allowing it to maintain positive rates on the largest tranche and cut rates further on the lower tranche.

Despite all these provisions to shield the banking sector from the impact of negative rates, the surprise factor backfired. Long-term interest rates declined, but bank shares declined sharply as well, and the yen appreciated rapidly, as discussed in the next chapter. The BoJ cut rates, but financial conditions tightened. The surprise rate cut set off a wider debate about whether excessively low interest rates, especially long-term rates, were putting the banking sector business model at risk.

The negativity of the reaction significantly raised the hurdle for further rate cuts. When, two months after the BoJ rate cut, the ECB cut its deposit rate to –0.4 percent and markets reacted adopting a negative view on the European banking sector, it became clear that it was the end of the road for negative rates. The ECB added a provision to cushion the negative impact on banks: it offered them long-term loans at the negative rate, thus offering banks the possibility of borrowing money at negative rates and investing it in any positive-yielding asset. In some sense, the ECB offered banks a profitable carry trade. Nevertheless, the political backlash from some coun-

---

46. Bank of Japan, "Introduction of 'Quantitative and Qualitative Monetary Easing with a Negative Interest Rate,'" Press release, January 29, 2016, www.boj.or.jp/en/announcements/release_2016/k160129a.pdf (accessed on March 29, 2017).

47. Two other provisions were added to maximize its impact: Reserves that banks generate by borrowing from the special BoJ lending facilities would be exempted from the negative rate, and excessive cash withdrawals would be penalized by increasing the amount of reserves subject to the negative interest rate.

tries, especially Germany and the Netherlands, was very strong, as very low interest rates, if sustained for a long time, would jeopardize the solvency of their banks and insurance companies.

Negative rates are not bad per se. With a very flat yield curve, they put in question the maturity transformation business of banks and financial institutions. Of course, monetary policy is set for the whole economy, not for the banking sector. But if a monetary policy strategy is to be sustainable, it has to ensure that financial stability is not put in jeopardy. The solution may be to combine negative rates with a rebalancing of asset purchases that lead to a steepening of the yield curve, an issue discussed in chapter 5.

Global Scarcity of Dollars: Birth of Central Bank Foreign Exchange Swaps

During the peak of the crisis, the major central banks tried to coordinate their actions in an attempt to show strength and increase their force. On October 8, 2008, at 7 AM Eastern Standard Time, all of the world's major central banks cut rates by 50 basis points in unison, reinforcing the move with a joint statement.[48,49] Central banks are very jealous of their independence and committed to maintaining the domestic focus of their mandates; such an explicit coordinated action had never happened before.[50] This time it was easier to justify that there was a domestic need to ease policy, as the recession had become global.

Global coordination became very intense in the area of liquidity provision in foreign currency. Very soon it became clear that the fact that central banks were willing to provide liquidity only in their domestic currency was a major problem for financial markets. Financial institutions across the globe had currency mismatches in their balance sheets (assets and liabilities denominated in different currencies), especially in dollars, and needed to have access to liquidity in those currencies. However, only financial institutions with access to the Fed system could enjoy dollar liquidity. Banks without a presence in the United States were out of the system and had to find the liquidity in the foreign exchange market, where it was becoming very scarce and very expensive.

---

48. Federal Reserve Board press release, October 8, 2008, www.federalreserve.gov/newsevents/press/monetary/20081008a.htm (accessed on March 29, 2017).

49. The BoJ had no room to cut rates but issued a statement supporting the action. The People's Bank of China was not involved in the coordination but also cut rates, by 27 basis points.

50. The 1985 Plaza Accord—signed by the governments of France, Germany, Japan, the United Kingdom, and the United States—to depreciate the dollar versus the deutsche mark and the Japanese yen, is an example of coordinated macroeconomic policy, not just interest rate cuts, and took place over an extended period of time.

Central banks were reluctant to provide liquidity in foreign currency, as they feared potential losses arising from foreign exchange volatility. As market pressures mounted, they capitulated. In September 2008 the six major central banks (the Fed, ECB, BoE, BoJ, Bank of Canada, and Swiss National Bank) launched an array of foreign exchange swap facilities to provide dollar liquidity, priced at 100 basis points over the overnight indexed swap (OIS) rate (the spread was intended to compensate for the risk the central banks were taking).[51] In May 2009 they also agreed to accept bonds issued by the governments of the United States, United Kingdom, Japan, Germany, and France as collateral. This move enabled financial institutions to manage their collateral more efficiently. The swap facility expired in February 2010, as market functioning improved; it was reintroduced in May 2010, when the European sovereign debt problems accelerated.

As the euro area crisis deepened, it became clear that the liquidity needs were not limited to the dollar market. Therefore, in November 2011 the six central banks agreed to establish temporary bilateral liquidity swap arrangements that enabled them to provide liquidity in each jurisdiction in any of their currencies. The pricing of these swaps was also reduced, to 50 basis points over the OIS. Those swap lines were initially authorized through February 2013. In October 2013 the six central banks agreed to convert them to standing arrangements (arrangements that remain in place until further notice).[52]

The announcement effect of these foreign exchange liquidity facilities was very powerful. Most of the facilities remained unused—yet another example of the insurance channel of policy. Central banks were hesitant to provide liquidity, or accept collateral, in foreign currency for fear of incurring losses. Once the system of foreign exchange swaps was established, markets calmed down and no losses were recorded.

Policy Strategies: Forward Guidance to Sell Insurance on the Economic Outlook

If you go to the doctor with a pain and he prescribes one pill a day and tells you to come back in a week, you might wonder whether you will recover. If he tells you to take the medication until you feel better, however, you might be more hopeful. Monetary policy should work the second way: it

---

51. Other central banks—including the Reserve Bank of Australia, the Banco Central do Brasil, Danmarks Nationalbank, the Bank of Korea, the Banco de Mexico, the Reserve Bank of New Zealand, Norges Bank, the Monetary Authority of Singapore, and Sveriges Riksbank—joined the scheme at various points.

52. Federal Reserve Board, "Central Bank Liquidity Swaps," www.federalreserve.gov/monetarypolicy/bst_liquidityswaps.htm (accessed on March 29, 2017).

should apply a remedy until the objective is achieved. Forward guidance became the strategy to provide this insurance.

The use of some forward guidance by central banks had become common before the crisis. There are strong arguments for it. Central banks do not have superior knowledge about how the world works, but they should be able to explain how they think. In addition, monetary policy becomes more effective the faster its transmission to the whole yield curve. Of course, the importance of forward guidance can be exaggerated. Before the crisis, some economists were arguing that in monetary policy "little more than expectations matters" (Woodford 2005). Words would be enough, no actions needed. Experience has shown that this is not true. Forward guidance without complementary actions is not credible and loses effectiveness. Words are necessary but not sufficient.

Successful guidance implies setting clear goals, committing to achieving them, adopting clear policy actions, and providing full accountability.[53] Can a simple policy rule provide such guidance? Policy rules came into vogue after the seminal 1993 article by John Taylor, which suggested that a simple rule that explained the level of interest rates as a function of a small set of variables, including neutral interest rates, the distance of inflation from the inflation target (the inflation gap), and the distance of output from potential output (the output gap), could explain the Fed's monetary policy.

These simple policy rules might be enough guidance when interest rates are positive, the economy is near full employment, and inflation is near target. However, they are very likely to be a very incomplete, if not erroneous, description of a goal-oriented policy when interest rates are closer to zero or the shocks affecting the economy are large, for two reasons. First, short-term interest rates cannot go much below zero, but the rule may indicate deeply negative rates.[54] The central bank has a wide array of other instruments at its disposal that the policy rule does not directly capture. Second, large shocks very likely generate large and time-varying changes in the underlying parameters of the reaction function—for example, the neutral real interest rate—that would make simple rules based on experience misleading. Forward guidance, with its fuller and more complete description of the nuances of the policy strategy, is a way to overcome the shortcomings of simple policy rules.

---

53. See Charles Evans, "Like It or Not, 90 Percent of a 'Successful Fed Communications' Strategy Comes from Simply Pursuing a Goal-oriented Monetary Policy Strategy," speech at the US Monetary Policy Forum, February 28, 2014.

54. For example, the rule described in Taylor (1999) would have suggested interest rates in the United States of –5 percent in 2009 (see Rudebusch 2009).

Forward guidance is also necessary because when growth shocks are very large or there is a risk of hitting the EZLB, the optimal policy prescription may demand that monetary policy be run in a slightly different way than usual. When interest rates are positive, the central bank cares equally about deviations in each direction of output from potential and inflation from its target (in technical terms, the central bank minimizes a quadratic loss function on the output gap and the inflation gap). Monetary policy then aims to set interest rates in a way that minimizes interest rate volatility and closes both the inflation gap and the output gap. In most cases these gaps are of similar magnitude; the central bank therefore sets interest rates to close them at a similar pace.

That practice may change when the size of the two gaps differs. If the output gap is much larger than the inflation gap—as happened during the crisis, for example, when the increase in unemployment was much larger than the decline in inflation—monetary policy should focus more on closing the output gap (in technical terms, the coefficient of the output gap in the policy rule may increase relative to the coefficient on the inflation gap). This practice—which Janet Yellen has called the "balanced approach rule"[55]—may imply a monetary policy stance that is more stimulative than in the past.

If, in addition, interest rates are close to zero, the central bank may care more about downside deviations of inflation and growth than upside deviations. The reason is the asymmetric nature of risks when rates are zero: Even if the central bank can deploy other instruments to ease policy, when interest rates are zero it is easier for the central bank to tighten policy if inflation or growth becomes too high than to ease policy if inflation or growth becomes too low. This difference implies that monetary policy becomes more inertial—changes to interest rates as output and inflation improve occur at a slower pace than when interest rates are at normal levels. As a result the central bank will want to keep policy easier for longer than when interest rates are positive.

In both cases, the standard policy rule would not cut interest rates enough and would raise them too soon. If markets followed the standard rule to price assets, the economy would not recover and inflation would remain too low. If the central bank did not communicate the change in approach, there would not be any assurances that the economy would return to equilibrium after a large shock.

Simple policy rules are thus good descriptions of how monetary policy works, but they are not invariant over time. In some special circumstances, the monetary policy strategy needs to deviate from the past, and the central

---

55. Janet L. Yellen, "Perspectives on Monetary Policy," speech at the Boston Economic Club Dinner sponsored by the Federal Reserve Bank of Boston, June 6, 2012.

bank needs to educate markets (and, when operating by committee, its own committee members) on this different strategy. Forward guidance becomes critical to communicate that monetary policy will do all that is needed to restore growth and inflation. It becomes the instrument to provide insurance on the economic outlook at times of change and uncertainty.

Forward guidance was widely used before the crisis, in speeches, statements, and monetary policy reports. The Fed introduced explicit guidance after cutting rates to 1 percent in August 2003, as a replacement of the simple biases it had used to signal the likely direction of rates: "In these circumstances, the Committee believes that policy accommodation can be maintained for a considerable period." As the Fed became more convinced that the next move in rates would be up, this guidance shifted in January 2004 to "the Committee believes that it can be patient in removing its policy accommodation" and in May 2004 to "the Committee believes that policy accommodation can be removed at a pace that is likely to be measured." The Fed provided guidance about both the timing of the beginning of the rate-hiking cycle and its pace.[56]

The BoE traditionally provided guidance through its inflation forecasts. It provides two inflation forecasts, one under constant interest rates and one under market interest rates. BoE watchers analyze the difference between the two to assess whether the BoE agreed with market pricing.

The ECB became fond of its "traffic light" system (essentially variations of the word "vigilance") to preannounce near-term interest rate increases. "Vigilance" typically meant a rate hike coming soon but not imminently, "strong vigilance" meant a rate hiking coming at the next meeting. The BoJ started providing forward guidance in 1999, signaling that rates would remain at zero until "deflationary concerns were dispelled."

As with asset purchases, central banks started using forward guidance cautiously—and with limited initial success. Despite some verbal guidance from the Fed (communicating that interest would remain unchanged for "some time"), markets were consistently pricing the return to positive rates about 6–12 months after the Fed cut rates to zero. Habits are very persistent. Markets had no history at the zero bound to base their outlook on and were using historical experience as a guide. They had to be educated about a new reality. Forward guidance evolved, becoming increasingly explicit and more closely linked to economic conditions. Most central banks transitioned from open-ended guidance ("some time") to time-contingent

56. Federal Reserve, press release, August 12, 2003, www.federalreserve.gov/boarddocs/press/monetary/2003/20030812/default.htm; press release, January 28, 2004, www.federalreserve.gov/boarddocs/press/monetary/2004/20040128; press release, May 4, 2004, www.federalreserve.gov/boarddocs/press/monetary/2004/20040504/default.htm.

guidance ("until December 2013") and state-contingent threshold guidance ("until the unemployment rate declines below 7 percent").

The Bank of Canada led the way. In April 2009 it introduced an innovation in forward guidance with explicit calendar guidance that suggested that interest rates would be on hold until a specific time (the second quarter of 2010). When it hiked rates (in April 2010, a quarter before the time implied by the calendar guidance), the new guidance focused on two elements. First, by stressing the large amount of slack in the economy and the long time it would take to absorb it, it signaled the likely gradual pace of rate hikes. Second, by stressing that the neutral rate was lower than in the past and that interest rates would be below neutral when slack was reabsorbed and inflation at target because of persistent headwinds, it indicated the likely lower endpoint of the hiking cycle. Most central banks would later follow this model.

The Fed started with some fuzzy temporal guidance in December 2008, signaling low rates for "some time," which in March 2009 became low rates for an "extended period." As the euro area crisis deepened, the Fed shifted to calendar guidance in August 2011, signaling that rates would be on hold until at least late 2013. This calendar guidance was modified twice, first in January 2012 (when the Fed announced that rates would be on hold until late 2014) and then in September 2012 (when it announced that rates would be on hold until mid-2015).[57]

Dissatisfaction with calendar guidance led to the adoption, in December 2012, of state-contingent guidance defining an "area of inaction" based on macroeconomic variables: an unemployment rate above 6.5 percent, an inflation rate of less than 2.5 percent one and two years out, and well-anchored inflation expectations. As long as the economy was in this area of inaction, markets should be confident that interest rates would not be changed. In addition, the FOMC stated that it "expects that a highly accommodative stance of monetary policy will remain appropriate for a considerable time after the asset purchase program ends and the economic recovery strengthens." Thus the Fed wanted to reassure markets that it would create a large enough cushion of growth before tightening policy. As with asset purchases, the strategy shifted toward providing insurance, with the Fed communicating that it would do whatever it took to achieve its mandate.

As the economy approached the point at which the thresholds were about to be breached, the guidance reverted to a more qualitative stance:

---

57. Federal Reserve, FOMC statement, December 16, 2008, www.federalreserve.gov/news-events/pressreleases/monetary20081216b.htm; FOMC statement, March 18, 2009, www.federalreserve.gov/newsevents/pressreleases/monetary20090318a.htm; Federal Reserve issues FOMC statement, December 12, 2012, www.federalreserve.gov/newsevents/pressreleases/monetary20121212a.htm.

Rates would be on hold "well past" the moment the unemployment rate crossed 6.5 percent. In March 2014 the Fed replaced the thresholds with qualitative guidance (similar to that adopted by the BoE, as described below) about the likely timing of the liftoff, the pace of rate hikes, and the terminal point. This verbal guidance was supplemented by the dot chart in the Survey of Economic Projections (SEP), which showed the path of interest rates consistent with the economic projections of each FOMC member. At that point the Fed was using a belt and suspenders approach, with state-contingent language in the statement combined with explicit rate guidance in the dot chart to guide markets.[58] When the time to raise rates arrived, the Fed introduced the concept of "gradual" rate hikes, to reinforce the message that the rate hiking cycle would be slow.

The ECB had refused to use explicit guidance on interest rates, out of concern that it would reduce its anti-inflation credibility. However, when global interest rates increased rapidly during the taper tantrum episode (the sharp increase in interest rates that followed Ben Bernanke's announcement that the Fed was considering tapering its asset purchases), the ECB adopted interest rate guidance in July 2013, stating that rates would stay on hold or lower "for an extended period of time." The strategy was defensive, aimed at avoiding an unwarranted tightening of financial conditions; it provided little additional information about the conditions that underpin the "extended period" (ECB 2013b, 2014).

This forward guidance was reinforced by the extension in May 2013 of the horizon of the fixed-rate full-allotment tenders to July 2014, with the implicit understanding that for as long as the ECB continued the full-allotment procedure, interest rates would not increase. When it finally launched QE, the ECB linked the guidance on rates to QE, stating that it expected rates "to remain at present or lower levels for an extended period of time, and well past the horizon of our net asset purchases." The ECB used a mixed forward guidance strategy for QE, combining calendar guidance with state-contingent guidance linked to the achievement of price stability: "These purchases are intended to run until the end of March 2017, or beyond, if necessary, and in any case until the Governing Council sees a sustained adjustment in the path of inflation consistent with its inflation aim."[59]

The BoE adopted state-contingent guidance in August 2013, replicating the "zone of inaction" the Fed had adopted earlier. It declared that interest

---

58. The Survey of Economic Projections remains an imperfect instrument, because it reveals discrepancies around a modal forecast, not uncertainty around a baseline case, and is not based on a homogeneous set of forecasts.

59. Mario Draghi, "Introductory Statement to the Press Conference (with Q&A)," Frankfurt, April 21, 2016.

rates would remain unchanged until the unemployment rate fell below a threshold (7 percent), subject to an inflation knockout (inflation not higher than 2.5 percent 18–24 months out) and a financial stability knockout (based on a decision by the Financial Policy Committee) (Monetary Policy Committee 2013). The intention was twofold: to give the economy room to grow in the face of very uncertain productivity growth, and to stress that there was much slack in the economy and that a period of rapid growth would therefore not lead to increases in interest rates.[60] As the unemployment rate approached 7 percent, the BoE moved in February 2014 to provide qualitative guidance on the policy reaction function that would prevail once the thresholds had been breached. Like the Fed, the BoE suggested that the liftoff of interest rates would be delayed and the hiking cycle gradual because of the large amount of slack and lower neutral rate.

The BoJ had been using forward guidance as a key policy tool since 1999. It introduced two variations during the crisis. During 2010–13, in the context of its strategy of "comprehensive monetary easing," it introduced forward guidance on interest rates: Rates would be at zero until inflation reached 1 percent. In April 2013 it shifted its strategy to QQE, which included, in addition to a new instrument (base money growth) and new asset purchases, forward guidance for asset purchases linked to a higher inflation rate with a temporal dimension (2 percent inflation to be reached in two years). In addition to this time-defined guidance, the BoJ added an open-ended second layer of guidance: It would continue to use QQE for as long as needed to maintain 2 percent inflation in a "stable" manner, with "stable" meaning that medium-term inflation expectations should be compatible with 2 percent inflation.

Central banks used words in many different ways. But words were not enough. The taper tantrum episode revealed that forward guidance and asset purchases were very complementary. After Bernanke hinted at the tapering of asset purchases, markets not only repriced the amount of expected asset purchases, they also aggressively brought forward the beginning of the rate-hiking cycle. This episode highlighted that what the Fed thought was the optimal sequencing for an exit strategy—first announce the tapering of asset purchases, then reinforce forward guidance for interest rates as needed—was wrong and that forward guidance for interest rates had to be reinforced first, in order to replace the positive impact on guidance of asset purchases. The reasoning of markets was simple: Markets believed that as long as a central bank was buying assets, it would not consider raising rates. The period during which asset purchases are undertaken is therefore

---

60. Spencer Dale and James Talbot, "Forward Guidance in the UK," VoxEU, September 13, 2013, www.voxeu.org/article/forward-guidance-uk (accessed on March 28, 2017).

taken as a "guarantee" that rates remain on hold (the signaling channel of asset purchases). Once asset purchases are over, uncertainty about guidance increases, no matter how strong the language, because the central bank can always change its mind.

Policy Communication: Opening the Doors of the Temple

Central banks used to be very secretive institutions. A 1987 book on the Fed, *Secrets of the Temple*, described it as a powerful center of political power, shielded from electoral scrutiny (Greider 1987). Alan Greenspan was legendary for the opaqueness of his comments and statements. His famous quip—"Since becoming a central banker, I have learned to mumble with great incoherence. If I seem unduly clear to you, you must have misunderstood what I said"[61]—summarizes the state of central bank communication a few decades ago. Constructive ambiguity was the preferred strategy.

This opaqueness started to change as central banks adopted inflation-targeting regimes that relied strongly on a credible inflation target. For the target to be credible, the Fed needed to explain how monetary policy operated.

The crisis led to a significant increase in transparency and communication across central banks. The need to enhance the credibility of their anti-deflationary strategies, the potential fiscal implications of some of their actions, and the controversy around the potential negative effects of asset purchases and negative interest rates led central banks to increase the quantity and quality of their communications. In 2009, at the peak of the crisis, Ben Bernanke even appeared on the CBS program *60 Minutes* to explain to the public what the Fed was doing.

The Fed continued the increased transparency initiated under Chairman Greenspan and strongly promoted by Chairman Bernanke. It expanded all FOMC meetings to two days, to allow more time for debate. It revamped the communication of its growth, unemployment, and inflation forecasts, increasing the frequency to four times a year, adding a year to the forecast, and providing a longer-run forecast that was intended to communicate the FOMC's view of the inflation objective, the nonaccelerating inflation rate of unemployment (NAIRU), potential growth, and the neutral interest rate. It also created the famous dot plot to communicate the path of interest rates each member of the FOMC considered compatible with his or her growth and inflation forecast. It added press conferences after the four meetings at which the new forecasts are released. FOMC members became more explicit

---

61. Comments before a Senate Committee in 1987, as quoted in the *Guardian Weekly*, November 4, 2005.

and detailed in their speeches, communicating in detail their outlook and, at times, their personal views about interest rates.

The BoE had a well-established and comprehensive communication framework that included the staggered publication of the minutes of the meetings, the detailed quarterly *Inflation Report*, and associated press conferences. Nevertheless, it introduced changes to the discussion of its forecasts in the *Inflation Report*, adding details about the estimated level of slack in the economy, the risks to the forecast, and the potential policy changes associated with those risks. It consolidated all the communications related to a given meeting into a single day, the Thursday of the week of the meeting (previously the statement was made on the day of the meeting, the *Inflation Report* was released a week later, and the minutes were reported two weeks later).

The ECB had been giving press conferences since its inception, as it felt a special need to explain the policies of a new institution to the very diverse public of the euro area. At the same time, it was the only major central bank that did not publish the minutes of its deliberations, having put a strong emphasis on its consensus decision making and therefore not considering it useful to disclose the debate that led to its decisions. In part because of the need to better explain its complex policy strategy, in part because of the politically conflictive nature of some of its actions, in 2014 it finally took the step of publishing the minutes of its meetings. It also reduced the frequency of its meetings, from 12 to 8, to diminish potential volatility induced by press conferences at which there was nothing new to communicate. Its new schedule matches the frequency of the Fed meetings.

A revamped communication strategy became an integral part of the new QQE strategy of Governor Haruhiko Kuroda. The BoJ focused on conveying a simple and clear message, designing QQE to be as memorable as the "2-2-2" approach: The BoJ would double the monetary base to achieve 2 percent inflation within about two years. In addition, to signal a clear break with the past, it changed the operational target from interest rates to the quantity of money (the monetary base). The BoJ expanded the information provided about the forecasts of the board members, with charts showing the aggregate probability distribution around median forecasts of growth and inflation and identifying individually the upside or downside risk associated with each board member's forecast.

Do or Do Not. There Is No Try

In Star Wars the old master Yoda had very clear advice for Luke Skywalker: "Do or do not. There is no try." Central banks reacted in many ways, along multiple dimensions, to contain the economic damage of the crisis. They left their comfort zones, many times grudgingly, going in directions no one could have imagined in 2007. They provided long-term liquidity, against very diverse collateral and in foreign exchange. They purchased a wide range of assets and, in many cases, became market makers of last resort. They cut rates to zero—and then to negative levels. They purchased more government bonds than countries had time to issue, de facto monetizing the fiscal deficit. They committed to keeping interest rates on hold for as long as needed. They made public the details of their deliberations, exposing themselves to heavy criticism.

However, the process to get there was often too slow and too cautious. Part of the reason why the central banks ended up implementing such a wide array of policies is that they were too conservative to start with. They were not doing, they were just trying. Their intellectual anchor created shackles that were difficult to shake. They worried too much about inflation and the potential side effects of low interest rates. The ECB's decision to raise rates by surprise in 2008, just a few months after a large US investment bank had been bailed out, reveals the extent of the asymmetric and narrow focus of central banks at the beginning of the crisis. The ECB's refusal to engage in QE at the beginning of the crisis generated a sharp tightening of financial conditions and very deep disinflationary momentum. As a result, it ended up having to implement a very aggressive QE program. The Fed's obsession with communicating its ability to exit from the initial QE program and reduce its balance sheet to precrisis levels, and its concerns about potential losses, blunted its effectiveness, forcing it to purchase more assets than it otherwise would have. The BoJ's excessive concern about losses from its purchases of government bonds led it to buy only at the front end of the curve, allowing long-term interest rates to rise too high. When it finally corrected, its balance sheet ballooned to levels well above what it had earlier feared.

Slowness and cautiousness also reflected intense learning by doing. This learning process led to a transition toward goal-oriented strategies—toward providing insurance on the economic outlook. The rules for asset purchases, and the forward guidance for both asset purchases and interest rates, transitioned from fixed quantities and dates to state-contingent rules (based on economic outcomes). At a time of high uncertainty, monetary policy worked best by providing insurance and committing to doing whatever it took to deliver its mandate.

Personalities mattered. Ben Bernanke was a scholar of the Great Depression. He was primed to fight deflationary forces and ready to engage in blue-sky thinking to find solutions. He did not have to be convinced that QE was the right policy to overcome deflation. Mervyn King's academic approach to central banking and economic analysis, and his well-known disdain for financial markets, led him to be overconfident about the virtues of a steady hand as the crisis unfolded. As a result, in September 2007 he presided over a run on Northern Rock, the first bank run in the United Kingdom since 1866. Jean-Claude Trichet had a more Germanic view of the world. He saw the crisis as an opportunity to use the ECB as a disciplinary instrument to make the euro area a more perfect monetary union via structural reforms in the crisis countries. His view introduced a deflationary bias into the ECB's strategy that changed only with the arrival of Mario Draghi. Masaaki Shirakawa was convinced that Japan's problems were structural, that there was little the BoJ could do to solve them. He therefore focused on keeping pressure on the government to consolidate the public finances and keeping monetary conditions tight to increase the incentive for structural reforms. His focus introduced a deflationary bias into the BoJ's strategy that changed only when Haruhiko Kuroda replaced him as governor.

As discussed in chapter 2, the environment was not favorable for central banks. Public opinion had been anchored in the anti-inflation debate of the last 40 years. It had a hard time accepting that the West could suffer a Japanese-style deflation and that very aggressive monetary policy was needed to avoid it. Politicians were not ready to understand that fiscal policy had to complement monetary policy and that fiscal austerity today could lead to weaker growth and higher debt levels tomorrow. Academics wanted to protect their pet theories to secure their moment of glory, regardless of the suitability to the problem at hand.

In the end, central banks were left alone. They were the only game in town. They knew what they needed to do but in most cases lacked both the will and the support to make it happen. Ben Bernanke's book is aptly titled *The Courage to Act*. It is scary to conclude that the Fed needs to increase the size of its balance sheet by several multiples in order to ease policy enough. It is human to fear the unknown, to decide to do a fraction of what needs to be done and see what happens, as the Fed did when it first launched QE. Humans like reference points, and the reference points are the experiences of the recent past. Learning is always a gradual process.

Central banks had many elements working against them. In an unfavorable environment, they wanted to be conservative as a means of self-preservation. They took some risks, at times not enough, but they all ended up providing insurance. The next chapter evaluates how well they did despite the headwinds.

4

Has Monetary Policy Worked?
Yes, No, Maybe

The problem with QE is that it works in practice, but it does not work in theory.[1]

—Ben Bernanke

If you go to the Mercato di San Lorenzo in Florence and quietly start buying up leather belts, it is possible that, after a while, the price of leather belts will go up, as merchants slowly realize that there is sudden excess demand. If you also announce loudly that you want to buy most of the supply of leather belts, the price of belts will surely go up—and the price of leather jackets or bags may rise as well. They are made of leather, are a nice accessory typical of Florence, and, given the scarcity of leather belts, tourists may decide to buy them as a souvenir instead. But why would the price of pizza at nearby stands go up? Why would the owners of food stalls selling panini consider hiring more people?

The same questions have been puzzling economists about QE. In theory, central bank asset purchases should have no effect on the economy beyond the prices of the specific assets being purchased. The central bank is just exchanging one kind of government debt (money) for another kind (government bonds). Unless investors have a strong preference for one versus the other, QE should make no difference. Of course, this view of monetary policy is mechanical. There is more to monetary policy than actions, as argued in chapter 3. Words and attitudes matter.

The puzzle has not been fully resolved. After almost a decade of zero rates, asset purchases, and forward guidance, there is still debate about whether monetary policy has been effective. The prevailing view is that it

---

1. Robin Harding, "US Quantitative Measures Worked in Defiance of Theory," *Financial Times*, October 13, 2014, www.ft.com/content/3b164d2e-4f03-11e4-9c88-00144feab7de (accessed on March 28, 2017).

has worked, in a rather conventional way, by reducing uncertainty, lowering real interest rates, and increasing asset prices. Monetary policy contributed to softening the impact of the crisis, boosting growth, and stabilizing inflation to some degree.

Skeptics argue that these monetary policy actions just inflated asset values and that the values will deflate once the asset purchases and their associated money flow end. According to this view, only structural policies can boost growth and restore price stability; cyclical policies can do little to offset the impact of a financial crisis (see, e.g., Hall 2013). All that monetary policy can do, at most, is buy time for governments to implement reforms. Worse, monetary policy can have negative side effects, creating moral hazard that delays reforms, blowing financial bubbles, or increasing inequality.

In the end, assessing whether monetary policy has been effective is an empirical question. Previous chapters have looked at the intellectual background before the crisis, the conceptual issues related to how monetary policy works, and the actions taken by central banks. This chapter examines the results. Precise measurement of the impact of specific policies always faces the problem of defining the counterfactual—what would have happened in the absence of the policy. Counterfactuals are not observable. But one can indirectly evaluate the success of monetary policy in four main ways:

- Did monetary policy decisions affect financial conditions in the expected way?
- Did policies ease to the extent recommended by simple benchmark rules?
- Did policies achieve their objectives in terms of inflation and growth?
- Has monetary policy had any negative side effects?

Did Monetary Policy Decisions Affect Financial Conditions in the Expected Way?

The most immediate way to assess the impact of monetary policy on financial conditions is to look at the evolution of indexes of financial conditions, which capture the level of dislocation of financial markets. A key impediment for the effectiveness of monetary policy early in the crisis was the clogging of the transmission mechanism: Central banks were cutting interest rates, but private interest rates were not declining in parallel—and often were increasing, as risk aversion and default worries contaminated financial markets (as discussed in chapter 3). Monetary policy initially focused on reducing these dislocations.

The Bloomberg Financial Conditions Index summarizes the behavior of a wide range of financial market indicators, mostly related to market functioning, relative to their precrisis long-term averages. It is constructed from the normalized values of the variables (demeaned and then divided by their standard deviation, with means and standard deviations calculated for 1994–2007); the composite index is normalized to precrisis levels. The index shows the z-scores that indicate the number of standard deviations by which financial conditions deviate from precrisis levels.

Figure 4.1 shows the dramatic worsening of financial conditions after the bankruptcy of Lehman Brothers and their subsequent improvement as central banks deployed an array of liquidity facilities that eliminated default risk in interbank markets, risky assets rallied, and bond yields declined. Financial conditions worsened again as the euro area crisis deepened, returning to normal levels only in late 2012, after Mario Draghi's "whatever it takes" statement. Financial conditions peaked in July 2014, around the time it became clear that the Fed would end its quantitative asset program later that year. They have declined toward average levels since then.

Impact of Asset Purchase Programs

Brief Summary of the Literature

Much research has been devoted to studying the impact of specific asset purchase programs. The main conclusion is that policies aiming to restore the functioning of disrupted markets have been very effective, with dislocations eliminated and market functioning broadly restored. Indeed, most programs have been discontinued (exceptions include the full-allotment nature of the ECB's monetary policy operations and the foreign exchange swaps among central banks).

There is broad consensus that policies were successful at lowering real interest rates, boosting asset prices, and reducing risk aversion. Assessment of the precise impact of policies aimed at lowering long-term interest rates has focused on both event studies and time series analysis (see, among many others, Gagnon et al. 2011, IMF 2013, and Joyce 2013).

While useful and illustrative, these studies are necessarily approximative and have several potential shortcomings. Most event studies compute the instant market reaction to the policy announcement, which may not be the same as the market reaction to the policy package, as in many cases the policy package was partly priced in before it was announced. They also assume that the market instantly prices in the full impact of the policy package, without allowing for either a delayed reaction by some market participants who update their portfolios less frequently or effects of a more persistent nature. Time series provide a useful cross-check on event studies, but to isolate the impact of the policy package they have to rely on identification assumptions over which there is little agreement. Studies cannot measure the buyer of last resort effect: Even if programs were rela-

Figure 4.1 Bloomberg Financial Conditions Index in selected economies, 1999–2016

z-score versus precrisis average level

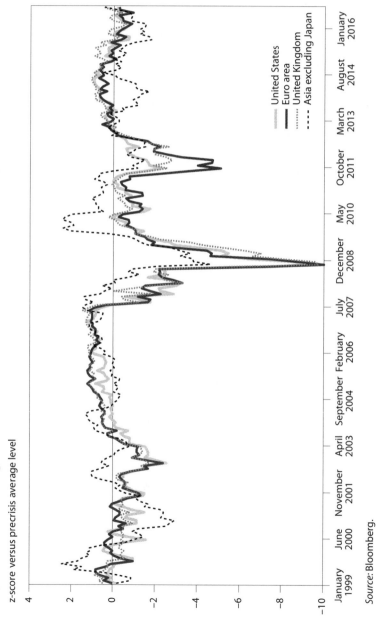

Source: Bloomberg.

tively small, markets assumed that in case of need, central banks would step up their purchases.

Given the difficulty of identifying the channels of transmission of QE, it is not surprising that there is wide disagreement about the precise impact of these programs (Reza, Santor, and Suchanek 2015; Borio and Zabai 2016). Few of these studies are comparable, as they focus on different time horizons and sizes. To overcome this problem, Philippe Andrade et al. (2016) computed the implied impact from a range of academic studies of an asset purchase program that represents 10 percent of GDP. The results show declines in long-term yields in the range of 23–175 basis points in the United States, 31–107 in the United Kingdom, 27–64 in the euro area, and 10–26 in Japan. Because it also lifted inflation expectations, the BoJ's QQE program is estimated to have reduced real interest rates by about 100 basis points (BoJ 2015).

Rafael De Rezende, David Kjellberg, and Oskar Tysklind (2015) study the impact of the Sveriges Riksbank's QE program on asset prices. They find a cumulative reduction on 10-year bond yields of about 30 basis points, comparable to the experience of other central banks. They provide a useful rule of thumb: Asset purchases worth about 4 percent of GDP lead to a reduction in long-term yields of about 30 basis points.

Some studies find that purchases of private assets were powerful early in the crisis, with QE1 in the United States reducing yields on mortgage-backed securities by about 150 basis points (Krishnamurthy and Vissing-Jørgensen 2011) and mortgage rates by about 50 basis points (Hancock and Passmore 2011). Some policies aimed at easing funding conditions in specific markets are considered to have been particularly successful. For example, the BoE's Funding for Lending Scheme (FLS), which is estimated to have lowered bank funding spreads by at least 100 basis points (Joyce 2013).

Because of the simultaneous nature of most of its policies, it is more difficult to identify the precise impact of ECB actions, but the overall assessment is that they were successful in lowering sovereign yields, reducing banks' credit risk and funding costs, and diminishing market segmentation. Marcel Fratzscher, Marco Lo Duca, and Roland Straub (2014) study the impact of ECB's programs (long-term refinancing operations [LTROs], the Securities Markets Program, Outright Monetary Transactions) on assets across countries. They find a strong impact in Italy and Spain (a reduction of 50–125 basis points on government yields, an increase of 5–10 percent in equity returns) and a much smaller impact on core euro area countries (almost negligible on bond yields, 0–10 percent on equity returns).

Viral Acharya et al. (2015) study the impact of the ECB's Outright Monetary Transactions announcement on euro area banks' behavior. They find that banks' credit risk declined as a result of the increase in the prices of their holdings of periphery sovereign bonds. The decline led to increased loan supply, especially for lower-quality borrowers. The combination of LTROs and QE also contributed to reducing the geographical segmentation of lending rates across euro area countries that opened up during the crisis (figure 4.2). The ECB's private asset program was less successful in boosting issuance and developing the market. Growth in the issuance of asset-backed securities in Europe was flat, failing to generate the expected expansion in supply.[2]

The impact of monetary policy actions during the crisis appears to be similar to the impact of monetary policy before the crisis. A study by the IMF (2013) compares the impact on government bond yields of policy surprises (defined as the change in the three-month interest rate one year forward) before and after 2007. It finds that the impact on asset prices was sizable in the United States, United Kingdom, and Japan but this impact is statistically greater only in the post-2007 period for US bond yields. Using an event study, Joseph Gagnon et al. (2011) find that the Fed's QE1 lowered bond yields by about 100 basis points, while a historical regression finds that a switch of Treasury duration equivalent to QE1 would have reduced bond yields by 50 basis points. These results indicate that asset purchases have a greater impact during a period of financial stress but that their impact is also sizable during normal times. The extent of the policy surprises was greater in the post-2007 period, when the policies were new and markets did not expect them in many cases, which explains why the absolute impact of policies was bigger as well.

The literature thus suggests that monetary policy is effective after short-term interest rates reach zero and does not necessarily suffer from diminishing returns. Impact depends on adopting the right strategy and implementing it in the right size.

Signaling, Portfolio Rebalancing, and Insurance

The next step after assessing the effectiveness of monetary policy is evaluating the specific avenues through which it has acted. The portfolio-rebalancing effect operates mostly by reducing the term premium on sovereign bonds. As the central bank communicates that it will be purchasing large quantities of bonds for an extended period, markets reduce the term premium they are willing to demand to hold these bonds—after all, there is a buyer of last resort. Demand for bonds increases, raising their price (and reducing their yield).

---

2. Christopher Whitall, "ECB's Attempt to Breathe New Life into Securitization Market Falls Flat," *Wall Street Journal*, February 1, 2016, www.wsj.com/articles/ecbs-attempt-to-breathe-new-life-into-securitization-market-falls-flat-1454315616 (accessed on March 28, 2017).

Figure 4.2   Corporate cost of borrowing in France, Germany, Italy, and Spain, 2003–17

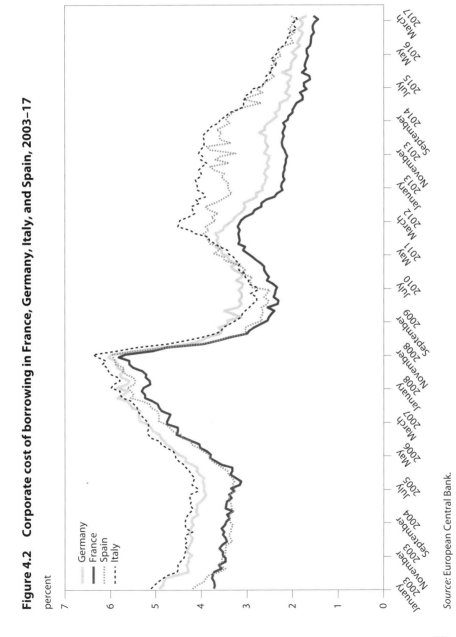

Source: European Central Bank.

Disentangling the term-premium effect from the signaling effect is not straightforward. When the central bank communicates that it is going to buy bonds until a set of economic conditions is met, it is also implicitly signaling that short-term interest rates will not be increased at least until it has achieved those conditions. Therefore, as long as the central bank is buying bonds, it is signaling that interest rates will not be increased. Some studies find that institutional factors can play a role in the relative importance of one channel versus the other (see, e.g., Christensen and Rudebusch 2012).

One way to separate the portfolio-rebalancing effect from the signaling effect is to look at financial market prices. Figure 4.3 compares the evolution of an estimate of the term premium on US 10-year rates (from Adrian, Covitz, and Liang 2014) with the evolution of the one-year interest rate two years forward (1y2y). With short-term interest rates pegged at zero, 1y2y is a good indicator of the market view about the timing of the next increase in interest rates and therefore of the signaling effect of policy.

The term premium and the 1y2y moved in parallel during most of the period, suggesting significant endogeneity between the two. Assurances about the path of short-term rates led to a lower term premium at the front end of the yield curve (as markets had high certainty that interest rates would not be increased); this assurance about short-term rates lowered the term premium at the long end of the curve as well, helping lower 10-year rates. At the same time, the sharp increase in long-term rates following the Fed's suggestion that asset purchases could end in the near future—the taper tantrum episode of mid-2013—also led to a rapid repricing of the timing and extent of the rate-hiking cycle, as the sharp move of the 1y2y curve suggests. When the Fed communicated that the QE program would end sooner than expected, the market brought forward the beginning of rate hikes. Once the central bank is no longer buying bonds, there is no certainty that it will not raise rates.

Only in 2014 did these two curves separate, in a possibly counterintuitive way. The Fed's tapering of the QE program led to an increase in short-term rates as the probability of near-term rate hikes increased, but the term premium declined sharply. The reason was that while the Fed was ending its bond purchases program, the ECB and the BoJ were increasing the size of their own programs. Their actions reduced the term premium for European and Japanese bonds and, by extension, US bonds. Over time it became clear that the term-premium effect was global, something that became even more apparent during 2015–16. Even as the Fed was raising rates, the term premium on US 10-year rates declined, pushed lower by the policies of the ECB and the BoJ.

This global term-premium effect became more intense as the yield curves in Europe and Japan dipped into negative territory. Investors in those

Figure 4.3 Signaling versus term-premium effects in the United States, 2007–16

percent

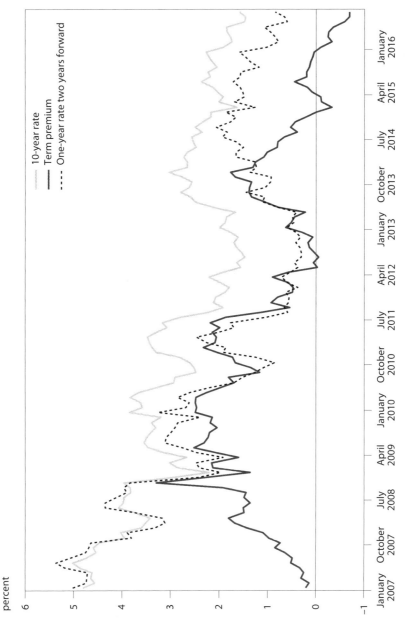

Sources: Term premium estimates are from Adrian, Crump, and Moench (2013). Rates are from Bloomberg.

regions had two options for avoiding negative interest rates: increasing the duration of their domestic fixed-income holdings or increasing their holdings of foreign bonds with positive yields. Both options increased demand for US Treasuries, lowering their yield and pushing the term premium to all-time lows.

Another channel of transmission of asset purchases is the insurance effect. An important role of monetary policy during the crisis was to provide insurance against the economic outlook. Several times in the last few years markets panicked, fearing that a new Great Depression was in sight. Monetary policy was seen as the only tool with which to fend it off, given the reluctance of politicians to use fiscal policy.

Several studies show that the decline in growth during 2008–09 was "impossible" using the data and models available in 2008 and that the decline in growth was incompatible with the model's relationship with inflation (see, among others, Chung et al. 2011 for the United States and Fawcett et al. 2015 for the United Kingdom). The decline in growth and employment was outside the 95 percent confidence interval of the forecasts generated by these models, but the inflation forecast was within the expected range. In other words, economists did not know why growth was collapsing or why inflation was not collapsing. This uncertainty about the underlying model of the economy required central banks to provide insurance to convince economic agents that, despite not fully understanding what was really driving the sharp recession, policy would return the economy to an expansionary mode.

The announcement of a large asset purchase program increased the conviction among investors that central banks were ready to do whatever was necessary to restore growth and inflation. Those actions had the effect of reducing overall tail risks, as evident from the reduction in stock market uncertainty implicit in the VIX Index (which captures the implied volatility of options on the S&P 500 Index), the lower probabilities of large exchange rate swings implicit in foreign exchange option risk reversals, and the lower probability of deflation implicit in the skewedness of inflation forecasts.

Spikes in risk aversion determined the timing of many of the main policy actions, as seen in figure 4.4, which shows the evolution of the VIX Index and the MOVE Index (which measures the implied volatility embedded in options of US interest rates across the yield curve). Both variables can be interpreted as measures of uncertainty about the evolution of the economy. All major announcements coincided with spikes in these variables and were reasonably successful in offsetting them, reducing uncertainty about the outlook. The lowest uncertainty point was right before the taper tantrum, when market certainty was high about the future path of the economy (low VIX Index) and the probability that interest rates

Figure 4.4 Impact of quantitative easing announcements on VIX and MOVE Indices, 2005–15

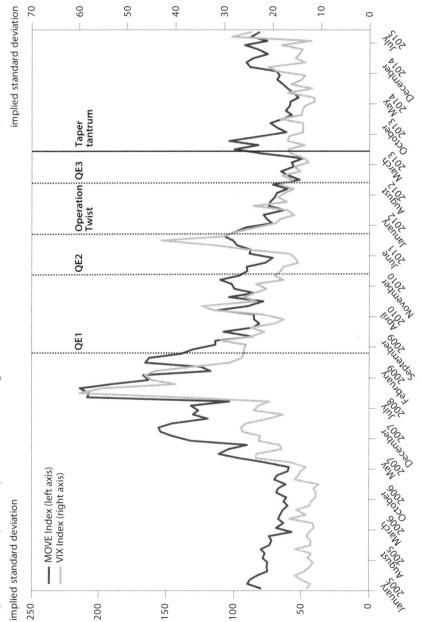

Source: Bloomberg.

would not change (the lowest point on the MOVE Index). To a large extent, this high certainty about the path of interest rates explains the size of the taper tantrum: Fixed-income markets were caught by surprise by the news that QE might end at some point and had to adjust quickly.

Several studies confirm this relationship between uncertainty and policy actions. Geert Bekaert, Marie Hoerova, and Marco Lo Duca (2010) show that a cut in the Fed funds rate is followed by a decline in the VIX Index, while an increase in the VIX Index elicits a response from the Fed, which reacts by cutting the target fed funds rate.

Asset Purchases and Asset Prices: A Longer-Term Event Study

Event studies can be useful for calibrating the precise impact of policy actions and policy surprises, but they risk missing the bigger picture about the medium-term evolution of financial variables and the comparison across different modalities of policy action and different times. One way to overcome this problem is to look at the relevant asset prices over longer periods, before and after the policy action.

Table 4.1 and the figures in appendix B summarize the results of a comparison of 2-year rates (a proxy for policy expectations), 10-year nominal rates, 10-year real rates, stock prices, and exchange rates at different time horizons before and after QE announcements. Table 4.1 shows the changes (in basis points for yields, in percent for stock prices and exchange rates) at different horizons around the event date, while the charts in appendix B complement the table by showing the evolution of the level of yields and of indexes of the stock market and the exchange rate. Because the different easing programs happened at increasingly lower levels of yields, analyzing only the rate of change could generate misleading or incomplete results.

The results suggest that QE worked the expected way. The median two-day change (from the market close of the day before the event to the market close of the day after the event [$t - 1$ to $t + 1$ in the table]) shows a 10 basis point reduction in nominal 10-year rates, an almost 2 percent appreciation of the stock market, and about a 1 percent depreciation in the exchange rate. The anticipatory effect was important: During the 90 days before the event, the median 2-year rate declined by about 12 basis points, the 10-year nominal rate by 27 basis points, and the real 10-year rate by 28 basis points; the stock market appreciated by more than 7 percent; and the exchange rate depreciated by 3.2 percent. The impact over the 90 days after the event was more muted, except for the real 10-year rate (which fell 14 basis points) and stock prices (which rose 10.7 percent). Two and 10-year nominal rates and exchange rates were stable 90 days after the event, seeming to suggest that the QE programs were effective, with a persistent effect on real interest rates and stock prices.

Table 4.1 Results of event study on quantitative easing (QE), 2009–15 (basis points, except where indicated otherwise)

Central bank/date/rate	t-90 to t-1	t-1 to t+90	t-90 to t+90	t-30 to t-1	t-1 to t+30	t-30 to t+30	t-5 to t-1	t-1 to t+5	t-5 to t+5	t-1 to t+1
				Federal Reserve						
QE1: March 18, 2009										
2-year rate	0.35	0.22	0.57	0.08	-0.06	0.02	0.07	-0.14	-0.06	-0.17
10-year nominal rate	0.93	0.82	1.75	0.25	-0.06	0.19	0.12	-0.35	-0.24	-0.40
10-year real rate	0.00	0.07	0.07	0.24	-0.20	0.05	0.01	-0.51	-0.50	-0.59
Stock index (percent change)	-14.29	18.02	3.74	-1.46	11.76	10.3	3.02	5.76	8.77	0.76
TWI (percent change)	7.40	-7.82	-0.42	-0.01	-1.87	-1.89	-7.56	3.62	-3.94	-3.73
QE2: November 3, 2010										
2-year rate	-0.19	0.36	0.17	-0.07	0.12	0.05	0.01	0.06	0.06	-0.02
10-year nominal rate	-0.32	0.96	0.64	0.08	0.42	0.50	-0.01	-0.04	-0.05	-0.10
10-year real rate	-0.64	0.80	0.16	-0.28	0.36	0.08	-0.04	0.03	-0.01	0.00
Stock index (percent change)	7.15	9.51	16.66	4.24	2.61	6.85	0.89	2.49	3.38	2.30
TWI (percent change)	-3.93	0.48	-3.46	-1.72	2.10	0.38	-0.59	0.11	-0.49	-0.90
Operation Twist: November 21, 2011										
2-year rate	-0.21	0.11	-0.10	-0.03	0.11	0.08	0.00	0.07	0.06	0.04
10-year nominal rate	-1.05	0.03	-1.02	-0.12	0.28	0.16	-0.11	-0.04	-0.15	-0.22
10-year real rate	-0.71	-0.14	-0.85	0.01	0.19	0.21	-0.07	0.08	0.02	-0.01
Stock index (percent change)	-7.46	3.46	-4.00	7.20	3.01	10.21	-1.11	-3.26	-4.36	-6.03
TWI (percent change)	2.40	3.46	5.86	2.91	-0.34	2.57	0.81	1.73	2.53	1.88

(table continues)

Table 4.1 Results of event study on quantitative easing (QE), 2009–15 (basis points, except where indicated otherwise) *(continued)*

Central bank/date/rate	t-90 to t-1	t-1 to t+90	t-90 to t+90	t-30 to t-1	t-1 to t+30	t-30 to t+30	t-5 to t-1	t-1 to t+5	t-5 to t+5	t-1 to t+1
					Federal Reserve					
QE3: November 12, 2012										
2-year rate	-0.04	0.00	-0.05	-0.01	0.01	0.00	0.00	0.01	0.00	-0.01
10-year nominal rate	0.04	0.00	0.03	0.04	-0.04	0.00	0.03	0.14	0.17	0.01
10-year real rate	-0.18	-0.16	-0.34	-0.08	-0.13	-0.21	0.01	-0.07	-0.05	-0.07
Stock index (percent change)	8.23	-0.35	7.88	1.96	-0.35	1.62	-0.31	1.93	1.62	1.84
TWI (percent change)	-3.46	0.92	-2.54	-2.75	0.03	-2.72	-0.51	-0.57	-1.08	-0.65
					Bank of England					
QE1: March 5, 2009										
2-year rate	-0.59	0.06	-0.52	-0.40	0.14	-0.26	-0.18	0.07	-0.11	0.00
10-year nominal rate	0.22	0.28	0.50	-0.07	-0.22	-0.29	0.02	-0.53	-0.51	-0.58
10-year real rate	-1.09	-0.29	-1.38	-0.24	-0.41	-0.65	0.14	0.01	0.15	-0.30
Stock index (percent change)	31.35	-21.74	9.61	5.82	-10.53	-4.71	-1.10	-1.90	-3.00	-3.16
TWI (percent change)	-3.24	4.65	1.41	-1.68	-0.20	-1.88	-0.68	-2.93	-3.61	-0.67
QE2: October 6, 2011										
2-year rate	-0.21	-0.18	-0.39	0.01	-0.05	-0.05	0.01	0.05	0.05	0.04
10-year nominal rate	-0.89	-0.34	-1.23	0.06	-0.05	0.01	-0.07	0.23	0.16	0.11
10-year real rate	-0.68	-0.43	-1.11	-0.26	0.00	-0.26	-0.04	0.06	0.03	-0.09
Stock index (percent change)	-16.62	10.73	-5.88	-1.15	8.33	7.18	-0.54	5.75	5.21	3.94
TWI (percent change)	1.61	3.15	4.75	0.49	1.31	1.81	-0.52	-0.85	-1.37	0.39

European Central Bank

QE: January 22, 2015

2-year rate	-0.12	-0.10	-0.22	-0.07	-0.06	-0.13	0.00	0.01	0.01	0.00
10-year nominal rate	-0.35	-0.36	-0.71	-0.08	-0.16	-0.24	0.07	-0.14	-0.07	-0.16
10-year real rate	-0.28	0.42	0.14	0.01	0.12	0.13	0.13	0.01	0.14	0.07
Stock index (percent change)	11.13	13.72	24.85	4.94	6.39	11.33	1.82	3.07	4.89	3.28
TWI (percent change)	-5.06	-5.36	-10.42	-5.43	-1.17	-6.60	0.54	-1.54	-1.00	-2.83

Bank of Japan

QE1: April 4, 2013

2-year rate	-0.03	0.07	0.04	0.02	0.05	0.07	0.02	0.04	0.06	0.02
10-year nominal rate	-0.27	0.30	0.03	-0.06	0.01	-0.05	0.01	-0.03	-0.02	-0.03
10-year real rate	-0.23	0.35	0.12	-0.04	0.02	-0.02	-0.02	0.05	0.03	-0.03
Stock index (percent change)	17.76	13.4	31.16	6.75	10.77	17.52	-0.31	6.72	6.41	3.81
TWI (percent change)	-3.77	-6.56	-10.33	0.83	-7.03	-6.21	5.28	-6.87	-1.59	-5.46

QE2: October 10, 2014

2-year rate	-0.01	-0.08	-0.09	-0.03	-0.03	-0.05	-0.01	-0.01	-0.02	0.01
10-year nominal rate	-0.05	-0.22	-0.27	-0.06	-0.04	-0.10	-0.03	0.00	-0.03	0.01
10-year real rate	-0.07	-0.14	-0.21	-0.06	-0.01	-0.08	-0.04	-0.02	-0.06	0.02
Stock index (percent change)	1.92	11.1	13.02	-2.13	8.41	6.28	-1.42	-2.62	-4.04	-1.15
TWI (percent change)	-2.44	-5.63	-8.08	0.06	-5.07	-5.01	1.12	1.40	2.52	0.43

(table continues)

Table 4.1 Results of event study on quantitative easing (QE), 2009–15 (basis points, except where indicated otherwise) *(continued)*

Central bank/date/rate	t–90 to t–1	t–1 to t+90	t–90 to t+90	t–30 to t–1	t–1 to t+30	t–30 to t+30	t–5 to t–1	t–1 to t+5	t–5 to t+5	t–1 to t+1
Mean and median across all events										
Mean										
2-year rate	-0.12	0.05	-0.06	-0.06	0.03	-0.03	-0.01	0.02	0.01	-0.01
10-year nominal rate	-0.19	0.16	-0.03	0.00	0.02	0.02	0.00	-0.08	-0.08	-0.15
10-year real rate	-0.43	0.05	-0.38	-0.08	-0.01	-0.08	0.01	-0.04	-0.03	-0.11
Stock index (percent change)	4.35	6.43	10.78	2.91	4.49	7.40	0.11	1.99	2.10	0.62
TWI (percent change)	-1.17	-1.41	-2.58	-0.81	-1.36	-2.17	-0.24	-0.66	-0.89	-1.28
Median										
2-year rate	-0.12	0.06	-0.09	-0.03	0.01	0.00	0.00	0.04	0.01	0.00
10-year nominal rate	-0.27	0.03	0.03	-0.06	-0.04	0.00	0.01	-0.04	-0.05	-0.10
10-year real rate	-0.28	-0.14	-0.21	-0.06	0.00	-0.02	-0.02	0.01	0.02	-0.03
Stock index (percent change)	7.15	10.73	9.61	4.24	6.39	7.18	-0.31	2.49	3.38	1.84
TWI (percent change)	-3.24	0.48	-2.54	-0.01	-0.34	-1.89	-0.51	-0.57	-1.08	-0.67

TWI = trade-weighted effective exchange rate

There are some interesting differences across countries and programs. The first programs had a larger impact on long-term rates—likely because of the surprise factor and the higher starting level of yields. In the case of the Fed, the four programs were designed in a different manner and with slightly different objectives, were executed at ever declining levels of both short- and long-term interest, and took place in different international contexts. QE1 occurred during a period of global worries about financial stability; it thus led to global flows across asset classes, from bonds into equities. QE2 took place in a more buoyant global environment (outside the euro area); it led to flows across countries, mostly into emerging markets.

These differences can be seen in the impacts of the programs. QE1 and QE3 were about neutral for two-year rates (a proxy for policy expectations); Operation Twist predictably led to higher two-year rates. QE2 shows a significant increase in two-year rates after the announcement, suggesting that markets were still behaving under precrisis rules of thumb and assuming the beginning of rate increases within two years of the easing action. The impact on 10-year rates suggests that fixed-quantity QE (QE1 and QE2) was less effective than Operation Twist or the open-ended QE3, as 10-year nominal yields increased after the announcement of both QE1 and QE2. The same pattern appears for 10-year real rates, which increased with QE1 and QE2 but declined with Operation Twist and QE3. Stock prices increased in all cases. The impact on exchange rates was markedly negative for QE1 and about neutral in the other episodes.

The BoE's QE programs took place in a different context, as the pound had already depreciated sharply before the policy action, driven by fears of sustainability of the UK economy, triggering a large increase in headline inflation. The result was a larger decline in real interest rates, while the pound appreciated steadily despite the QE programs.

Despite the ECB's reluctance to engage in QE, and the concerns that it might not work in the euro area, the ECB's QE program worked in a textbook manner. Both short- and long-term interest rates fell, stock prices rose, and the currency weakened.

The BoJ QE program (QQE1) and its extension (QQE2) had diametrically opposed impacts on interest rates. QQE1 led to an initially sharp and persistent increase in short- and long-term interest rates, as the Japanese financial sector took a long time to adjust to the very large increase in purchases of government bonds, in both size and duration. Stock prices rallied and the currency depreciated on impact, as expected, and interest rates eventually declined. QQE2 led to the expected decline in both short- and long-term interest rates.

Overall, the evidence suggests that, if implemented with conviction, and in the required size, asset purchase programs worked in the expected manner, easing financial conditions. A different question is whether, as their size or duration increases, their side effects could become detrimental, an issue addressed below.

A Closer Look at the European Central Bank: Did It Engage in Selective Quantitative Easing?

The previous chapter described the two phases of the ECB's policies. During the first phase, the ECB refused to do what other central banks were doing—buying government bonds. It focused more on exerting pressure on countries to reform than on creating the conditions for price stability. Despite its overarching price-stability mandate, it prioritized the transformation of some of the euro area economies, even at the risk of achieving its inflation objective. As a result, government bond yields increased dramatically in the crisis countries, and financial conditions tightened in a significant manner for the euro area as a whole. This tightening of financial conditions since 2010 was a major reason behind the euro area's double-dip recession and the decline in inflation and inflation expectations. During this period the ECB had strong political support in Germany, where, if anything, it was criticized for being too soft.

The second phase of ECB policies started with the arrival of Mario Draghi as president in 2011. He refocused monetary policy on the achievement of price stability, an effort that eventually included QE and the purchase of government bonds. German political criticism of the ECB skyrocketed during this phase.

The drastic change in tone in Germany as the ECB moved from tighter to easier financial conditions may not be a major surprise—after all, as discussed in chapter 2, the ordoliberalism pervasive in German economic thinking dictates that structural policies are the only source of growth and cyclical policies can only create distortions that impede the correction of structural deficiencies. The more critical voices were highlighting the high risk Germany was incurring as Target 2 balances increased with the expansion of the ECB's balance sheet.

It is possible that Germany's opposition was just ideological. It is also possible that the reality was a bit more complex. During the first phase of ECB policies, when interest rates for some euro area countries were reaching almost double-digit levels and their economies were sinking into a deep recession, Germany, and to a lesser extent France, were enjoying financial conditions similar to those in the United States and United Kingdom. From the standpoint of German financial conditions, the ECB was doing QE. It was not buying sovereign bonds, but German long-term real interest rates were as low as rates in the United States and United Kingdom.

Figure 4.5 shows the evolution of 10-year real interest rates, calculated as

Figure 4.5   Real 10-year interest rates in selected economies, 2004–16

percent

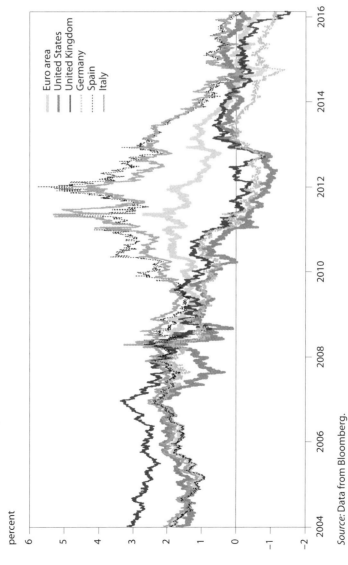

Source: Data from Bloomberg.

the 10-year swap rates minus 10-year expected inflation rates implied in inflation swaps, for the United States, the United Kingdom, a GDP-weighted average of the euro area, Germany, Spain, and Italy. It shows the sharp increase in real interest rates in the euro area, especially in Spain and Italy, after 2010, which was reversed only after the Outright Monetary Transactions (OMT) program was announced. Real interest rates in Germany (and in France, not shown) moved in sync with US and UK rates most of the time. The default risk that was being priced in Spanish or Italian bonds reflected the fear of a debt restructuring as a precondition for an assistance program. Debt restructuring had happened with Greece, and markets feared it could happen again. Because Germany and France were seen as too big to fail—if they failed, the euro failed, and no country in the euro area could force Germany or France to bail in investors—their bonds were considered risk-free assets.

At the global level, arbitrage was keeping the interest rates of US Treasuries, British gilts, and German bunds in sync. As the Fed and the BoE were engaging in QE and reducing long-term interest rates, they were also driving German long-term rates lower. Their actions—not structural reforms or confidence from fiscal adjustment—are a main reason why the German economy performed relatively well during the euro area crisis. The German economy was enjoying a very sharp monetary easing that some of its neighbors were not.

From a German standpoint, there was no need for QE. Interest rates were low enough—others were doing the job for them. Could the low interest rates in Germany explain, to a large extent, Germany's strong and determined anti-QE position? Would Germany have shown the determined anti-QE stance had investors flown away from German bunds, leading to skyrocketing interest rates in Germany?

We will never know. But a few anecdotes are telling. In 2007–08, at the depth of the crisis in the German banking sector, the Bundesbank pushed for aggressive policy easing and liquidity support, rescued its banks without resort to bail-ins, and was the first euro area central bank to provide emergency liquidity assistance. Only after its own problems were solved did Germany's stance on monetary easing and bail-ins become very hawkish. The German government did not hesitate to use the crises in Greece and Cyprus for its own political benefit in domestic elections (see Michaelides and Orphanides 2016). And it complained about negative interest rates because they hurt its domestic financial sector.

Forward Guidance and Asset Prices: Are Words Enough?

Voltaire once claimed that you can kill a flock of sheep by witchcraft provided you feed them enough arsenic at the same time (Robinson 1966). If the word of central banks were fully credible, words alone could accomplish goals. But in the real world, words need to be accompanied by action, or the promise of action, to have an effect. In theory, the witchcraft practiced by central banks would consist of setting short-term rates at the right level and communicating their future intentions. Markets would take these intentions at face value and price the yield curve accordingly. Therefore, central banks should also be able to ease policy even when interest rates are zero. All they would need to do is communicate that they plan to keep interest rates unchanged for a very long period or until a set of conditions is met. Markets would then price this scenario, which would imply a much lower level of long-term interest rates. Mission accomplished.

But markets do not trust words—and history makes it hard for markets to think otherwise. Central banks have spent decades communicating that they never precommit, that when circumstances change they change their policies. Makes sense. In most cases, retaining flexibility is a valuable strategy. How can central bankers then convince markets that "this time is different," that they will not change their mind for a long while? Beyond the fact that there could always be unexpected events, the leadership of central banks changes. Chairs, presidents, and committee members come and go, with sometimes dramatic results. Mervyn King constantly dismissed financial markets; Mark Carney, who replaced him, takes messages from markets seriously. Jürgen Stark resigned from the ECB's executive board because he did not agree with the expansionary policies the ECB was adopting, especially the idea of buying government bonds. John Taylor, a perennial potential candidate for Fed chair, has constantly criticized the Fed for keeping interest rates too low. Central banker statements have, at most, the shelf life of their leaders. Frameworks support words, but they also change. Most major central banks changed their policy frameworks to adapt them to the new reality of very low inflation and very low interest rates (see chapter 3).

Words are not enough—but they are critical to the success of policies, especially at the zero bound. If central banks do not communicate well, their policies will not work. If they do not believe in their own policies, markets will not believe them either.

Forward guidance when rates are zero could be effective for two main reasons. First, the time horizon over which rates will be on hold may be longer than it was in the past. Before 2007 the average time between the end of a rate-cutting cycle and the beginning of the subsequent rate-hiking cycle was about 9–12 months; markets took this benchmark as a guide to price interest rates. The new horizon of policy easing may be longer than can be communicated with standard tools. For example, the inflation forecast published in the BoE's *Inflation Report* was effective to communicate rates on hold over two years but not beyond.

Second, the central bank wants to communicate that it is moving to a different reaction function because the trade-off between inflation and growth has changed. After sharp recessions, the level of GDP is much lower and the output gap much greater than in standard recessions. The economy thus needs much faster GDP growth than in the past to generate inflation. In addition, nominal downward wage rigidity—the fact that workers will resist cuts in nominal wages, preferring a longer period of stable wages— contains the decline in inflation that the sharp decline in growth should generate. As growth picks up, inflation will thus remain low for a much longer period than in past cycles. Central banks need to communicate that a return of strong growth is not going to be followed, as in the past, by the same increases in interest rates.

When clearly communicated, the anchoring effect of central bank guidance can be very powerful. But central banks need to be careful. If their guidance merely reflects the fact that weaker economic conditions warrant keeping rates on hold for longer or lower, its communication can backfire, as the public could interpret it as the central bank acknowledging a weaker outlook but doing nothing about it (see Woodford 2012 for an elaboration of this point). Transparency can be a double-edged sword. Clear communication requires a similarly clear commitment to do what it takes to achieve the targets.

Forward guidance was already used before 2007, with mildly positive results. The academic research shows that the BoJ's guidance influenced market expectations about the path of short-term rates and reduced long-term rates (Okina and Shiratsuka 2004). The Fed engaged in strong forward guidance during the 2004–06 rate-hiking cycle, in an attempt to avoid a repetition of the sharp increase in interest rates that happened in 1994, when the Fed started policy tightening. The "measured pace" sentence in its statements during 2004–06 was very effective in anchoring market expectations around a pace of rate increases of 25 basis points per meeting and had some impact on the shape of the yield curve (Bernanke, Reinhart, and Sack 2004).

Forward guidance was widespread during the crisis. Figure 4.6 shows the amount of interest rate increases priced at each point in time for the subsequent 3 years. The Fed's calendar guidance and thresholds eased financial conditions in the United States, United Kingdom, and euro area by delaying the market's pricing of the first tightening across all markets. This guidance was "active easing," as it lowered the view of the markets about the near-term path of interest rates for a given path of growth and inflation. The next steps in guidance were mostly about "passive easing," to avoid an undesired increase in interest rates. For example, the debate at the BoE about the introduction of thresholds in the summer of 2013 served to contain, at least initially, the contagion of the US taper tantrum to the United Kingdom. However, the final publication of the levels of the

Figure 4.6 Interest rate increases priced over 36 months in the United States, United Kingdom, and euro area, 2007–15

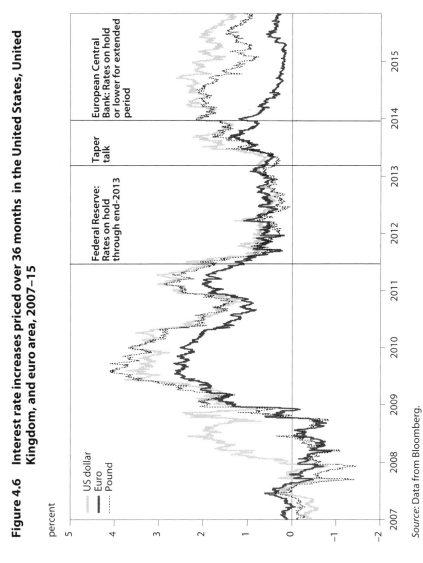

percent

Federal Reserve: Rates on hold through end-2013

Taper talk

European Central Bank: Rates on hold or lower for extended period

Source: Data from Bloomberg.

BoE thresholds (which featured a higher level of unemployment threshold than the market had expected) pegged the expected path of BoE hikes back to the Fed's. The ECB's forward guidance issued in 2014 was effective in separating the expected path of ECB action from that of the Fed.

Several academic studies show that the impact of forward guidance was positive (see Charbonneau and Rennison 2015 for an overview). Jeffrey Campbell et al. (2012) find that the Fed's forward guidance had a significant effect on long-term Treasuries and corporate bond yields. Eric Swanson and John Williams (2013) show that the responsiveness of Treasury yields to economic news fell to almost zero after the Fed introduced time-contingent guidance in late 2011. Katherine Femia, Steven Friedman, and Brian Sack (2013) show that forward guidance changed market expectations about the level of unemployment that, for a given level of inflation, will lead to the first rate hike, thus generating an easier policy stance. William English, David López-Salido, and Robert Tetlow (2013) show that the threshold guidance allowed the Fed to approximate an optimal control rule that is welfare improving with respect to an inertial Taylor rule and better filtered the signal from the noise as far as the direction of monetary policy (e.g., by neutralizing the impact of hawkish dissenting commentary). Uncertainty about the path of rates, measured from options markets, fell to the lowest levels ever in April 2013, when the Fed's forward guidance was in full force. Markets were convinced that the Fed would not change its policy stance for a very long time: The MOVE Index (a proxy for uncertainty about the path of rates) was at its lowest level (see figure 4.4). Clemens Kool and Daniel Thornton (2012) find that forward guidance helped improve the forecasting of short-term rates. Eric Engen, Thomas Laubach, and David Reifschneider (2015) show that forward guidance was successful in shifting the market's view of the Fed's reaction function toward one more focused on employment stabilization but that it failed to convince analysts that the lift-off would ever be more than two years away. Stephen Hansen and Michael McMahon (2016) find that the Fed's forward guidance has had more impact on market variables than the Fed's view about economic conditions.

The BoE's forward guidance became more intense with the change in leadership and the new BoE remit. However, the BoE's decision to introduce a threshold system to communicate an extended period of interest rates on hold was clouded by a large initial mistake forecasting the unemployment rate—an episode that reveals the potential downside of forward guidance. When it unveiled its new guidance, the BoE announced that it would keep rates on hold at least until the unemployment rate fell below 7 percent, a period it expected to last about two years. In the event, the economy, especially the labor market, strengthened at an unprecedented pace and the 7 percent threshold was hit about six months after the new guidance was issued. Many observers saw the development as a failure of forward guidance, because it introduced confusion and dented the forecasting credibility of the BoE.

Nevertheless, the threshold guidance was useful, because it prevented a sharp increase in market interest rates as a result of this acceleration in growth (Filardo and Hofmann 2014). Had markets interpreted this strengthening in the labor market under the standard behavior of the BoE before 2007, they would have priced a very rapid increase in interest rates. Because the economy was operating near potential growth and inflation was close to target, the behavior of the BoE before the crisis could be approximated well by a rule that suggested that interest rates would increase when the rate of growth of GDP accelerated or the Purchasing Managers' Index (PMI) increased sharply.[3] The acceleration in job creation and the decline in the unemployment rate in the second half of 2013 were the fastest in recent history. Fortunately, the threshold system allowed the BoE to communicate clearly the difference between the level of GDP and the rate of growth of GDP. Despite the rapid rate of GDP growth, the level of GDP was still well below precrisis levels; there was therefore much slack to absorb, which allowed the BoE to tolerate rapid GDP growth for longer than usual. The threshold system also provided insurance against inflation stickiness arising from hikes in fees and regulated prices, which kept inflation artificially elevated for an extended period, and ensured discipline and unity of message inside the Monetary Policy Committee, at a time when discrepancies could have been very damaging for the effectiveness of monetary policy.[4]

Once the threshold was crossed, the BoE moved to the second phase of forward guidance, transitioning from signaling what it would not do (raise rates until the threshold was crossed) to what it would do (raise rates gradually when conditions were right). Interest rates barely moved during this transition, suggesting the new communication had been effective.

Perhaps the best proof of the effectiveness of the threshold system is that, in the end, the BoE did not raise rates. The economy slowed, and inflation stayed subdued once all the transitory effects had faded away. The next BoE action was a policy easing as a result of the downturn triggered by the Brexit referendum.

The ECB's effectiveness of forward guidance was initially more limited. Unlike guidance from the Fed and the BoE, the ECB's initial guidance, is-

---

3. Ben Broadbent, "Conditional Guidance as a Response to Supply Uncertainty," speech at the London Business School, London, September 23, 2013.

4. Spencer Dale, "Inflation Targeting and the Monetary Policy Committee's Forward Guidance," speech at the International Journal of Central Banking Annual Conference, Warsaw, September 6, 2013.

sued in July 2013, did not send a clear message of shifting to a different reaction function that signaled easier policy. It simply confirmed that the inflation outlook had weakened and that the expected rate path should be consistent with this weakness. The ECB's guidance did not ease policy, it just prevented, by signaling an easing bias, a tightening of policy from the global sell-off in interest rates resulting from the Fed's tapering and the increase in money market rates stemming from the repayment of the LTROs during 2014 (ECB 2014). It was nevertheless effective, as it broke the link between US and euro area short-term rates, reduced uncertainty about the expected path of short-term rates, and muted the responsiveness of short-term rates to macroeconomic news (Picault 2015). However, the ECB's guidance was passive easing, intended to offset an undue tightening driven by exogenous factors or respond to a worsening of the economic outlook rather than engaging in active easing to increase the amount of accommodation for a given economic outlook. This reluctance to engage in active easing was a pervasive feature of ECB policy. This changed after the introduction of QE, when forward guidance became a very effective element of active easing—especially with the interest rates guidance, signaling that interest rates would stay unchanged until "well past" the end of asset purchases.

Overall, when used in an active manner and accompanied by other actions, forward guidance has been effective in easing financial conditions. The next chapter shows that its use during the attempted normalization of interest rates had a more mixed record.

Do Negative Interest Rates Ease, or Tighten, Financial Conditions? The Change in the Reference Point

Marketers usually include a high-priced item as a reference point that makes everything else look cheaper. A restaurant does not care if it barely sells any $50 chateaubriand if including it on the menu helps sell lots of $39.95 hanger steaks with a large markup. The trick is that they would not be able to charge $39.95 for the hanger steak if it were the most expensive item on the menu. The reference point dominates everything. Change the reference point, and everything else changes.

Reference point bias is well known in behavioral economics; it is critical to understanding how markets work. Assets have to be priced under uncertainty, and need reference points, or anchors, to be priced. In the case of fixed-income assets, the reference point is the short-term interest rate, which, until recently, had been truncated at zero. This meant that, assuming some positive risk premium, long-term interest rates were unlikely to reach zero. This created a strong reference point that defined the buying and selling targets for market participants. With interest rates truncated at zero, 10-year interest rates at, say, 1 percent, were considered to be "very low." Few people would think 10-year rates of 1 percent would be a good buying opportunity. Indeed, at 1 percent, shorting 10-year rates would seem to make sense: The risk reward was attractive and asymmetric, as potential loss was well defined and limited, truncated at or near zero.

When central banks cut rates to negative levels, they changed the reference point. Rates are no longer truncated at zero, and pricing ranges (the buying and selling targets) are no longer asymmetric. Market participants are no longer sure that 10-year rates cannot fall to zero or become negative.

From an economic standpoint, there is nothing special about negative interest rates: Arithmetically, the difference between +0.1 and –0.1 is 20 basis points. But mentally, and for the behavior of financial markets, the difference is massive. Cutting rates to –0.1 changes the reference point, which changes everything.[5]

The change in reference point affects not just long-term rates but all assets. If long-term rates can be negative, what happens to the outlook for the profitability of banks, the actuarial balance of pension funds, and the solvency of insurance companies? What should the manager of a large bond fund do—buy a bond yielding 0.1 percent or wait and risk that the next bond issued carries a negative coupon?

Early in the crisis, central banks thought that negative interest rates were a way to contain capital inflows. They worked when they were used in isolation, by small countries like Denmark or Switzerland, whose rates do not affect global interest rates. But what happens when large countries use them?

Size matters. When Japanese long-term yields became negative, they affected the pricing of German and US yields via global arbitrage. When investors wondered how low 10-year German yields could go, they looked at Japan. The lowest yield among the large countries became the new anchor. Traders who wanted to short 10-year bonds yielding 1 percent now had a tougher time convincing their risk managers that the trade had an attractive risk-reward ratio. What if rates fell to –0.2 percent? And once at –0.2 percent, where the 10-year Japanese government bond was, what prevented them from falling to –1 percent? Some analysts were suggesting the BoJ could cut rates all the way to –2 percent (Credit Suisse 2016). This qualitative change in the reference point is the most important effect of negative interest rates.

It may be too early to draw conclusions about the impact of negative interest rates. The sample of events is not large, and markets are still trying to understand this new reality. Table 4.2 and the figures in appendix C show

---

5. Grisse, Krogstrup, and Schumacher (2017) investigate this reference point effect and conclude that negative interest rate announcements have affected yields globally by changing market views about the lower bound.

Table 4.2 Results of event study on negative rates, 2014–16 (basis points, except where indicated otherwise)

Central bank/date/rate	t–90 to t–1	t–1 to t+90	t–90 to t+90	t–30 to t–1	t–1 to t+30	t–30 to t+30	t–5 to t–1	t–1 to t+5	t–5 to t+5	t–1 to t+1
Bank of Japan										
January 29, 2016										
2-year rate	–0.03	–0.2	–0.23	–0.002	–0.19	–0.21	–0.012	–0.154	–0.17	–0.13
10-year nominal rate	–0.06	–0.3	–0.36	–0.004	–0.29	–0.34	–0.001	–0.195	–0.21	–0.17
Stock index (percent change)	–3.50	–20.40	–23.90	–2.20	–19.40	–21.60	0.50	–1.30	–0.82	4.83
TWI (percent change)	2.70	7.38	10.10	1.86	4.27	6.14	–0.60	0.80	0.16	–1.68
December 18, 2014										
2-year rate	–0.094	–0.71	–0.80	0.03	–0.59	–0.56	–0.01	–0.03	–0.04	–0.01
10-year nominal rate	–0.265	–0.37	–0.64	–0.13	–0.33	–0.46	0.00	0.04	0.04	–0.01
Stock index (percent change)	–1	5.82	4.82	–2.2	–9.76	–11.96	–3.0	4.42	1.42	2.28
TWI (percent change)	0.1	9.36	9.46	–0.3	18.65	18.35	–0.1	–0.53	–0.63	–0.50
Swiss National Bank										
January 15, 2015										
2-year rate	–0.22	–0.34	–0.56	–0.09	–0.15	–0.24	–0.04	–0.27	–0.31	–0.24
10-year nominal rate	–0.33	–0.54	–0.87	–0.24	–0.74	–0.98	0.00	–0.52	–0.52	–0.36
Stock index (percent change)	13.0	3.00	16.00	5.0	–6.00	–1.00	1.0	–11.00	–10.00	–14.0
TWI (percent change)	–2.0	14.00	12.00	–2.0	12.00	10.00	0.0	18.00	18.00	20.00

European Central Bank

June 4, 2014

2-year rate	-0.064	-0.12	-0.19	-0.08	-0.04	-0.12	-0.01	-0.02	-0.03	0.00
10-year nominal rate	-0.173	0.503	-0.68	-0.03	-0.17	-0.19	0.08	-0.03	0.05	-0.08
Stock index (percent change)	1.80	1.50	3.30	1.90	1.30	3.30	-0.20	1.80	1.60	1.10
TWI (percent change)	-0.50	-2.70	-3.20	-1.30	-0.70	-2.00	0.10	0.5	-0.50	0.10

September 4, 2014

2-year rate	-0.08	-0.01	-0.09	-0.05	-0.05	-0.09	0.00	-0.05	-0.04	-0.05
10-year nominal rate	-0.48	-0.21	-0.68	-0.18	-0.03	-0.21	0.06	0.04	0.11	-0.03
Stock index (percent change)	0.30	-0.20	0.20	4.23	-2.71	1.40	1.20	-0.20	0.80	0.80
TWI (percent change)	-0.20	-1.30	-3.56	0.69	-2.38	-3.10	0.50	-0.60	0.04	-0.90

Mean and median across all events

Mean

2-year rate	-0.10	-0.28	-0.37	-0.04	-0.20	-0.24	-0.01	-0.11	-0.12	-0.09
10-year nominal rate	-0.26	-0.18	-0.64	-0.12	-0.31	-0.44	0.03	-0.04	-0.11	-0.13
Stock index (percent change)	2.12	-2.06	0.08	1.35	-7.31	-5.97	-0.10	-1.26	-1.40	-1.00
TWI (percent change)	0.02	5.35	25.01	-0.21	6.37	5.88	-0.08	3.63	3.33	3.4

Median

2-year rate	-0.08	-0.20	-0.23	-0.05	-0.15	-0.21	-0.01	-0.05	-0.04	-0.05
10-year nominal rate	-0.27	-0.30	-0.68	-0.13	-0.29	-0.34	0.00	0.00	0.04	-0.08
Stock index (percent change)	0.30	1.50	3.30	1.90	-6.00	-1.00	0.50	-0.20	0.80	1.10
TWI (percent change)	-0.20	7.38	10.10	-0.30	4.27	6.14	0.00	0.50	-0.40	-0.50

TWI = trade-weighted effective exchange rate

the evolution of asset prices (2-year rates, 10-year rates, stock indexes, and trade-weighted exchange rates) around central bank reductions of interest rates to negative levels. The initial impact (the two-day effect) is as expected: Long-term interest rates declined, the stock market rallied, and the currency depreciated. However, the reduction in long-term interest rates was, in some cases, extraordinarily large: When the BoJ cut the overnight rate by 10 basis points, the 10-year Japanese government bond rate fell 17 basis points in two days. Markets panicked that, once the door had been opened for negative interest rates, the BoJ could cut rates much more. With that new reference point in mind, 10-year rates at 0.75 percent looked very attractive. As the front end of the yield curve was dipping into negative levels, investors moved out into longer maturities, pushing long-term yields lower. At some point the yield curve up to the 20-year maturity point was at negative interest rates. In its *Comprehensive Assessment*, the BoJ concluded that cutting rates from 0 percent to –0.1 percent had led to a decline in 10-year government bond rates of 23 basis points (BoJ 2016). This very large impact may have been the result of the surprise effect (the BoJ, intentionally, did not warn markets in advance). The impact in places where communication was forthcoming, such as the euro area, was less abrupt. The impact on 10-year rates after the ECB cuts to negative rates was three to eight basis points.

Long-term rates declined after central banks cut rates below zero. But it is not clear that the cuts eased financial conditions. The experience of Japan is illustrative. Markets panicked about the viability of Japanese banks facing a very flat yield curve, selling off stocks. As a result of fear about the solvency of the Japanese financial sector, foreigners liquidated their holdings of Japanese assets, causing the yen to appreciate. Part of this fear was unwarranted: Financial institutions benefit greatly from the capital gains associated with the decline in long-term interest rates. But at the same time, a persistent period of zero or negative long-term interest rates exposed the Japanese financial sector to rollover risk: When their current holdings of bonds expired, they would have to replace them with bonds yielding zero or negative coupons, with little further room for price gains. The capital appreciation benefit is a one-off event that cannot be repeated. Markus Brunnermeier and Yann Koby (2017) coined the term "the reversal rate"—the interest rates at which bank profitability will fail, reducing retained earnings and thus capital, which eventually could dampen lending. A similar phenomenon happened in the euro area: the more negative bund yields became, the more European bank stocks underperformed the stock market index.

Confidence in Abenomics, and QQE, faltered with the introduction of negative rates. The index of Japanese financial conditions compiled by Goldman Sachs shows that overall financial conditions tightened, rather than eased, after the introduction of negative rates (figure 4.7).

Figure 4.7 Index of Japanese financial conditions, 2007–17

index (August 1, 2007 = 100)

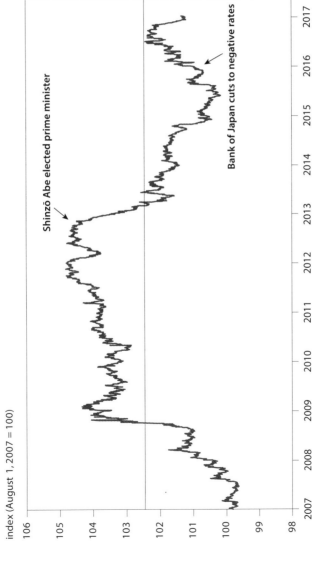

Sources: Data from Bloomberg and Goldman Sachs Investment Research.

The behavior of markets after the BoJ decision shows the potential limits of monetary policy. The limits to negative rates are not determined by the preference for cash, but by behavioral biases. A main channel of transmission of monetary policy at low interest rates is the portfolio-rebalancing effect (see chapter 3). Central bankers assumed that as they pushed long-term interest rates lower, investors would move to riskier assets. But the Japanese experience with negative rates shows an important flaw in this reasoning: If long-term rates can go negative, there is no strong reason to move out of bonds. If there are expected capital gains from holding bonds, why move into riskier assets, such as stocks, where there can be principal losses? Negative interest rates can disrupt the portfolio-rebalancing effect and just push long-term rates lower. If, because of the specific structure of the financial system in a country, negative rates hurt banks, insurers, and pension funds and no longer contribute to the portfolio-rebalancing effect, are they easing policy? It is not clear anymore.

Currency Wars and the Fear of Floating

As soon as the major central banks started to ease monetary policy aggressively, cries of currency debasement and accusations of competitive devaluations became widespread. Some emerging markets, such as Brazil, were particularly vocal, coining the term *currency wars* to accuse the United States of engaging in a strategy of competitive devaluation. This debate became particularly acute after 2010, when the combination of monetary easing in the United States and the United Kingdom and the euro area crisis triggered a redirection of capital flows into emerging markets. Several emerging markets engaged in currency intervention and the imposition of capital controls to stem these inflows and the associated appreciation of their currencies. The QE programs of the Fed became a main focus of attention, with critics arguing that asset purchases had an outsized impact on currencies. Many analysts started to forecast the evolution of exchange rates as a function of the relative size of the central banks' balance sheets, as if the monetary channel remained alive for exchange rates, even if it had disappeared for interest rates.

The reality is that many factors affect exchange rates. The broad trends in exchange rates have not validated the currency wars view. The sharp depreciation of sterling occurred before the BoE started QE; it reflected a downward reassessment of the sterling equilibrium rate. Given the large current account deficit and very large banking sector relative to the size of its economy, fears about the sustainability of the UK economy—and therefore the value of its currency—were substantial. Once these fears subsided, sterling appreciated, even as the BoE intensified its asset purchases.

Fluctuations of the dollar reflected worries about the sustainability of the US economy and expected yield differentials, but, from a medium-term perspective, the broad range of the dollar has remained consistent with fundamentals. The euro was initially driven by the risk of breakup and the flows (in both directions, as outflows were driven by crisis uncertainty and inflows by repatriations of assets abroad by euro residents) that this risk generated, not by monetary policy; it remained overvalued by most equilibrium measures. The euro depreciated only when the ECB decided to aggressively ease monetary policy, cutting rates and launching QE. QE led to a depreciation of the currency, but only as a result of a correction of wrong fundamentals, as interest rates were too high in the euro area.

Similarly, the launching of Abenomics triggered a large depreciation of the yen that corrected a large overvaluation by adopting a more adequate policy mix.[6] It did not trigger the rapid increase in exports that some were expecting (or fearing). A key reason is that over the years, Japanese firms had moved a large share of their production facilities abroad in order to benefit from lower costs and produce on-site rather than export. This trend partly explains the weakness of Japanese domestic investment over the years, as Japanese firms preferred to invest abroad, where demand prospects were more buoyant. The depreciation of the yen increased the profits of Japanese multinationals and made investment in Japan more attractive relative to investing abroad. The impact of the weaker yen was thus stronger investment in Japan, not stronger exports.

Contrary to the accusations of competitive devaluations, the academic evidence suggests that QE did not have an outsized impact on exchange rates. Exchange rates react to the term structure of interest rates, not just the short-term rate. Several studies show that once they are properly calibrated in terms of their equivalent effect on short-term interest rates, the impact of asset purchases on asset prices, including exchange rates, has been similar to the impact of cuts in short term interest rates (see, e.g., Glick and Leduc 2013, Swanson and Williams 2013, and Rosa and Tambalotti 2014). Furthermore, the impact of monetary policy on exchange rates has a broadly neutral impact on foreign economies, because there are two offsetting channels. On the one hand, US exports may increase as a result of the weaker dollar. On the other hand, US domestic demand—and therefore imports—may increase, as a result of lower interest rates. Ben Bernanke refers to Fed estimates showing that a US monetary easing that lowers US Treasury yields by 25 basis points results in a depreciation of the dollar of 1 per-

---

6. Calculations using the fundamental equilibrium exchange rate (FEER) (see Cline 2015) suggest that both the euro and the yen were at about fair value in 2012 and became substantially undervalued as a result. However, the FEER is based on multilateral current account adjustment and may exaggerate the extent of undervaluation given the muted reaction of exports.

cent over three years, increases US net exports by about 0.15 percent of US GDP (because a weaker dollar leads to higher exports), but reduces US net exports by a similar amount through the associated increase in imports (because lower interest rates generate stronger US demand) (Bernanke 2015a). If the reduction in interest rates in the United States facilitates a reduction in interest rates in emerging markets, the net impact on emerging markets' growth could be positive (see IMF 2011 and Kamin et al. 2016).

In addition, changes in exchange rates in the last several years have been mostly in the "right" direction, correcting disequilibrium situations. Figure 4.8 shows the deviation from equilibrium of a GDP-weighted basket of G-10 and emerging-market currencies versus the dollar. The definition of equilibrium corresponds to the Goldman Sachs Dynamic Equilibrium Exchange Rate (GSDEER) model, which has a long history and covers a wide array of countries (Goldman Sachs 1997). Both G10 and emerging-market currencies became overvalued versus the dollar during 2006–08, possibly reflecting worries about the sustainability of the US economy, but this overvaluation did not increase during the QE period; it was corrected as the US economy recovered. Based on this measure, the dollar became overvalued after mid-2014, reflecting the better economic performance of the United States versus the rest of the world and the likely widening of interest rate differentials.

The major central banks did not try to engage in competitive devaluations. There were no currency wars with emerging markets. Exchange rates remained within broad ranges consistent with fundamentals, reflecting mostly cyclical divergences. Countries engaging in QE did not experience export booms or large increases in their export share—if anything, they experienced a decline in exports versus countries that did not engage in QE (Rose 2017).

Global capital flows to emerging markets did add a layer of difficulty to their macroeconomic management. But the right response to these flows was not a different monetary policy in the United States, Europe, or Japan but better macroeconomic management in the receiving countries, especially macroprudential policies but also a better policy mix. The best example is Brazil, the country that complained the most. Instead of tightening fiscal policy to cool down a very overheated economy, which would have allowed it to lower interest rates and slow capital inflows, it opted for capital controls and a fiscal expansion to continue to boost growth. It addressed the symptom (capital inflows), not the disease (the bad policy mix). The result has been a long and deep recession in Brazil.

A more subtle issue is that, as the time spent at the zero bound has increased, the major central banks have shown a behavior that resembles the "fear of floating" displayed by many emerging markets. Fear of floating refers to the behavior of economies that, despite having floating exchange

Figure 4.8 GDP-weighted over- or undervaluation of G-10 and emerging-market currencies, based on Goldman Sachs Dynamic Equilibrium Exchange Rate (GSDEER) model, 2000–16

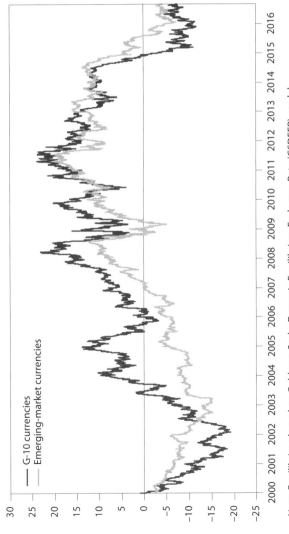

deviation from equilibrium of GDP-weighted basket of currencies versus dollar (percent)

G-10 currencies
Emerging-market currencies

Note: Equilibrium based on Goldman Sachs Dynamic Equilibrium Exchange Rate (GSDEER) model.
Sources: Data from Bloomberg and Goldman Sachs Investment Research.

rates, routinely intervene in currency markets—verbally, with monetary policy actions, or with outright intervention. Rather than allowing their currency to float and then react with policy accordingly—reducing interest rates if the currency appreciates, for example—they engaged in preemptive actions to prevent currency moves. Such behavior manifests itself, for example, in interest rate moves (both actual and communication about future moves) based on expected currency moves or routine verbal intervention.

Such actions are perhaps logical. When all countries are at the zero bound, exchange rate movements "distribute" demand across countries. All of the main central banks have accentuated their commentary about exchange rates and their verbal interventions, ranging from increased commentary in speeches about the impact of exchange rate fluctuations on inflation, output, and financial conditions to explicit changes in their forward guidance on interest rates in an attempt to arrest the appreciation of their currency. The rapid and persistent decline in oil prices, which put downward pressure on measures of inflation expectations and increased the deflationary risk of currency appreciation, compounded this sensitivity toward exchange rates.[7]

This distributional effect of demand could be more accentuated for countries with reserve currencies, as the excess demand for their safe assets leads to appreciation of their currencies (as is the case of Switzerland or the United States). The Fed was very active in this regard, highlighting the impact of the appreciation of the dollar on inflation, stressing the impact of the dollar on financial conditions and its equivalent effect in terms of interest rate increases, and systematically lowering its forward-looking path of the neutral interest rate to reflect a potentially stronger currency.[8] Reducing the expected path of interest rates, as communicated in the dot plot, became a preferred Fed instrument for reacting to the appreciation of the dollar after mid-2014.

As a result of this sharpened focus on exchange rates as policy objectives, the main currencies have been confined to a wide band since early 2015, reminiscent of the "target zone" exchange rate systems of the 1990s. Whenever the dollar, the euro, or the yen has approached the bands of these corridors, central banks have reacted—mostly with words, but also at times

---

7. The BoE's Minouche Shafik, for example, has stated that the strong appreciation of sterling since 2013 is exerting significant downward pressure on inflation and will continue for several years to come (Minouche Shafik, "Treading Carefully," speech at Institute of Directions, December 14, 2015).

8. See Lael Brainard, "Economic Outlook and Monetary Policy," speech at conference on "North America's Place in a Changing World Economy," 57th National Association for Business Economics Annual Meeting, Washington, October 12, 2015; and William C. Dudley, "The US Economic Outlook and the Implications for Monetary Policy," speech at Bank of Indonesia-Federal Reserve Bank of New York Joint International Seminar, Bali, July 31, 2016.

with actions. This focus on exchange rates raised the issue of policy coordination at the G7 and G20 levels, something that will surely become more prominent if inflation rates remain well below target for a long period.

Did Policies Ease to the Extent Recommended by Simple Benchmark Rules?

Monetary policy has affected asset prices and financial conditions, mostly in the desired and expected manner. The second step of an evaluation of the performance of monetary policy is comparing the level of interest rates versus some measure of what the "right" interest rates should have been.

The effective lower bound makes it impossible to directly compare the level of interest rates with the "right" level, as the "right" short-term interest rate was likely to be negative and, as discussed in chapter 3, the central bank has instruments other than short-term rates at its disposal. Therefore, some approximations are needed in order to assess the "true" underlying stance of policy.

A first step is to estimate the historical relationships between changes in 10-year rates and changes in the short-term rates and between asset purchases and changes in 10-year rates, in order to establish an approximate relationship between asset purchases and short-term interest rates. Academic research shows that the Fed's QE1 led to a reduction in the 10-year rate of about 50 basis points (with uncertainty bands around it of 30–100 basis points). Regressing the 10-year rate on the fed funds rate over the precrisis period indicates that this reduction in 10-year rates was equivalent to a 200 basis point reduction in the fed funds rate (Chung et al. 2011 and Thorton 2011). In testimony before Congress February 9, 2011, Chairman Bernanke argued that the Fed had calibrated QE2 to be equivalent to a cut of 75 basis points in the fed funds rate, which it calculated required a $600 billion QE program.[9] The rule of thumb therefore was that $100 billion of purchases was equivalent to a bit more than a 10 basis point cut in the fed funds rate cut. If all the Fed purchases had taken place at the same time, the impact of the $3.5 trillion program would have been equivalent to a rate cut of close to 400 basis points. This approximation is very rough, as the impact of the purchases should decay over time; as the stock effect declines as the issuance of Treasuries increases steadily, Fed holdings should become a smaller portion of the total stock.

A more sophisticated methodology to assess the impact of monetary policy at the effective lower bound is the estimation of shadow interest rates, which approximate short-term interest rates from the shape of the

---

9. Ben S. Bernanke, "The Economic Outlook and Monetary and Fiscal Policy," testimony before the Committee on the Budget, US House of Representatives, Washington, February 9, 2011.

yield curve (Wu and Xia 2016). This methodology estimates an underlying relationship, based on historical evidence, between the different points of the yield curve and the short-term interest rate and identifies the short-term rate that would have delivered such a yield curve at each point in time.

Figure 4.9 shows the results of these estimates for the United States, United Kingdom, and euro area. The shadow rate declined to negative territory in the United States in 2009, reaching a low of near –3 percent in early 2014. In the United Kingdom the rate was more volatile. It was initially negative, then became positive in late 2011, reaching 2 percent in early 2012 (reflecting the BoE's debate in 2011 about the likelihood of interest rate increases) before dropping to about –1 percent in early 2014. In the euro area the interest rate initially fluctuated around zero, indicating the lack of active policy easing (and the rate hikes in 2011, of course); it dropped to negative territory when deposit rates were cut to negative levels and QE launched. The ECB has achieved the most negative shadow interest rate of the three main central banks, falling well below –4 percent.

Once the "true" interest rate has been established, one needs to define what the "right" interest rate should have been. One way to approximate this rate is to define a policy rule, which would define the "right" short-term interest rate as a function of the neutral real interest rate (r^*) and deviations of inflation (π) and unemployment (u) from its objectives (π^* and u^*):

$$r = r^* + \pi + \alpha\,(\pi - \pi^*) + \beta^*\,\text{Okun}^*\,(u - u^*) \tag{4.1}$$

where Okun is the coefficient of Okun's law, which relates the unemployment gap to the output gap. Swedish economist Knut Wicksell famously wrote: "There is a certain rate of interest on loans which is neutral in respect to commodity prices, and tends neither to raise nor to lower them" (Wicksell 1936, 102). The r^* in equation (4.1) corresponds to the Wicksellian natural rate, which can be operationalized as the real interest rate that would prevail if the economy were at maximum employment and inflation were at target, absent transitory shocks. Conceptually, the existence of a natural rate means that the central bank can achieve its objectives only by ensuring that the market real interest rate is equal to the neutral real interest rate over the longer run. The problem is that the neutral real interest rate is an unobservable variable and therefore needs to be inferred or estimated.

Why Have Neutral Interest Rates Declined?

One way to proxy for the unobservable neutral interest rate is to look at market rates. Figure 4.10 shows the evolution of the 10y10y real forward yield, a measure of what financial markets expect the annual real interest rate to average over the 10-year period that starts 10 years from the cur-

Figure 4.9 Shadow interest rates in the United States, United Kingdom, and euro area, 2004–15

percent

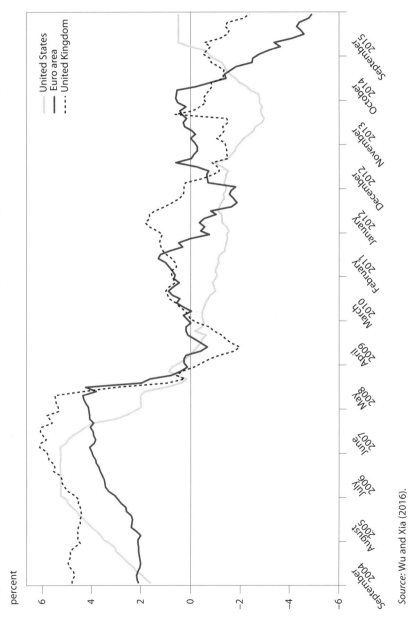

Source: Wu and Xia (2016).

Figure 4.10 Average real 10y10y interest rates, 2003–16

percent

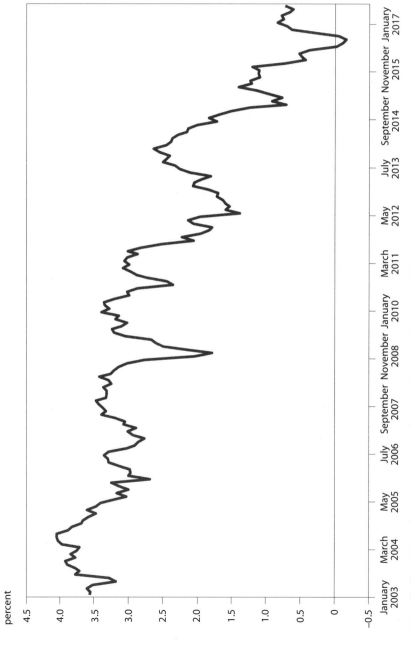

Note: 10y10y is 10-year interest rate 10 years forward. Unweighted average yield for Australia, Canada, the euro area, Japan, New Zealand, the United Kingdom, and United States.

Source: Data from Bloomberg.

rent date. By going deep into the future, this measure tries to eliminate the influence of the business cycle to replicate the Wicksellian concept. The unweighted average yield for Australia, Canada, the euro area, Japan, New Zealand, the United Kingdom, and the United States declined between 2003 and 2016, from 3–4 percent before the crisis to a bit below zero by mid-2016, when it ranged from –0.85 in Japan to 0.75 percent in New Zealand.

Two possible factors explain this decline in the observed long-term real rate. The first is that the long-run neutral real interest rate has declined. The second is that investors expect looser monetary policy for a very long period, conditional on an unchanged long-run neutral real interest rate. However, inflation expectations have also shown a steady decline, suggesting that, if anything, markets expect monetary policy to be too tight, not too loose, in the future. Therefore, the decline in market real rates is more likely to be associated with an expected decline in the neutral real rate.

The existence of term premia can contaminate market approximations of the neutral rate. An alternative and complementary approach to finding the neutral interest rate is to estimate it using macroeconomic relationships. Academic research on the United States shows a wide dispersion of results, with estimates for r^* in 2016 ranging from –2 percent to 1.25 percent (see Justiniano and Primiceri 2010 and Kiley 2015). The most popular methodology is the one originally described in Laubach and Williams (2003), which estimates r^* for the United States as an unobservable variable derived from the relationship between interest rates, output, and domestically generated inflation. Holston, Laubach, and Williams (2016) estimate a simplified version of r^*, using inflation rather than domestically generated inflation, for a variety of countries. Figure 4.11 shows their results for the United States, United Kingdom, and euro area. To illustrate the high sensitivity of these models to small changes in the assumptions and because Fed officials often mention it in speeches, figure 4.11 also shows the results for the United States using the Laubach and Williams (2003) results.

For the United States, the neutral rate declined steadily, from more than 2.5 percent in 2000 to a bit above or below zero after 2009, depending on the model used. The spread between the two estimates is 25–70 basis points for 2009–16.

For the euro area the evolution is similar, albeit less smooth, until the onset of the euro area crisis in 2010, when r^* for the euro area collapsed toward a low of –0.5 percent. Adjusting this figure for the average spread between the two estimates yields an r^* for the euro area of about –1 percent in 2016.

For the United Kingdom the pattern is different. Before the crisis r^* was more stable; after the crisis the dip was less acute and stabilized early, at a higher level of about 1.5 percent.

Figure 4.11   Estimated neutral rate of interest in the United States, United Kingdom, and euro area, 1972–2016

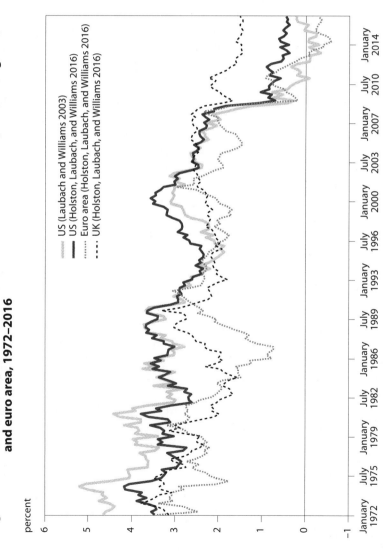

percent

— US (Laubach and Williams 2003)
— US (Holston, Laubach, and Williams 2016)
······· Euro area (Holston, Laubach, and Williams 2016)
- - - UK (Holston, Laubach, and Williams 2016)

Sources: Laubach and Williams (2003) and Holston, Laubach, and Williams (2016).

The reasons for this secular decline in observed or estimated neutral real interest rates are not well understood. Many factors are potentially at play. Conceptually, the optimality condition for savings in the standard growth model yields a relationship between the real interest rate and technological progress, population growth, and factors shaping preferences for desired savings and investments.[10] Before the crisis the steady aging of the population, the perceived plateau in technological progress and educational attainment, and the increase in savings in emerging markets may have driven the neutral rate lower. The secular increase in the supply of labor and the decline in the labor share in GDP resulting from the combined effect of globalization, skills-biased technological progress, and weaker labor bargaining power may have reduced the demand for capital and the real interest rate over time.

The crisis and its aftermath may have exacerbated the decline. Worries about the hysteresis effects of the crisis, and the failure of productivity growth to rebound, have dragged down the estimates of future potential growth. Fiscal austerity has increased public savings, and worries about the inability of economic policy to deliver sustainable growth have depressed investment. A crisis-induced increase in the demand for safe and liquid assets may have increased the "convenience yield" (the special safety and liquidity attributes of safe assets such as Treasuries [see Krishnamurthy and Vissing-Jørgensen 2011]) of government bonds and reduced the neutral interest rate. The tightening of financial regulations, a typical reaction to a large financial crisis, depressed risk taking and likely investment. Everything else equal, the widening of inequality leads to higher savings, as the rich have a greater propensity to save. Larry Summers famously summarized most of these factors in his secular stagnation speech, which is worth watching.[11]

Attempts at more precise estimates of the sources of the decline in neutral rates have led to a variety of results (Pescatori and Turunen 2015, Rachel and Smith 2015, Fischer 2016)—notably, different researchers claim to be able to explain most of the decline with their preferred factor, something that cannot be true in aggregate. For example, Lukasz Rachel and Thomas Smith (2015) estimate that changes in desired savings and investment account for about two-thirds of the decline in global neutral interest rates since the 1980s, with the rest caused by lower expectations of potential

---

10. Specifically, the optimality condition for savings along a balanced growth path implies that the real interest rates is a function of the intertemporal substitution for consumption, the rate of labor augmenting technological progress, the rate of population growth, and the rate of time preference.

11. Mundell-Fleming Lecture by Lawrence H. Summers, November 3, 2016, www.imf.org/external/mmedia/view.aspx?vid=5196724125001.

growth. Etienne Gagnon, Benjamin Johannsen, and David López-Salido (2016) estimate that demographic changes over the last decades explain most of the decline in US real interest rates. Marco Del Negro et al. (2017) argue that the increased demand for safe assets explains a very large part of the decline in neutral real interest rates.

Whether this trend will continue is the subject of a strong debate. There are reasons to be optimistic. It is possible that the decline in the estimated r^* in recent years reflects an identification problem. The US economy suffered two negative shocks—first a sharp fiscal contraction and then a sectoral recession in the energy sector. Not "knowing this," the Laubach-Williams model allocates the failure of GDP to accelerate despite the low level of interest rates to a decline in r^*. In addition, core inflation in the US has suffered from transitory shocks, related mostly to healthcare legislation but also to the decline in oil prices, which temporarily reduced inflation. The model allocates this failure of inflation to increase to a lower r^*. As the impact of this transitory shock fades, r^* should naturally increase.

It is also possible that recent weakness in productivity growth is temporary. Historically, productivity growth has shown long cycles, with periods of weak growth followed by periods of stronger growth. A combination of mismeasurement of GDP at the time of rapid generation of new products and services, cyclically depressed investment, and a slowdown in technology adoption driven by weak demand could be keeping productivity growth temporarily depressed, setting the stage for a rebound. Despite the gloom, technological progress seems to be buoyant: there is strong evidence that firms at the frontier in each industry have been increasing productivity at a healthy pace, while the rest of firms have lagged significantly, thus reducing average productivity growth. This slowdown in the diffusion of best practices—which could reflect increased inequality among firms or lack of competition—could reverse over time (Baily and Montalbano 2016).

The pessimistic view of r^* is best summarized by Summers' secular stagnation hypothesis, which would suggest a continuation of the low real interest rates absent a policy reaction. The secular stagnation hypothesis conjectures that, in a world in which economic policy is constrained, the economy can remain in a state of persistent insufficiency of demand. In such a case, lack of demand—and its mirror image, an excess of savings—would keep neutral real interest rates very low for a long time. Of course, this need not be the case. A determined fiscal expansion that boosts demand, a reduction in risk aversion as time heals the wounds of the financial crisis, an increase in investment in emerging markets that rebalances their excess savings, and the peaking in the effective labor supply that will arise from the aging of populations would all argue for a reduction in the excess of savings over investment and a reversal toward higher neutral real interest rates. A fiscal expansion would also ease the shortage of safe assets that is putting downward pressure on bond yields.

Whatever happens, this decline in neutral real interest rates and the fear that secular stagnation may be the most likely outcome is already affecting policy. A good example is the behavior of the FOMC, which has steadily reduced its estimates of the current and future neutral interest rate over the last few years. Not only has it reduced its estimates of the neutral long-run fed funds rate (from 4 percent when it was first published in 2012 to 3 percent in 2017), it has also steadily lowered the pace at which it expects to reach it. Figure 4.12 shows the evolution of the implicit median dot for the end of 2017 (as published in successive editions of the *Summary of Economic Projections*) using the Taylor policy rule, which decomposes interest rates into the neutral rate and the contribution of the inflation gap and the unemployment gap.

Assuming an inflation objective of 2 percent, a NAIRU equal to the estimate of long-term unemployment in the *Summary of Economic Projections*, and coefficients 0.5 for the inflation gap and 1 for the unemployment gap, as per Taylor (1999), one can solve for the implicit neutral rate. Figure 4.12 shows a steady decline in the FOMC estimate of the neutral interest rate by the end of 2017, from close to 1.5 percent in the December 2014 estimation to about –0.6 percent in the June 2016 estimation. This decline has been the main reason why the FOMC has been steadily lowering the path of interest rates in the dot chart.

Uncertainty about the equilibrium rate could have important implications for monetary policy. Athanasios Orphanides and John Williams (2002, 2006, 2007) argue that if the central bank does not have a good estimate of what the equilibrium real rate should be, it may be better able to achieve its objectives by putting more inertia into its decisions than it otherwise would. The intuition is simple: If there is uncertainty about the level of r^*, the central bank should adopt a policy rule that takes the current interest rate as given and focuses on the required change in interest rates rather than the desired level.

James Hamilton et al. (2015) simulate several alternative paths for the fed funds rate. They find that when uncertainty about the equilibrium rate is greater, a policy that follows an inertial rule and raises rates later but— provided the recovery does gather pace and inflation picks up—somewhat more steeply may deliver a higher value of the objective function. This preference for inertia implies a very gradual approach to raising interest rates and, in case of doubt, erring on the side of being behind the curve.

Once the shadow interest rate and the neutral rate are calculated, they can be combined in a policy rule such as the one in equation (4.1) and monetary policy assessed. Figure 4.13 shows the results of calculating policy rules

Figure 4.12   Implicit neutral interest rate in the 2017 dot of the Federal Open Market Committee's 2017 dot plot, 2014–16

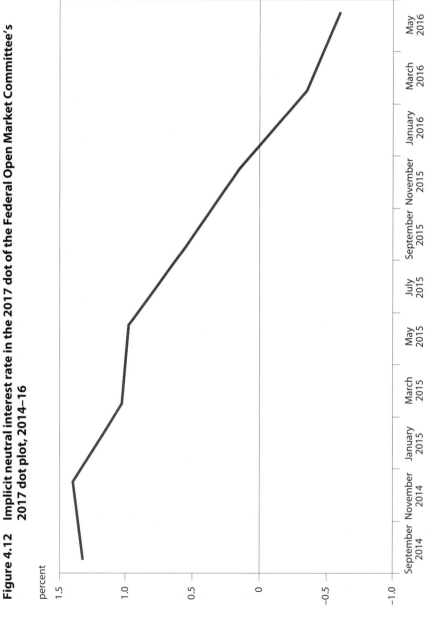

Source: Data from the Federal Reserve.

Figure 4.13   Estimated policy rule for the Federal Reserve, Bank of England, and European Central Bank

a. Federal Reserve

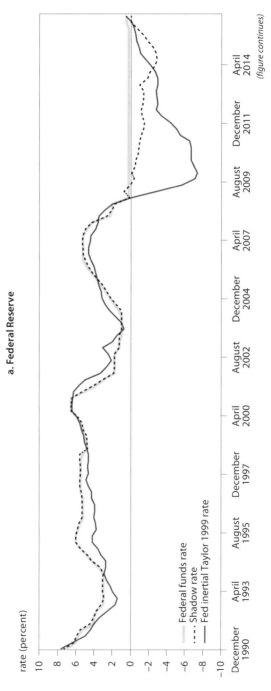

rate (percent)

Federal funds rate
Shadow rate
Fed inertial Taylor 1999 rate

(figure continues)

Figure 4.13   Estimated policy rule for the Federal Reserve, Bank of England, and European Central Bank (*continued*)

b. Bank of England

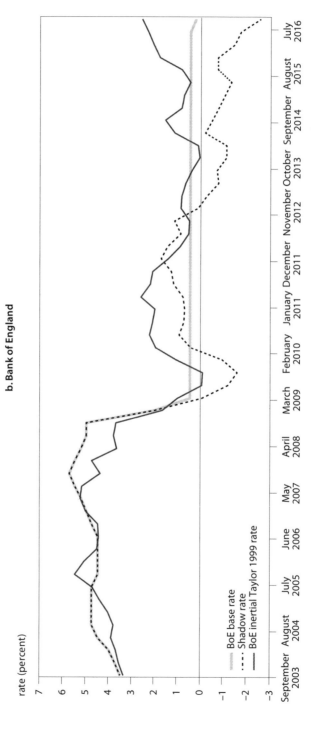

rate (percent)

BoE base rate
Shadow rate
BoE inertial Taylor 1999 rate

c. European Central Bank

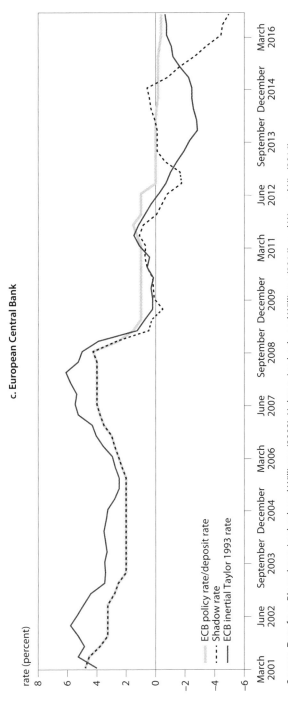

Sources: Data from Bloomberg; Laubach and Williams (2003); Holston, Laubach, and Williams (2016), and Wu and Xia (2016).

139

using equation (4.1) for the Fed, ECB, and BoE and comparing them to their respective shadow interest rates. For the United States, r^* is from Laubach and Williams (2003); for the euro area and the United Kingdom it is from Holston, Laubach, and Williams (2016). Inflation corresponds to the central bank's preferred measure of core inflation, to eliminate the noise generated by the large fluctuations in commodity prices. The time-varying NAIRU is the one estimated by the Congressional Budget Office for the United States, the BoE for the United Kingdom, and the OECD for the euro area.

In the case of the Fed and the ECB, it appears that policy has not been eased enough. The inertial Taylor 1999 rule for the United States, which provides the best fit precrisis (with an inertial coefficient of 0.6) suggests that the fed funds should have been cut toward –8 percent at the peak of the crisis. The estimates of the shadow fed funds rate decline only slowly, reaching a low of –3 percent.[12] The shadow rate estimates suggest that the easing was too gradual, reaching its maximum level several years into the crisis—which corresponds to the more aggressive form of easing (open-ended QE), adopted only in late 2012.

An inertial Taylor 1999 policy rule suggests that the BoE did about right. During 2010–11 it (rightly) ignored the level shift in inflation created by the tax hikes; the shadow rate and Taylor prescription converge once the impact of the tax hikes wears off. During 2013–15 policy was below the prescription of the Taylor rule, likely because of the risk to inflation from the euro area, the decline in oil prices, and (later) Brexit.

The Taylor rule for the ECB (Taylor 1993) shows that the ECB should have eased much more aggressively after 2011. The gap between the shadow rate and the Taylor rule estimate is about 200 basis points. The estimated optimal policy rate is higher (less negative) than for the United States, despite the deeper and longer recession, because, in most estimates of the NAIRU for the euro area, there is an implicit assumption that most of the increase in unemployment was structural. Whether this was the case is debatable; these real-time estimates of the amount of slack in the euro area may be underestimating the extent of spare resources. The failure of core inflation to rebound and the repeated downward revisions to the ECB's inflation forecast are initial signals of this underestimation of available slack.

Overall, the conclusion is that monetary policy was eased aggressively but, in the United States and euro area, by less initially than what a policy rule would have advised.

---

12. An alternative calibration of the "true" interest rate, following the rule of thumb that $600 billion of purchases are equivalent to about a 75 basis point rate cut in the fed funds, would yield an equivalent rate cut of about 500 basis points, closer to the indication of the Taylor rule.

Did Policies Achieve Their Objectives in Terms of Inflation and Growth?

Monetary policy has been working overtime since 2007. By some counts central banks around the world have made more than 600 rate cuts and purchased several trillion dollars' worth of assets. But what matters is not the amount of inputs but the quality of outputs. The previous section established that monetary policy affected financial conditions in the expected way and that the amount of easing was large, although it happened later and in a less aggressive fashion than suggested by simple policy rules, at least in the United States and euro area. But these estimates are approximations. The proof of the pudding is in the eating. Has all this monetary policy action been enough to restore growth and inflation?

The simple answer would be yes. By end of 2016 GDP had surpassed its precrisis peak in all regions (figure 4.14). Despite a very deep recession and a very large decline in oil prices, core inflation remained positive and inflation expectations remained, in general, stable. Given that monetary policy was the main (and in many cases the only) economic policy in play, these outcomes suggest it was successful.

A more detailed answer is more nuanced, and the verdict becomes less positive. The level of GDP remains well below what would have been a continuation of the precrisis trend, and the recovery has been weaker than in previous cycles. Part of this weakness reflects structural factors, such as the slowdown in productivity growth, which predated the crisis; the decline in labor force participation in the United States; and the persistent risk of the breakup of the euro area. But monetary policy has also played a role. Inflation has failed to rebound enough to be consistent, on average, with the inflation targets of the main central banks. And inflation expectations seem to be anchored at a lower level than before the crisis (see the extensive discussion on inflation in Miles, Panizza, Reis, and Ubide 2017).

There is a clear academic consensus that monetary policy has had a positive impact on growth and inflation, but the range of econometric estimates on its impact is wide. One reason for this wide range could be that the impact of the different channels through which monetary policy operates varies over time. In addition, as monetary policy becomes more multidimensional, its impact on growth and inflation becomes less directly observable and requires econometric identification schemes. There is little consensus on how to introduce such identification restrictions. Martin Weale and Tomasz Wieladek (2015), for example, use four identification schemes to identify QE shocks in structural vector autoregressions.

Despite the variety of strategies, the results are robust, with most of the literature finding a positive effect on growth and inflation. The IMF (2013) reviews a wide range of research and concludes that a 100 basis point

Figure 4.14   GDP index in the United States, United Kingdom, euro area, and Japan, 2000–16

index (2000 = 100)

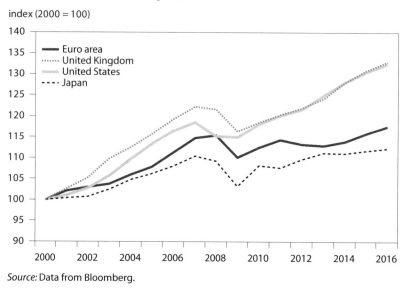

Source: Data from Bloomberg.

decline in long-term yields has an average impact on growth of about 2 percentage points over two years (with a range between little impact and about 8 percentage points) and an average impact on inflation of about 1.5 percentage points (with a similarly wide range). The range of econometric exercises with different identification schemes that Andrew Haldane et al. (2016) run reveals that a 1 percent GDP increase in the central bank balance sheet leads to real GDP increase of 0.13–0.64 percent and a 0.1–0.6 percent increase in inflation.

Research shows that the signaling channel seems to have a larger impact on growth and inflation than the portfolio balance channel (IMF 2013). This result could be reflecting the fact that the signaling channel transmits a more persistent change in financial conditions than the portfolio-rebalancing channel—it signals more determination to achieve the targets and possibly a change to a more dovish reaction function by the central bank. Jeremy Stein argues that the declines in the expected path of interest rates generated by the signaling channel lower the hurdle rate for investment and should boost capital spending, but that reductions in the term premium created by the portfolio-rebalancing channel lead firms to engage in liability management (i.e., change the relative composition of their funding between stocks and bonds) but not new capital spending.[13]

---

13. Jeremy Stein, "Evaluating Large-Scale Asset Purchases," speech at the Brookings Institution, Washington, October 11, 2012.

This differential impact on firms of these two channels on transmission of monetary policy could partly explain the very large volume of share buybacks by corporations, their large holdings of cash, and the relative underperformance of investment during the recovery (see the detailed analysis on the underperformance of investment in IMF 2015a).

It could also help explain the difference in performance between risky financial assets and real investment. The portfolio-rebalancing effect supports risky financial assets in the near term, but the decline in the term premium, unless it is seen as permanent, may not lead to new real investment projects with a multiyear expected life. Portfolio managers with a one-year horizon for their decisions may be more reactive to asset purchases that reduce the term premium than corporate boards that need to decide on multiyear investment projects. In this case, however, what is the difference between easing via a lower term premium and standard rate cuts? This is where the insurance channel of monetary policy makes a major difference.

During normal recessions, central banks cut rates and economic agents assume that the rate cuts will be enough for the economy to return to its normal, prerecession state. Rate cuts thus increase future expected demand, increasing investment. When interest rates are at zero, and the central bank eases policy only by reducing the term premium, economic agents no longer trust that the economy will return to its normal, prerecession state. The uncertainty about expected future earnings increases, and that offsets the reduction in the term premium. Unless central banks provide credible insurance, unless they take some risk and offset the risk aversion that afflicts the private sector, short-term pricing of financial assets may react but longer-term real investment lags. When uncertainty is high, the option value of waiting increases. Ben Broadbent argues that uncertainty about growth could add as much as 10 percentage points to the hurdle rate for an investment.[14]

Of course, other factors unrelated to the monetary policy transmission mechanism could explain this underperformance of investment and preference for cash during the recovery. They include persistently high risk premia; the fear that, being at the zero lower bound, economic policy has few options to react to an unexpected shock, increasing the probability of recession; more active tax-avoidance strategies; and increased competition in the technology sector that requires abundant cash for acquisitions.

---

14. Ben Broadbent, "Uncertain Times," speech on monetary policy at the *Wall Street Journal*, London, October 5, 2016.

Price Stability at Risk: The Weakness of Inflation and Inflation Expectations

Central banks have been unlucky. Not only were they left alone by governments to deal with a very large recession, they also had to deal with a very large move in oil prices, which created a major headwind to their mission of restoring price stability. From the peak in mid-2014 to the trough in early 2016, oil prices, measured by the West Texas Intermediate (WTI) contract, declined by about 75 percent. As a result, headline inflation turned negative almost everywhere. At a time of fears about recession and deflation, negative headline inflation, even if transitory, becomes an additional and powerful downside risk to inflation expectations. Not all consumers are sophisticated analysts; often they react to changes in the prices that are salient or with which they interact most often. The price of gasoline at the pump, for example, affects the formation of inflation expectations even two years out (Armantier et al. 2016).

Regardless of oil and commodity prices, core inflation has been low. The average core inflation during 2007–16 was 1.6 percent in the United States, 1.8 percent in the United Kingdom, 1.3 percent in the euro area, and –0.1 percent in Japan. Core inflation has been very subdued in the United States for a long time, with the year-on-year growth of the deflator of core personal consumption expenditures below 2 percent since 2008 (except a few months in 2012). Core inflation in the euro area reached 2 percent in 2011 and 2012 as a result of large indirect tax hikes (mostly VAT) in some countries, but it plunged toward zero as these effects disappeared from the price indexes and stabilized at about 1 percent. In the United Kingdom, inflation has been more resilient as a result of a series of price-level shocks related mostly to taxes and fees and the volatility of the currency. Once these effects are taken into account, core inflation has remained below 2 percent. In Japan it is difficult to assess the true trend in inflation, because of large movements in the exchange rate, taxes, and inflation expectations, but the core inflation index developed by the BoJ (comparable to the core inflation indexes in the rest of the G7) increased from negative levels early in the crisis to near 1 percent in 2016 (the sharp spike above 2 percent in 2014–15 reflected the 2014 VAT hike). The experimental daily index of the University of Tokyo accelerated toward 1.5 percent during 2016.[15]

What has kept inflation low? At the most fundamental level, inflation is a function of two main variables: the amount of slack in the economy and inflation expectations (in addition, of course, to exogenous factors,

15. See UTokyo Daily Price Index, www.cmdlab.co.jp/price_u-tokyo/daily_e (accessed on March 30, 2017).

such as exchange rates and commodity prices).[16] The previous section showed that growth has recovered since the recession but that there is probably some slack in the economy, especially in the euro area. The transformation taking place in global labor markets may be exacerbating the downward pressure from economic slack. The combination of technology, globalization, and weak labor bargaining power has probably pushed labor markets toward an equilibrium in which more jobs are being created but at lower wages. This phenomenon may explain the weakness in wage growth in the United States and United Kingdom, despite the strength of their labor markets, and could be a preview of what may happen in the euro area, where the depth and length of the recession and the further liberalization of labor markets may keep wage growth tepid for a very long time. The dualism in labor markets fostered by labor market liberalization can generate heavy downward pressure on wage growth. Temporary jobs pay less than comparable permanent jobs. If the composition of jobs growth is tilted toward temporary jobs, the composition effect will lead to weaker aggregate wage growth. Japan is leading the way in rethinking this issue. Income policies, especially "equal pay for equal work," are at the forefront of Abenomics and of the advice the IMF is offering Japan to continue its progress toward 2 percent inflation (IMF 2016b).

At the same time, one could ask the opposite question: What has kept inflation so high? The size of the recession was almost unprecedented; a priori one could have forecast a much larger decline in inflation. Three reasons come may explain this "missing deflation." First, inflation expectations were well anchored when the recession hit. Despite the size of the recession, professional forecasters had little doubt, at least initially, that inflation would return to target over the medium term, as discussed below. Second, the steady appreciation of commodity prices until 2014 kept inflation expectations higher. In fact, the probability of five-year average inflation being higher than 2 percent remained elevated in the United States and United Kingdom (and to a lesser extent the euro area) until 2014 (figure 4.15). In this sense central bankers were lucky. Imagine the tone of the discussion if commodity prices had not rebounded after the dip in 2008, pushing headline inflation into very negative territory at the time unemployment rates were shooting higher. Fears of deflation would have been much more extreme (see the discussion in Miles, Panizza, Reis and Ubide 2017). Third, the downward rigidity of wages was widespread. Mary Daly, Bart Hobijn, and Brian Lucking (2012) show that the numbers of workers receiving zero wage increases almost doubled during the recession. This downward rigidity may

---

16. Janet L. Yellen, "Inflation Dynamics and Monetary Policy," Philip Gamble Lecture, University of Massachusetts, Amherst, September 24, 2015.

Figure 4.15   Market-implied probability of five-year average inflation rate in the United States, United Kingdom, and euro area exceeding 2 percent, 2009–16

probability (percent)

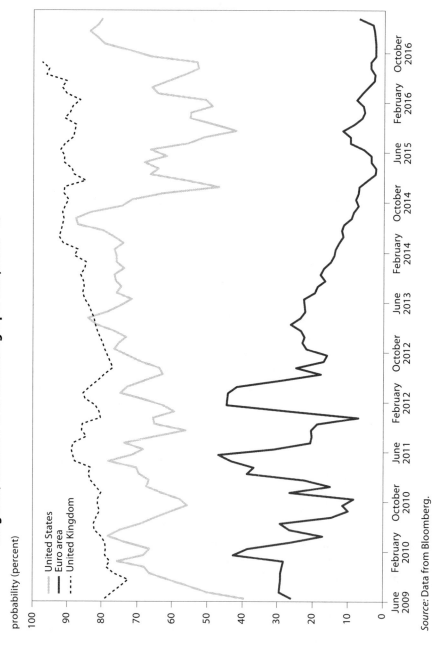

Source: Data from Bloomberg.

have delayed the adjustment and increased the unemployment rate, but at the same time it may have helped contain the decline in inflation. The downward rigidity in markups (profit margins) also may have helped. Firms may have prioritized the preservation of cash flows (because, with financial markets in turmoil and the banking sector tightening lending conditions, the value of cash increased) over preserving market share by lowering prices, which may have reduced the extent of price reductions and thus the negative impact of the recession on inflation.

In addition to slack and wage growth dynamics, the other critical element for the evolution of inflation is inflation expectations, especially if the impact of economic slack on inflation has declined (the Phillips curve has become flatter) over the years. Inflation expectations seem to have declined, or at least the downside risks have increased, with respect to the period before 2007. There are two main ways to measure them, market-based measures and surveys.

Market-Based Measures of Inflation Expectations

Market-based measures infer inflation expectations from measures of inflation break-evens (the spread between nominal and real yields) or inflation swaps. Because transitory factors, such as changes in the price of oil, can affect near-term inflation, the standard method of looking at inflation expectations is to look at medium-term horizons, such as five-year average inflation starting five years in the future (5y5y inflation).

Figure 4.16 shows the evolution of 5y5y inflation, extracted from inflation swaps, for the United States, United Kingdom, euro area, and Japan. In the United Kingdom, inflation swaps are priced off of the retail price index excluding mortgage interest payments (RPIX), not the harmonized index of consumer prices (HICP). The BoE's 2 percent inflation target refers to the HICP, and the spread between the HICP and RPIX has typically been about 100 basis points. Therefore, an inflation expectation of 3 percent from the inflation swaps market is compatible with the 2 percent inflation target.

Until mid-2014 the BoE, and to a lesser extent the Fed and the ECB, were successful in keeping inflation expectations well anchored around precrisis levels that were compatible with their mandate—although euro area inflation expectations were always anchored at a lower level than in the United States or United Kingdom, probably the effect of the ECB's asymmetric inflation objective. After mid-2014 markets started to doubt the resolve of the Fed and the ECB to restore inflation at mandate-consistent levels, and 5y5y break-evens started to drift lower. In the case of the ECB, markets started to expect a very long period of below-target inflation. The BoJ was able to buck this trend and increase inflation expectations

Figure 4.16   Market-expected five-year inflation rate, five years forward, in the United States, United Kingdom, euro area, and Japan, 2007–17

percent

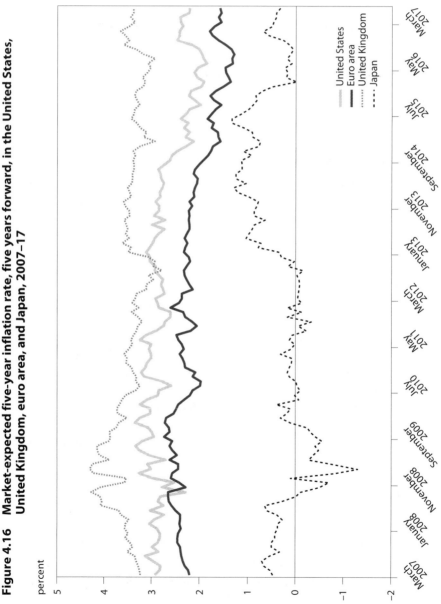

United States
Euro area
United Kingdom
Japan

Source: Data from Bloomberg.

with respect to precrisis levels. In fact, with the launching of QQE, 5y5y settled around 1 percent, until dragged lower during 2016 by the global decline in break-evens and the market disappointment with the BoJ's negative rate cut.

The 5y5y indicator, while useful, masks the details of market expectations about inflation and, in particular, when inflation is expected to return to the target. Central banks typically have a diffuse horizon—over the medium term—in order to have flexibility to manage shocks. This feature is welcome, but at the same time it is important that it not become a window to tolerate excessively high or low inflation for too long.

One way to explore this issue is to look at the term structure of forward inflation. Figure 4.17 shows the term structure of annual inflation rates—expected annual inflation one year from now, two years from now, and so forth—as of March 2017 for the United States, United Kingdom, and euro area, compared with the average during 2005–06 (data are not available for Japan before 2007). The period 2005–06 is used as a benchmark because it is a period in which there was consensus that central banks had achieved price stability and their credibility was beyond doubt. This benchmark shows that inflation expectations were very stable then; markets expected inflation to be at levels compatible with the inflation mandate over the medium and long run.

Based on these figures, markets were suggesting in early 2017 that neither the Fed nor the ECB will be likely to deliver the same level of inflation as before the crisis. In the case of the Fed, the market saw the Fed delivering inflation about 50 basis points lower on average. For example, the one-year inflation five years forward was 2.2 percent, down from 2.8 percent during 2005–06.

In the case of the ECB, the spread with respect to the precrisis average is wider and closes only toward the end. According to markets, annual inflation will be below 1.5 percent until 2023. The figure also shows the term structure the week before the January 2015 ECB meeting, at which the ECB finally announced its QE program. At that point, markets were expecting inflation to be below 1 percent for four years. Markets were not confident that the ECB was willing to deliver on its mandate. It is possible, though, that the global negative term premium or pessimistic expectations for oil prices affected these market expectations and biased them downwards.

Other central banks seem to be more credible. For example, the market expectation for the BoE is solidly anchored at levels above those prevailing before the crisis. The fact that the BoE was willing to tolerate a long period of above-target inflation—headline inflation was 5 percent—while at the same time expanding QE may have solidified the antideflation credibility of the BoE.

Figure 4.17   Term structure of market-implied expectations of inflation in the United States, United Kingdom, and euro area

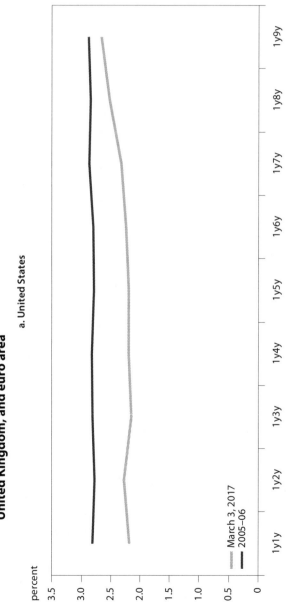

a. United States

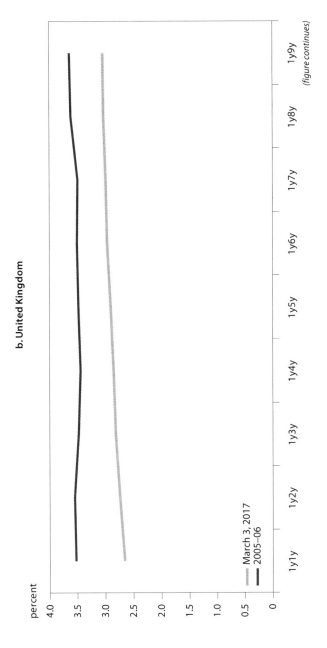

b. United Kingdom

(figure continues)

Figure 4.17 Term structure of market-implied expectations of inflation in the United States, United Kingdom, and euro area (*continued*)

c. Euro area

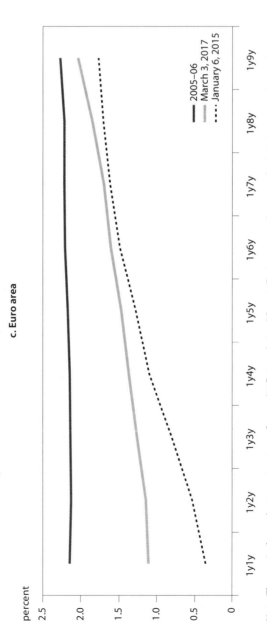

Note: The x-axis shows the term structure of annual inflation derived from inflation swaps. For example, 1y1y is expected annual inflation starting in 1 year, 1y2y is expected annual inflation starting in 2 years, and so on.

Source: Data from Bloomberg.

Actions matter. The ECB's delay in responding to downside risks to inflation may have long-term consequences. In a staff assessment of its QE program, the ECB implicitly agreed that price stability had been at risk: "After decreasing noticeably during 2014, long-term inflation expectations returned toward levels consistent with the ECB's definition of price stability" (Andrade et al. 2016, 7). If expectations "returned" toward levels consistent with price stability, it means they were not at levels consistent with price stability before. This deanchoring of inflation expectations in the euro area led to a situation in which near-term developments in inflation had an impact on long-term inflation expectations. Since mid-2014 the correlation between near-term and long-term inflation expectations increased, as they did before Draghi's "whatever it takes" speech, suggesting that markets had doubts about the ECB's ability to restore inflation to target levels.[17] ECB research shows that longer-term inflation forecasts had become more sensitive to shorter-term forecasts and to actual inflation data. It also finds that the ECB's inflation projections had become more important for short- and medium-term professional forecasts and that the role of the ECB inflation target for those forecasts had diminished (Łyziak and Paloviita 2016).

The deterioration of the credibility of the ECB's price-stability mandate during the pre-QE period can be seen in the evolution of inflation floors. Figure 4.18 shows the average market-implied probability of inflation falling below zero over five years. It reached high levels before the January 2015 meeting, suggesting that lack of action would have consolidated deflationary expectations in the euro area.

After the ECB launched QE inflation breakevens remained low, not just in the European Union but also in the United States. The decline in US inflation expectations was out of sync with the strong recovery in the labor market. Something else may have been going on. A range of factors can drive the behavior of inflation break-evens, including expected inflation, liquidity risk, the term premium, and inflation risk.

The Federal Reserve Bank of Atlanta estimated a model to extract these factors. It concluded that the decline in the inflation and liquidity premia of Treasury Inflation-Protected Securities (TIPS) drove the decline in US 5y5y break-evens since early 2014, suggesting that inflation expectations embedded in inflation break-evens may have remained more stable than they appear.[18] David Elliot et al. show that changes in contemporaneous

17. Cecchetti, Natoli, and Sigalotti (2015) find that negative short-term inflation surprises affected long-term inflation expectations but positive short-term surprises did not, further supporting the assessment of an increased risk of downward deanchoring of inflation expectations.

18. Federal Reserve Bank of Atlanta, "Are Long-Term Inflation Expectations Declining? Not So

Figure 4.18 Market-implied probability of negative five-year average inflation rate in the United States, United Kingdom, and euro area, 2009–16

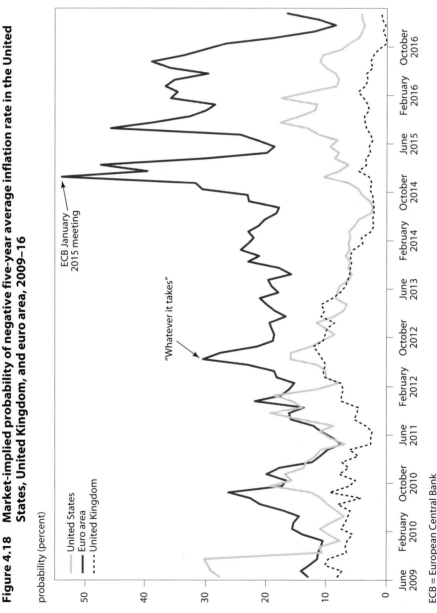

probability (percent)

ECB = European Central Bank
Source: Data from Bloomberg.

oil prices affected forward inflation break-evens, with the impact felt along the inflation term structure, up to five to six years in the future.[19] Their calculations showed that a 10 percent change in oil prices reduced 5y5y in the United States by 4 basis points. The IMF (2016a) calculates that lower oil prices accounted for about a third of the decline in 5y5y break-evens in the United States and about a fifth in the euro area between mid-2014 and 2016.

The decline in oil prices was large, but the persistency of its impact on medium-term inflation expectations during that period is puzzling, as it is difficult to argue that oil price changes today, no matter how large, determine annual inflation five years from now. Three explanations are possible.

First, the persistency may be showing a decline only in the inflation risk premium, as actual inflation volatility has declined and lower oil prices may reduce worries about future inflation. But one could argue that the sign should be the opposite: If oil prices are expected to stabilize or revert to the mean, the inflation risk premium should be higher in the future.

Second, it is possible that a common factor—such as increased worry that central banks will not have enough room to cushion recessions in the future—is driving oil prices and inflation risk premia and that aggregate demand (and thus oil prices) and inflation will therefore be permanently lower. This possibility would be a cause for concern for central bankers.

Third, the inflation-indexed market is notoriously illiquid, with highly volatile risk premia. It is therefore possible that arbitrage does not perform its stabilizing role (Shen 2006) The fact that market-based inflation expectations appear to be poor forecasters of inflation, at least over shorter-term horizons, reinforces this possibility. In forecasting contests, market-based inflation expectations have less forecasting power than survey data or naïve "no change" models that forecast unchanged inflation (Bauer and McCarthy 2015).

Survey-Based Measures of Inflation Expectations

Liquidity-driven distortions in market-based measures of inflation led central bankers to emphasize that market-based measures were measures of inflation compensation, not just inflation expectations, and to stress

---

Fast, Says Atlanta Fed," Macroblog, January 15, 2016, www.macroblog.typepad.com/macroblog/2016/01/are-long-term-inflation-expectations-declining-not-so-fast-says-atlanta-fed-1.html (accessed on March 27, 2017).

19. David Elliot, Chris Jackson, Marek Raczko, and Matt Roberts-Sklar, "Does Oil Drive Financial Market Measures of Inflation Expectations?" Bank Underground (blog), Bank of England, October 20, 2015, www.bankunderground.co.uk/2015/10/20/does-oil-drive-financial-market-inflation-expectations (accessed on March 28, 2017).

that it was useful to cross-check the information with survey data. Survey data reflect a different type of inflation expectation. They provide not a probability-weighted outcome, as in market data, but a baseline (most likely) forecast without any sense of uncertainty around it. The dispersion of forecasts indicates different views or beliefs, not uncertainty around the individual baseline forecasts.

Surveys of professional forecasters show that long-term inflation expectations have been better anchored around mandate-consistent levels: For all four major central banks, longer-term inflation expectations have been near target in these surveys. The Tankan survey of inflation expectations of firms in Japan showed average five-year-ahead inflation at 1.7 percent in early 2014. It seems that with QQE, the BoJ had been able to convince the Japanese corporate sector about its commitment to 2 percent inflation. This figure declined to 1.3 percent by mid-2016, mirroring the decline in headline inflation that occurred during 2016.

It is possible that part of the decline seen in survey data corresponds to a narrowing of possible outcomes. For example, the gradual decline in US inflation expectation survey data reflects the fact that fewer respondents expected very high inflation. It is possible, however, that the degree of anchoring of the inflation target may have declined. The IMF (2016a) shows an increase in the sensitivity of survey-based inflation expectations to current inflation news, especially in countries where monetary policy has little room to ease.

This discrepancy between the measures of inflation expectations derived from inflation swaps and the measures derived from surveys may confirm that lower market inflation expectations reflect a decline in the inflation term premium rather than a decline in the level of inflation expectations. But surveys also have their issues. For example, forecasters have been more prone than markets to overestimate inflation in recent years. Part of the reason has surely been the sharp decline in commodity prices, but core inflation rates have also been overestimated. For example, the estimate of the euro area 2017 inflation rate from the ECB's third quarter 2013 Survey of Professional Forecasters was 2.0 percent, much higher than the 1.2 percent in the third quarter 2016 survey (ECB 2013a, 2016). Such a large forecasting mistake, at the three- to four-year horizon, can only reflect an overestimation of core inflation. It is also possible that the survey data are biased: Professional forecasters may have a higher belief in inflation targets because most of them are economists. In addition, most forecasting methods assume a return to equilibrium, thus biasing forecasts toward the inflation target.

Overall, the message that comes across is that central banks have been able to contain the downside pressure on inflation but have been unable to fully return inflation expectations to precrisis levels. It seems that economists and markets are seeing the inflation targets as ceilings, not midpoints. Their view may be the rational reaction to the reluctance by central banks, especially the Fed and the ECB, to explicitly target a transitory overshooting of inflation to compensate for a long period of undershooting. Once again the paradox of risk is evident: The result of central banks being too conservative and reluctant to temporarily overshoot the target is a permanent increase in the downside risks to inflation.

What If Monetary Policy Had Targeted the Price Level, Not Inflation?

A debate that arose early in the crisis is whether central banks should abandon inflation targeting and adopt a price level–targeting framework in order to better fight deflationary pressures. The main difference between the two frameworks is that with inflation targeting, "bygones are bygones" (a miss in inflation one year does not need to be clawed back the subsequent years); in contrast, with price level targeting a miss one year requires some compensation in subsequent years. Inflation targeting thus introduces a random walk element into the inflation path (inflation can drift away from a given value), while price level targeting is "history dependent" (Woodford 2003).

Price level targeting is a good strategy against deflationary demand shocks, because it reduces uncertainty over inflation: During a period of below-target inflation, it commits the central bank to aim for a period of above-target inflation. If a negative shock pushes the economy to below-target inflation and zero interest rates, boosting inflation expectations is one of the remaining instruments to lower real interest rates. Under inflation targeting, inflation expectations would remain, at best, anchored at the target (say, 2 percent). Under credible price level targeting, inflation expectations would increase temporarily above the trend inflation implicit in normal times in the price level target (e.g., if the trend inflation implicit in the price level target is 2 percent, inflation expectations would increase above 2 percent), as the central bank would have to compensate for the below-target inflation and catch up with the trend. Under a variety of models, and assuming full credibility of the price-targeting regime, these higher inflation expectations generated by a price level target increase current inflation and aggregate demand; this ability to overcome the zero bound implies that the central bank can target a lower level of inflation, with additional welfare gains (see, among others, Eggertsson and Woodford 2003 and Coibion et al. 2012).

However, central banks have rejected the idea of explicitly shifting to a price level–targeting framework, mostly because of its negative features in other situations (e.g., when a negative supply shock leads to higher inflation and lower growth, forcing the central bank to tighten into a downturn); the cost of transition; and the communication issues it would entail (it is easier to communicate an inflation target than a price level target). And a disciplined inflation targeter would aim to compensate periods of below-target inflation with periods of above-target inflation, mimicking price level targeting.

Have the main central bankers behaved, de facto, like price level targeters? To assess their performance, one has to make a decision about the starting point of the price level target. Ideally, it would be when the economy was at price stability and zero output gap. An assessment of the performance of monetary policy cannot therefore set 2007 as the starting point.

One option is take a longer-term view and start from the moment when a policy framework was introduced (e.g., 1998 for the ECB and BoE). For the sake of comparability, this starting point is also used for the United States. Figure 4.19 shows the evolution of the price level in the United States, United Kingdom, and euro area compared with a 2 percent trend. (This exercise cannot be conducted for Japan because it has been shifting its inflation target over time. It is clear, however, that it would have missed the price level target.)

In all three cases, headline inflation performed reasonably close to the 2 percent trend; a price level–targeting regime would therefore not have made a big difference. In contrast, core inflation is below the price level target in all three cases, probably reflecting the need to keep it lower to offset the high commodity price inflation of the past decade. The gap is widest in the euro area, the region where inflation expectations are also the lowest. The ECB's tolerance for low inflation looks worrisome.

This raises an important question looking forward: Assuming stable commodity prices, central banks will have to rely more than in the past on domestically generated inflation in order to achieve 2 percent inflation. Most of the inflation will have to come from core inflation. In fact, core inflation may have to overshoot the target to compensate for external disinflationary pressures (or just lack of inflationary pressures). Central banks will thus have to run their economies with less slack than in the past. They will have to generate more growth to achieve their price-stability mandates and probably achieve levels of unemployment below the NAIRU.

What If Monetary Policy Had Targeted Nominal GDP?

Another alternative framework with which to evaluate monetary policy is nominal GDP targeting. Under this framework the central bank seeks to keep nominal GDP along a predetermined level or growth path. Nominal GDP targeting derives from Milton Friedman's idea of targeting money

Figure 4.19 Core and headline inflation in the United States, United Kingdom, and euro area, 1998–2016

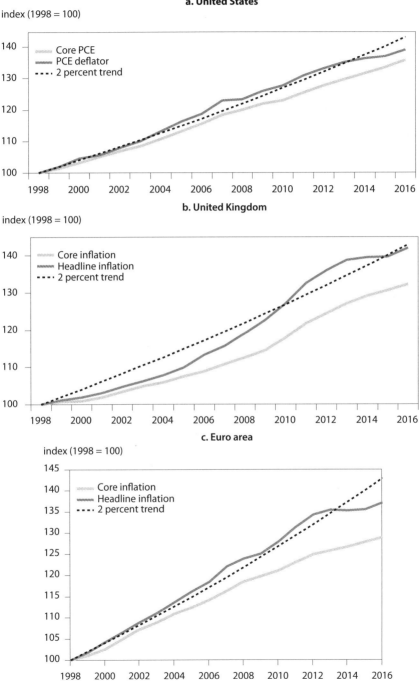

a. United States

index (1998 = 100)

b. United Kingdom

index (1998 = 100)

c. Euro area

index (1998 = 100)

PCE = personal consumption expenditures

Source: Data from Bloomberg.

growth (Friedman 1965). Back in the 1960s broad money and nominal GDP had a stable relationship; targeting money growth was therefore akin to targeting nominal GDP growth. However, the elimination of interest rate ceilings made the demand for money sensitive to interest rates and thus unstable, breaking the steady relationship between money and nominal GDP.

The crisis has brought back the concept of nominal GDP targeting, not as a money growth rule but as a broad framework for reinforcing forward guidance and evaluating the success of policy in a way that can be easily understood by the public (see, for example, Woodford 2012 and Hetzel 2015). Essentially, the central bank could publish a benchmark path for the level of nominal GDP and commit to it, explaining deviations from this path and the actions that it plans to undertake to achieve it. If monetary policy is expected to deliver stable inflation and sustainable real growth, nominal GDP targeting would be a way to combine both objectives into a single variable. It faces similar criticisms to price level targeting: Being a level target, it could introduce excessive volatility in the face of a negative supply shock that increased inflation. In addition, nominal GDP does not differentiate among the different ways to achieve the target (a 4 percent nominal GDP target, for example, could be achieved with 2 percent growth and 2 percent inflation but also with 0 percent growth and 4 percent inflation; the welfare implications of the two scenarios are very different). In addition, nominal GDP targeting includes variables that are outside the control of monetary policy, such as population growth. One could argue that monetary policy can affect productivity growth via hysteresis effects or its impact on investment. But it cannot be argued that it affects population growth. Therefore, a better way to evaluate monetary policy under this yardstick would be the evolution of nominal per capita GDP, to allow comparisons across countries with very different demographic trends, such as the United States and Japan.

As with price level targeting, a critical issue in assessing the performance of a nominal GDP target is the selection of the starting point for the calibration of the precrisis trend. Figure 4.20 shows the results of comparing the evolution of actual annual nominal GDP per capita with a series that shows the extrapolation, after 2007, of the average growth rate during 1995–2007. The 1995–2007 period starts at the time of the first information technology revolution and the entering of China into the global trading system, thus capturing the key elements of the precrisis environment.[20] In all cases a gap opened versus the precrisis trend, but this gap was much smaller in Japan than in the other countries. As of the end of 2016,

20. The vertical axis in figure 4.20 has been made the same for all four economies, to better compare across them the relative size of the gap between the actual nominal per capita GDP growth and the long-term trend.

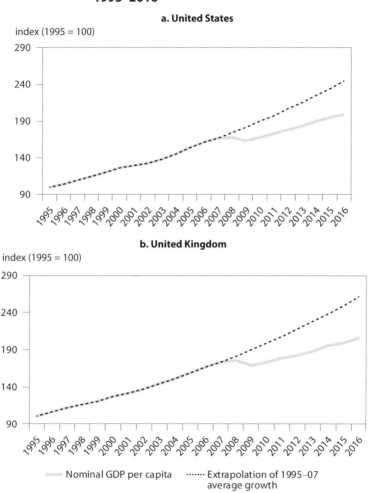

Figure 4.20   Nominal per capita GDP in the United States, United Kingdom, euro area, and Japan, 1995–2016

a. United States

index (1995 = 100)

b. United Kingdom

index (1995 = 100)

▬▬▬ Nominal GDP per capita   ⋯⋯ Extrapolation of 1995–07 average growth

(figure continues)

only Japan has closed the gap, while nominal GDP per capita remains well below the extrapolation of the precrisis trend in the United States (18 percent), the euro area (23 percent), and the United Kingdom (21 percent).

Two interesting, and perhaps surprising, results stand out. First, Japan was the best (or least bad) performer, minimizing the reduction in the growth of nominal per capita GDP. One could argue, of course, that when the prior trend is weaker than elsewhere it may be easier to keep up with it. But the data also show that Japan's economic performance, typically obscured by its weaker demographics when comparing absolute levels of GDP, was resilient despite its low inflation.

Figure 4.20   Nominal per capita GDP in the United States, United Kingdom, euro area, and Japan, 1995–2016 *(continued)*

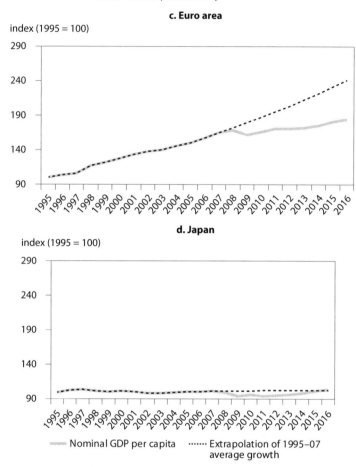

c. Euro area

index (1995 = 100)

d. Japan

index (1995 = 100)

Nominal GDP per capita   ······ Extrapolation of 1995–07 average growth

Note: Vertical axis is the same for all four economies in order to better illustrate the relative size of gap between actual nominal per capita GDP growth and longer-term trend.

Source: Data from Bloomberg.

Second, the nominal per capita GDP gaps in the United States, United Kingdom, and euro area are of similar magnitude—a surprising result given the deeper and longer recession in the euro area. Two reasons may explain this result: the different growth trends before the crisis (faster in the United States and United Kingdom than in the euro area) and divergent population trends, which exaggerate the euro area's underperformance when analyzed in absolute GDP terms.

Has Monetary Policy Had Any Negative Side Effects?

People fear the unknown, especially when it brings up memories of bad events. When central bankers started to ease policy rapidly—cutting rates, buying assets, and expanding their balance sheets—the immediate reaction was of caution. Careful, many warned, low interest rates and rapid money growth can create inflation and asset bubbles and weaken the discipline of governments. Worry about the potential side effects of monetary policy became a major headwind for central bankers. The implied message was that either monetary policy was the wrong approach for dealing with the recession or central bankers would not have the ability to deploy the right dose of stimulus or the willingness to take it away at the right moment.

This chapter has shown that monetary policy has had positive effects, although it should have been more aggressive. Have negative side effects materialized?

Inflation Is a Monetary Policy Phenomenon, Not a Monetary Phenomenon

Since Milton Friedman first said it, in 1963, one of the basic tenets of economics has been that inflation is "always and everywhere a monetary phenomenon." Money growth was directly related to inflation over the medium term; controlling money growth was the way to control inflation. For monetary believers, the large expansion of the major central banks' balance sheets posed the risk of an uncontrolled increase in inflation.

Events have not borne out these predictions. Central bank balance sheets have ballooned, yet inflation has barely moved. The size of the balance sheet of the central bank has become an irrelevant quantity, with no informational content about the stance of monetary policy or the evolution of inflation. Inflation is a monetary policy phenomenon, because monetary policy is in charge of stabilizing inflation. However, it is not a monetary phenomenon in the Friedman sense. The money multiplier no longer works. In fact, some economists argue that the concept of the money multiplier should have been eliminated from economic textbooks years ago.[21] Technology (which allowed for a diversification of transactions outside money aggregates) and inflation targeting (which stabilized inflation expectations) severely damaged the money multiplier; QE finally killed it.

The basis of the monetary roots of inflation is the quantity theory of money, which argues that nominal output is a function of the money supply and that this function depends on the velocity of money (the ratio

---

21. Simon Wren-Lewis, "Kill the Money Multiplier!" Mainly Macro blog, July 30, 2012, https://mainlymacro.blogspot.com/2012/07/kill-money-multiplier.html.

of nominal GDP to the money supply). The velocity of money can be understood as the rate of turnover of the money supply—the number of times one dollar is used to purchase goods and services included in GDP. If real output is fixed, and the velocity of money is constant, then an increase in money leads to an increase in inflation. Central banks increase the money supply by increasing reserves, which creates base money, which is on-lent to the private sector via the banking sector. In a fractional reserve banking system, the same dollar of reserves can be lent several times, as banks do not have to hold a dollar of reserves for each dollar they lend. The ratio of base money to the total amount of money circulating in the economy is the money multiplier.

A large body of literature studies the relationship between money and inflation. It finds a relationship between money growth and long-run inflation for countries with high inflation levels (say, above 10 percent). The relationship is much weaker, or nonexistent, for countries with low inflation (see, for example, De Grauwe and Polan 2005). The main reason for this weak relationship is the instability of the demand for money, which has made the quantity theory of little practical use for central banks (see the discussion in Cline 2015). The main exception has been the ECB, which initiated its operations in 1998, giving particular preeminence to monetary issues in its inflation analysis. It set an intermediate M3 target in addition to its inflation objective (mostly to give the appearance of continuation with Bundesbank policies). After a few years, however, it acknowledged the minimal usefulness of the M3 intermediate target and relegated the monetary pillar to a secondary role in its framework of analysis.

Despite this evidence, the quantity theory remained the basis for initial attempts at QE. The pure QE framework argues that increases in base money stimulate aggregate demand, as excess reserves in the banking system are eventually on-lent, boosting consumption and investment. The BoJ used this rationale to justify its QE policy during 2001–06, which explicitly targeted the level of excess reserves in the banking system.

The BoE also based the initial design of its QE program on the quantity theory, explicitly aiming at increasing base money in order to increase nominal GDP. The BoE assessed that the shortfall in nominal GDP versus the precrisis trend was about 5 percent and therefore decided that "the increase in the level of money balances should be of a similar magnitude to the required increase in nominal GDP."[22]

However, the experience of the last decades has shown that the money-inflation link is broken. The second part of the Milton Friedman quotation provides the explanation: "Inflation is always and everywhere a monetary

---

22. See the minutes of the March 2009 BoE meeting (Monetary Policy Committee 2009, 9).

phenomenon, in the sense that it cannot occur without a more rapid increase in the quantity of money than in output." For this mechanism to be successful, the money multiplier (the relationship between base money and broad money) and the velocity of money (the relationship between broad money and nominal GDP) have to remain stable. The mechanism breaks down during periods of intense deleveraging. As a result, despite a rapid increase in base money, broad money has not expanded, and the money multiplier has collapsed. As the velocity of money has remained stable, nominal GDP growth has been very subdued (see Cline 2015) (figures 4.21 and 4.22).

However, a question remains: What may happen if the money multiplier is restored and broad money starts growing rapidly? One worry would be that the large amount of excess reserves could "leak" rapidly and lead to rapid growth in lending, creating accelerating inflation that central banks may not be able to control. This fear lacks basis. It ignores the fact that the total amount of reserves in the system is determined by the central bank's balance sheet, because the central bank's liabilities must equal its assets. Therefore, as long as the central bank holds a large stock of assets acquired under QE, the system as a whole will have correspondingly large excess bank reserves. And with the system of paying interest on excess reserves, any level of excess reserves can be compatible with stable inflation. The link between money and inflation has been completely severed.

In some sense, it is a distinction without a difference. In the previous regime, the Fed would lend reserves on demand at the fed funds rate. Now the reserves are already there, but the Fed controls the interest rates it pays on them. In both cases the Fed controls the opportunity cost of lending, which is the key determinant of lending. Inflation, and monetary policy, is not about quantities, it is about interest rates (and risk premia). Defining asset purchase programs on the basis of quantities has been an operational necessity, to make it understandable to the general public. But the ultimate objective has been to set the right asset prices to achieve the desired level of financial conditions. Quantities have been an instrument, not an objective.

Therefore the question is not whether all these reserves will "leak" into the economy in an uncontrolled way but what amount of interest paid on excess reserves will be enough to achieve price stability. It is possible that once the economic recovery is consolidated the needed short-term interest rate will be higher than in the past, as banks will now be paid interest on their reserves, tempering the typical decline in profitability that accompanies monetary tightening. It is possible that, at some point, central banks may need to raise rates faster than in the past to stabilize inflation. The link between money and inflation has been broken by the new monetary policy regime, but no one knows exactly how.

Figure 4.21   Money multiplier in the United States, United Kingdom, euro area, and Japan, 2000–14

broad money as percent of monetary base

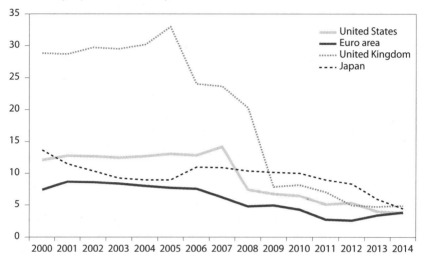

Source: Data from International Monetary Fund.

Figure 4.22   Velocity of money in the United States, United Kingdom, euro area, and Japan, 2000–14

ratio of nominal GDP to broad money

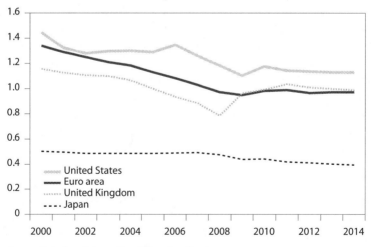

Source: Data from International Monetary Fund.

Is Monetary Policy Sowing the Seeds of the Next Financial Crisis in Order to Restore Economic Growth?

A key narrative of the cause of the crisis was that loose monetary policy led to excessive risk taking and a financial bubble. It was perhaps therefore normal that, as central banks started to ease policy, worries appeared that in order to restore growth and inflation, monetary policy was sowing the seeds of the next financial crisis. To assuage these fears, central banks have created financial stability committees and developed enhanced and comprehensive methodologies for surveilling risks (see, for example, Adrian, Covitz, and Liang 2014).

This enhanced monitoring of financial risks has not convinced some critics of recent monetary policy actions. They argue that by reducing interest rates to very low levels (negative in real terms), monetary policy fosters excessive risk taking and a search for yield, creating financial vulnerabilities along the way. The Bank for International Settlements (BIS) has led the charge, arguing that monetary policy should pay more attention to the financial cycle, because financial busts have greater consequences for growth than standard recessions generated by economic overheating (see, for example, Borio 2014). Since 2009, the argument goes, monetary policy has been too easy, creating vulnerabilities that will lead to the next financial crisis; interest rates should be increased as soon as possible to stabilize the credit cycle. The results of this BIS research program may have been too one-sided, though. An independent review of BIS research argues that "the internal culture should be more open to challenge and research should avoid focusing on generating results to support the 'house view'" (Allen, Bean, and de Gregorio 2016, 1).

Conceptually, the financial cycle view faces a fundamental dilemma: how to calibrate monetary policy to address such a long-term cycle. Which variables should inform the daily actions of central banks? Growth and inflation forecasts are subject to high uncertainty, but credit forecasts are subject to even higher uncertainty.

There are two important counterarguments to this line of reasoning. First, there is nothing special about the impact of negative real interest rates on the level of risk taking. Low interest rates need not be "too low," just as a low price of a good or service is not necessarily too low. The central bank aims at setting the right level of financial conditions for the economy, which can require positive or negative real interest rates. Moreover, the relationship between the level of interest rates and financial risk taking is tenuous. Some research finds that the riskiness of new loans extended by banks is inversely proportional to the level of interest rates, but this relationship weakens in less well-capitalized banks and during periods of financial distress, and it is possible that what this relationship is measuring is bank forecasts of a decline in the riskiness of the loans as a result of the low interest rates (Dell'Arricia, Laeven, and Suarez 2016).

Second, one of the main channels of transmission of unconventional policies is portfolio rebalancing, which aims at inducing economic agents to move further out on the risk curve to offset the excessive risk aversion generated by the crisis. Therefore the success of these policies should include a return of risk taking to at least long-term average levels. It is contradictory to adopt a monetary policy strategy that focuses on promoting risk taking and at the same time caution about excessive risk taking. In the end, policy becomes less effective and has to be deployed with more intensity. Worries about risk taking may lead to having to take more risk—the paradox of risk.

Search for yield can be defined in many ways, but it always involves investors taking higher risk in order to obtained higher expected returns. But it is critical to differentiate higher risk taking from too much risk taking, the same way low rates must be distinguished from too low rates. Behavioral biases, such as herd behavior, myopia, and the use of the wrong heuristics, can lead to too much risk taking. Regulatory constraints, such as limits to asset holdings or differentiated capital charges, can lead some financial market participants who have mandated return targets, such as insurance companies and pension funds, to move out in the risk spectrum. These behavioral biases and regulatory constraints may generate excessive risk taking, especially if the individuals or institutions are not well prepared to manage these risks. They should be managed with macroprudential policies and reforms in the sectors affected, rather than with interest rates, however, as discussed below. The complaint in Europe that low interest rates are a source of financial instability because they affect the profitability of German banks and Dutch insurers should lead to changes in the business models of those institutions, not to higher interest rates.

A Recovery in Risk Aversion

It is difficult to make a case that there has been a sharp increase in financial risk taking beyond a broad recovery toward more normal levels. There have surely been pockets of overvaluation in some specific markets, but this is normal after a long period of expansion. Central bankers have cautioned extensively in this direction, at times confusing levels of risk taking (which are still low) with rates of change (the increase in risk taking, which is much needed).

But pockets of expensive asset prices are not the same as financial stability risks. It is a standard pattern after financial crisis that measures of equity risk premia remain high for an extended period; this episode is no exception. Figure 4.23 shows the equity risk premium of four major stock market indexes (the S&P 500, the Euro Stoxx 50, the FTSE 100, and the Nikkei 225). The equity risk premium is calculated as the earnings/price ratio minus the yield on nominal 10-year bonds, following Blanchard and Gagnon.[23] It shows that equity risk premia recovered since the peak of the crisis but remained, in 2016, above the 2004–06 average in the United States, euro area, and Japan.

This result is robust to different methodologies for estimating the equity risk premium. Fernando Duarte and Carlo Rosa (2015) calculate the first principal component (a statistical technique to extract the common component across time series) across a large variety of methods to estimate the equity risk premium in the US stock market. They conclude that, although below the crisis peak, it was still well above precrisis levels in 2015. Price earnings ratios are in the upper quintiles of their historical distributions, but should be put in context. For example, the Shiller cyclically adjusted price earnings (CAPE) ratio shows US equities at valuations near precrisis levels and above long-term averages. However, this index is somewhat distorted: Because it uses the average of the last 10 years of earnings, it is biased upward by the very sharp recession of 2008 and the historically unprecedented decline in corporate profits during 2008–09 (which reduces the denominator [earnings] and thus boosts the ratio). Moreover, price/earnings ratios are also expected to be higher, because sectors with traditionally higher ratios, such as health care and technology, have become larger shares of stock indexes, thus biasing the historical comparisons. Lower inflation and lower neutral interest rates also support higher price/earnings ratios.

Similarly, credit spreads contracted as a result of the improvement in economic and financial conditions and the sharp reduction in bankruptcies but stabilized above the levels reached in 2005–07. In 2015 credit spreads increased sharply as a result of the collapse of oil and commodity prices (a large share of high-yield credit has been financing the development of shale oil in the United States; the oil price decline thus increased bankruptcies and defaults in that sector).

Credit spreads are an important indicator to watch. David López-Salido, Jeremy Stein, and Egon Zakrajzek (2015) argue that low credit spreads forecast weaker growth two years later, as a result of reversion to the mean in credit market conditions. Credit quality deteriorates during good times, because the contraction in spreads disproportionally favors issuance by low-

---

23. Olivier Blanchard and Joseph Gagnon, "Are US Stocks Overvalued?" Peterson Institute for International Economics: RealTime Economic Issues Watch (blog), February 1, 2016, www.piie.com/blogs/realtime-economic-issues-watch/are-us-stocks-overvalued (accessed on March 28, 2017).

Figure 4.23 Equity risk premia of four leading stock indexes, 2001–16

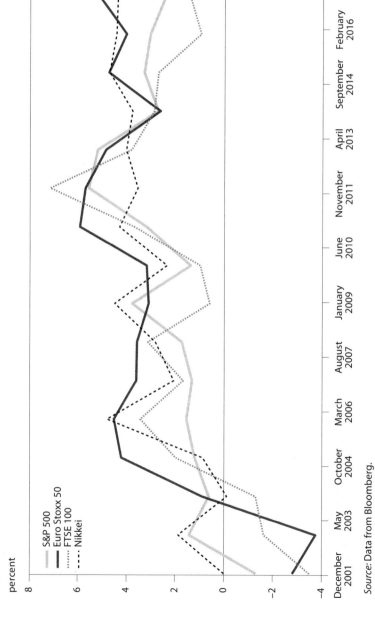

percent

Source: Data from Bloomberg.

quality firms. Based on this result, Robin Greenwood and Samuel Hanson (2013) argue that issuer quality is a better indicator of financial vulnerabilities than aggregate credit market growth. It is the quality, rather than the amount, of credit that matters. In this regard critics have argued that ECB purchases of corporate bonds may have pushed yields too low. Average euro-denominated corporate bonds fell to a low of 0.60 percent in late August 2016, and a few firms were able to issue at marginally negative yields.[24]

Risk taking in the banking sector has remained very subdued, in part because of regulatory tightening. Lending standards have barely recovered their long-term averages. For example, data from the New York Federal Reserve Bank shows that in the United States the median average FICO score of mortgages issued increased from 700 precrisis to about 750 in 2016.[25] As a result, it is more difficult to get a mortgage. Small businesses have suffered a larger share of the tighter average lending standards. The volume of small loans ($1 million or less) as a share of all commercial and industrial loans fell from 35 percent before the crisis to about 20 percent in 2016[26]—despite the fact that levels of bank capital increased and leverage in the banking sector remains low (e.g., the loan-to-deposit ratio of US commercial banks remains at historical lows).

Some areas of concern have been the leverage loan market, commercial real estate prices, and agricultural land prices in the United States, where activity and price appreciation have been robust. The boom in shale oil in the United States, and its subsequent bust, could be partly associated with easy financial conditions, as it was financed largely in the high-yield market. It is an example of a rational bubble: A new technology leads to overinvestment until it finds its new equilibrium level.

At the global level, the increase in leverage in the corporate sector has been noticeable. In 2015 the debt-to-earnings ratio rose to the highest level since 2003, potentially increasing the vulnerability of the corporate sector—though the possibility is less of a concern in an environment in which neutral interest rates are lower than in the past. Most of this increase in debt has been used for mergers and acquisitions and share buybacks

---

24. Gavin Jackson, "Henkel and Sanofi Sell First Negative Yielding Euro Corporate Bonds," *Financial Times*, September 6, 2016, www.ft.com/fastft/2016/09/06/henkel-and-sanofi-sell-first-negative-yielding-euro-corporate-bonds/ (accessed on March 30, 2017).

25. FICO is a measure of the riskiness of the borrower; the higher the number, the less risky the borrower. New York Federal Reserve Bank, "US Economy in a Snapshot," www.newyorkfed.org/medialibrary/media/research/snapshot/snapshot_sept2016.pdf (accessed on March 30, 2017).

26. Craig Torres, "As Wall Street Thrives, America's Little Guy Chokes on Paperwork," Bloomberg, February 27, 2017, www.bloomberg.com/news/articles/2017-02-27/as-wall-street-thrives-america-s-little-guy-chokes-on-paperwork (accessed on March 30, 2017).

rather than to fund new investments. It could become a problem in the future if risk premia increase sharply, as firms would have to service a larger stock of debt without new revenue streams (see, for example, IMF 2015b).

At the macro level, however, the ratio of credit to GDP remains low. The credit-to-GDP gap (the gap between the actual ratio of credit to GDP and its long-term trend) has been identified as a potential indicator of excessive credit growth. Basel III adopted it as a key variable to guide the buildup of the countercyclical capital buffer. This gap remains negative in the United States, United Kingdom, and euro area (a simple average of Germany, France, Spain, and Italy, as the data for the whole euro area are available only since 2009) and just barely positive for Japan (figure 4.24). The message from credit markets is that vulnerabilities remain low in these economies.

Another source of potential worry is housing markets. They have slowly recovered, but their annual appreciation remains subdued, with the global real average price still below the precrisis peak (figure 4.25). This average masks divergent behavior across countries and regions. Prices are very high in high-end markets in New York or London, where demand is global and the supply very limited, and countries where housing prices did not decline during the crisis and housing prices and indebtedness remain at very elevated levels, such as Australia, Canada, and New Zealand. But these prices are not the consequence of monetary policy in the United States, Europe, or Japan; they reflect policy choices in those countries. The appreciation of housing prices in Germany is one of the arguments used to criticize the ECB's expansionary monetary policy. Although real housing prices increased about 30 percent between 2007 and 2016, to a large extent the increase reflects a healthy recovery after a long period of flat growth. Rapid appreciation should not be confused with overvaluation.

Figure 4.26 shows a measure of overvaluation, computed as the average of the deviation of price to rent, and the price to disposable income per person, from their respective long-term averages (using data from the *Economist* database).[27] Based on this measure, as of late 2016 housing prices were undervalued in Germany, Italy, and Japan; about at equilibrium in the United States and Switzerland; and overvalued in France, Spain, the United Kingdom, Canada, Australia, and New Zealand.

Reaching the Limits of Portfolio Rebalancing

As long-term interest rates continued to fall during 2016, reaching negative levels in several countries, the sovereign bond market became a po-

---

27. See "Foreign Buyers Push up Global House Prices," *Economist*, March 11, 2017, www.economist.com/news/finance-and-economics/21718511-bolthole-money-welcome-comes-unintended-consequences-foreign-buyers (accessed on March 30, 2017).

Figure 4.24 Credit-to-GDP gap in the United States, United Kingdom, euro area, and Japan, 1980–2013

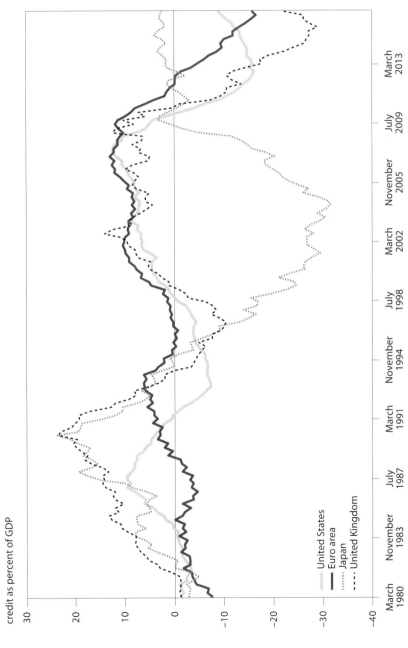

credit as percent of GDP

United States
Euro area
Japan
United Kingdom

Source: Bank for International Settlements.

Figure 4.25   Global index of housing prices, 2000–16

index (2000 = 100)

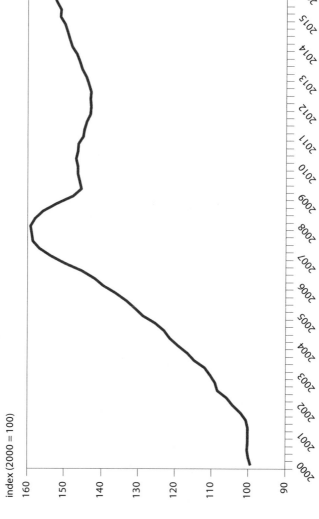

Source: International Monetary Fund.

Figure 4.26 Housing price valuations in selected countries, 2016

percent

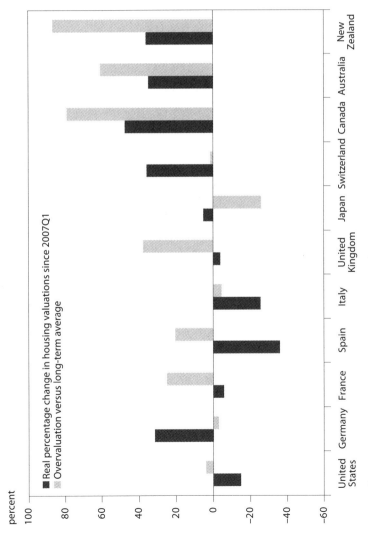

■ Real percentage change in housing valuations since 2007Q1
▨ Overvaluation versus long-term average

Source: The Economist.

tential source of financial sector vulnerability. With central banks cutting rates to negative levels, the search for duration intensified.

A striking feature of the postcrisis period is that investors have been very reluctant to buy equities. Figure 4.27 shows the cumulative flows into US bond and equity mutual funds and exchange-traded funds (ETFs), indicating that, despite the efforts of central bankers, retail investors have preferred bonds over equities. This result should not be surprising. Equities face the risk of principal losses. Therefore, in order to hold equities, investors require assurances that growth will be durable and some reasonable expectation that equity prices will increase, combined with unattractive prospects for bond returns. Instead, investors have been facing the opposite outlook, doubts about growth—and therefore about equity prices— and expectations of higher bond prices, thanks to the bond purchases of the central banks. This investor behavior is a strong argument for central banks to focus their purchases on riskier assets, in order to more effectively reduce the cost of capital for the private sector, as argued below.

The ability to generate positive returns from negative-yielding bonds by taking advantage of the cross-currency basis swaps has created a strong link between negative-yielding Japanese government bonds and US Treasuries, which pushed US long-term rates lower during 2016 (see, e.g., Iida, Kimura, and Sudo 2016). (Investors can, for example, buy Japanese government bonds yielding negative rates and swap them into dollars, taking advantage of the spread between the dollar Libor and the yen Libor to generate the positive yield. In August 2016 a US investor could buy a three-month Japanese bill yielding –0.24 percent, achieving a yield of 1.24 percent with this transaction.[28])

The existence of the cross-currency basis is an interesting puzzle, as it implies that covered interest parity—the notion that the interest rate differential between any two currencies in the money markets should equal the differential between the forward and spot exchange rates—does not hold. If the "basis" is not zero, an investor could profit by borrowing a currency in the cash market and lending it in the foreign exchange market via a swap (e.g., selling dollars for euros today and repurchasing them back at the forward rate).

However, the basis has been positive since 2007 (figure 4.28), first as a result of the crisis, later mostly as a result of the limits to arbitrage generated by the tightening of financial regulation, which has added a higher cost

28. Brian Chapatta and Andrea Won, "World's Biggest Bond Traders Undeterred by Negative Yield," Bloomberg, August 21, 2016, www.bloomberg.com/news/articles/2016-08-21/pimco-china-show-no-fear-of-negative-yields-in-market-gone-awry.

Figure 4.27   Cumulative bond and equity inflows into US mutual funds and exchange-traded funds, 2009–17

billions of US dollars

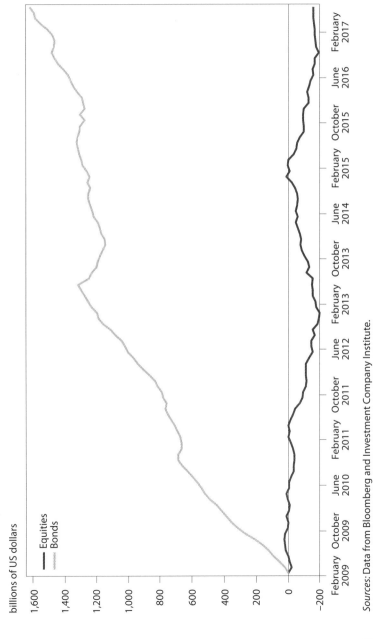

Sources: Data from Bloomberg and Investment Company Institute.

Figure 4.28 Euro, yen, and pound cross-currency basis swaps (one-year maturity), 2006–17

basis points

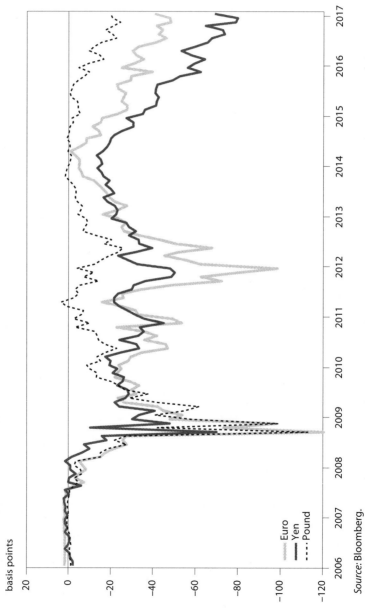

Source: Bloomberg.

to banks' balance sheets.[29] With the Fed raising rates while the ECB and the BoJ are still easing, there is an excess demand for dollars that is not being arbitraged away. The expectation is that as central banks end their QE programs (and thus the discrepancy in terms of the amount of liquidity across regions declines), this basis will gradually disappear. We shall see.

This search for duration in sovereign bond markets has increased the sensitivity of global portfolios to interest rate risk: The losses of a portfolio associated with a large move in interest rates are larger the longer the maturity of the bonds in the portfolio. If long-term rates were to increase sharply, this heightened sensitivity could feed into itself and amplify the increase—what in technical terms is called a VaR (value at risk) shock, in which a sharp increase (decrease) in interest rates leads to forced bond sales (purchases) that amplify the increase (decline) in rates. This type of shock occurred in Japan in 2003, during the taper tantrum in the United States in 2013, and in Germany in 2015, when long-term rates increased by more than 100 basis points in a short period.

The persistent decline in long-term rates and the flatness of the yield curves are also putting pressure on the long-term viability of business models in the financial sector. Banks are faced with a compression of net interest margins, which lowers the value of bank stocks and raises the cost of capital. Market valuations show these concerns. By late 2016 the price/book value ratio was consistently below 1 in the euro area, United Kingdom, and Japan (i.e., markets valued these banks below their book value) and barely at 1 in the United States. Regulatory tightening in the financial sector and a return on equity that has been well below precrisis levels probably contributed to these weak valuations, which reflect deep pessimism about the future of banks' business models.

Insurers face reinvestment risk (maturing bonds with high coupons have to be reinvested in much lower coupons), which could increase worries about their ability to meet their commitments. Pension funds face growing funding deficits if they stick to fixed-income investments. These valid concerns should be managed mostly with changes to the business model of financial institutions. Central banks should watch the slope of the yield curve when they manage their asset purchase programs, however, and be mindful that they may need to actively manage the yield curve, as discussed in the next chapter.

Another consequence of the persistent decline in the income stream provided by bonds has been an increased investor preference for dividend-

---

29. See Claudio Borio, Robert McCauley, Patrick McGuire, and Vladyslav Sushko, "Bye-Bye Covered Interest Parity," VoxEU, September 28, 2016, www.voxeu.org/article/bye-bye-covered-interest-parity (accessed on March 30, 2017).

paying stocks. A stock can be viewed as an infinite-duration bond; if it pays a reliable dividend, its cash flow profile is similar to that of a very long-term bond. By mid-2016 the dividend yield on stocks in most countries was higher than the yield on bonds. This excess demand for dividend-paying stocks raised their valuations to high levels. For example, Unilever's price/earnings ratio reached 28 in the summer of 2016, the highest in 16 years—adjusted for inflation, its shares were worth more than its cumulative earnings of the previous 32 years.[30]

The increase in the duration of global portfolios, pressure on the business models of financial institutions, and excess demand for dividend-paying stocks suggest that there are limits to the intended "forced" rebalancing of portfolios away from bonds and into other assets. They also suggest that monetary policy may be more effective, and create fewer distortions, if it directly buys riskier assets (such as equities or packaged loans) and relies less on induced portfolio rebalancing.

It is, again, the paradox of risk. By focusing on buying assets with less risk, central banks may be creating avoidable pockets of risk.

Interest Rates Have Been Low, but Not Too Low

Financial crises are scary events; they leave deep and long-lasting scars, especially on the behavior of markets. Historically, markets take a long time to recover their average levels of risk premia after systemic events and deep recessions. Olivier Blanchard (2016) shows that the equity premium after the Great Depression remained very elevated for a long time, as did the risk premium on the Japanese stock market after the stock market bubble burst in the early 1990s (Yamaguchi 2013). Domestic investors in Japan have been persistently underinvested in their stock market since then.

The reaction to a crisis is similar to the posttraumatic stress disorder that follows stressful events. Market participants remain risk averse, and economic policy must compensate for this lack of risk taking, just as it must temper periods of excessive risk taking. This responsibility is not limited to monetary policy. For example, Abenomics tried to change the risk-averse behavior of Japanese investors not only by having the BoJ purchase assets but also by increasing the asset allocation to equities of the major public pension funds, like the Government Pension Investment Fund (GPIF), in order to serve as a role model for the rest of the private sector.

Since the 2008 crisis, when markets were surprised by the unexpected interconnections across assets that led to massive losses in the global

---

30. Mike Bird, "Risk Grows in Safe Stocks," *Wall Street Journal*, August 22, 2016, www.wsj.com/articles/risk-grows-in-safe-stocks-1471914253 (accessed on March 30, 2017).

banking sector, markets have become oversensitive to the possibility that another "small" shock could generate a systemic crisis. This sensitivity has kept risk aversion higher than it would otherwise have been, as became clear in early 2016, when worries about the US high-yield market, Chinese capital outflows, and questions about the European banking sector combined to create a sense of panic as investors started to look for unexpected connections.

Hypersensitivity to another crisis has kept levels of risk taking low. Of course, financial crises often appear where no one is looking; whether pockets of excessive risk have been created will be known only after the fact. Complacency is always a risk. As far as can be assessed, the stance of monetary policy contributed to higher asset prices, as intended, but by mid-2017 it had not led to excessive risk taking—the Fed's assessment was that the financial vulnerability of the US economy was "moderate compared with past periods."[31] From a financial stability standpoint, interest rates have been low, but not too low.

Has Monetary Policy Created Moral Hazard and Runaway Fiscal Deficits?

Another major criticism of zero rates and balance sheet policies has been that they create moral hazard for governments and lead to irresponsible fiscal policies. The large size of some of the asset purchase programs as a share of annual fiscal deficits and debt issuance created concerns that central banks were monetizing deficits and that doing so would erode fiscal discipline. Not surprisingly, the Bundesbank and the German government have been strong proponents of this line of reasoning as an argument against policy easing.[32]

From a conceptual standpoint, Ricardo Reis (2016) looks at the way in which a central bank can, in theory, alleviate the fiscal burden of the government. The channels are various, including inflation, seigniorage, and use of the central bank's balance sheet. He concludes that the scope for potential alleviation is limited.

The historical record suggests that worry about fiscal moral hazard was unwarranted. Fiscal tightening was sharp during the period of zero interest rates and QE. In fact, fiscal policy has likely been tightened too

---

31. Stanley Fischer, "An Assessment of Financial Stability in the United States," speech at the IMF Workshop on Financial Surveillance and Communication: Best Practices from Latin America, the Caribbean, and Advanced Economies, June 27, 2017, Washington, www.federalreserve.gov/newsevents/speech/fischer20170627a.htm.

32. Miroslav Zajac, "ECB's Weidmann Slams Brakes on QE Path, Calls It 'Moral Hazard,'" WBP Online, November 17, 2014.

Figure 4.29 Cyclically adjusted primary balance in the United States, United Kingdom, euro area, and Japan, 2007–16

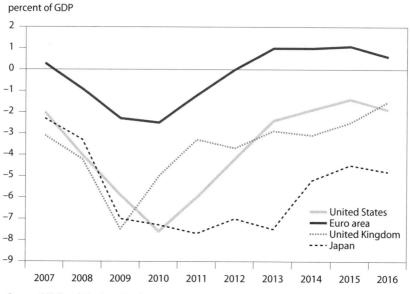

percent of GDP

Source: IMF *Fiscal Monitor*, October 2016.

much. Based on the cyclically adjusted primary balance, which corrects the evolution of the deficit for the impact of the cycle and of changes in interest rates, fiscal policy tightened in all four economies shown in figure 4.29 (a more positive number implies a tighter policy), in some cases sharply.[33] Except in Japan the cyclically adjusted primary balance was less negative in 2016 than in 2007—and even in Japan, which incorporated fiscal expansion as part of the Abenomics package, fiscal policy tightened via the 2014 VAT hike. Fiscal policy was contractionary.

It is true that lower interest rate payments were mostly spent rather than used to reduce public debt. Paolo Mauro et al. (2015) conclude that although this argument is qualitatively correct, the quantitative impact was minor. Using data for a large cross-section of countries and episodes, they find that everything else equal, if the marginal cost of sovereign borrowing declines by 1 percentage point in a country with an initial debt-to-GDP ratio of 100 percent, the primary surplus deteriorates by 0.28 percent of GDP. Therefore, the potential softening of the resolve to reduce fiscal deficits does not seem to justify the opposition to achieving the right monetary policy stance.

---

33. To a very large extent, market pressure forced the tightening in Spain and Italy.

In fact, the negative impact of the fiscal contraction on growth has potentially been quite strong. Christopher House, Christian Proebsting, and Linda Tesar (2016) argue that the fiscal multiplier could have been as high as 2 (i.e., a reduction in the deficit of a given size reduces GDP growth by twice as much) and that debt-to-GDP ratios may have increased in some European countries as a result of this negative impact of fiscal austerity on GDP.

Fiscal policy does not occur in a vacuum. The concern about moral hazard and expansionary fiscal policies assumed that monetary policy would be successful in restoring growth and inflation and that fiscal policy would contribute to overheating the economy and later generate fiscal dominance. It ignored the fact that when interest rates are at zero, and the economy is undergoing a long period of deleveraging and risk aversion, the government has to step up and compensate for the private sector's lack of demand and risk taking.[34]

By 2016, almost a decade after the beginning of the financial crisis, economists had started to shift their view on fiscal policy. More and more central banks started to call for a more active fiscal policy. The consensus is forming in the developed world that more active fiscal policy contributes to raising productivity, enhancing the effectiveness of monetary policy, and helping reduce inequality (Ubide 2016).

Has Monetary Policy Widened Income Inequality?

One negative side effect that was not foreseen as monetary policy started to be eased aggressively was its potential impact on income inequality. Asset prices have more than doubled since QE started, but wage growth has been subdued and the stock of credit has not yet reached the precrisis peak. Commercial real estate prices have appreciated sharply, while residential real estate prices have stagnated. With interest rates at record lows and below-inflation rates, savers' incomes have declined in real terms. Most of the benefit has accrued to the better off.

The fact that it has makes some sense. Corporate profits, asset prices, and sectors of the economy that are sensitive to interest rates are always the first to improve during upswings—and by more than wages. They are also the first to react to a tightening of monetary policy. The process is to a very large extent symmetric (profits and asset prices decline faster and by more than wages during recessions), reflecting the higher risk, and thus the higher reward, of entrepreneurs and investors versus workers.

---

34. In IS/LM (investment-savings/liquidity-money) terms, when the economy is in the flat part of the LM curve, the IS curve has to move.

However, the claim that monetary policy has widened income inequality is wrong along several lines, however. Inequality has increased while monetary policy has cut rates and undertaken asset purchases, but correlation is not causation. The increase in inequality predates the crisis. A combination of factors—including changes in taxation, the globalization of trade and production, skills-biased technological change, and a widening in the inequality of firm sizes—fostered it. In addition, a comparison has to be made against a counterfactual in which there was either no or a different policy stimulus. With interest rates at zero, the options were doing nothing, buying different assets, or implementing fiscal policy. If the alternative was doing nothing, the conclusion is obvious: The recession would have been much more intense, and inequality would have increased more, as recessions hit the poorer harder.[35] Let's not forget that the most important driver of inequality is unemployment. To the extent that monetary policy contributed to reducing it, it has contributed to reducing inequality.

If the alternative was buying different assets, such as foreign exchange, to depreciate the currency, the boost to growth and employment would have been less than under QE and headline inflation would have increased, cutting real wages and disproportionally hurting the poor, who rely on wage income and cash transactions. Higher inflation benefits debtors (as the real value of their debts diminishes), thus helping the middle class, who tend to have large mortgages, while hurting lenders, who are typically wealthier (Doepke, Selezneva, and Schneider 2015).

If the alternative was depending more on fiscal policy, the effect depends on the composition of the fiscal policy package. Conceptually, there should be a positive correlation between the progressivity of a fiscal package based on taxes and transfers and its effectiveness in stabilizing output and inflation, likely related to the fact that the poorer are more liquidity constrained and have a higher propensity to consume any fiscal stimulus. For spending packages, the impact is less clear and depends on the sectoral composition. Josh Bivens (2015) compares the impact of the Fed's QE with an alternative fiscal policy package in 2010 that includes a two-year payroll tax cut, extension of emergency unemployment compensation, and accelerated depreciation. He finds that the impact on growth, inflation, and income distribution is similar to the Fed programs. Although higher prices of risky assets boost inequality (because the holdings of risky assets increase with the level of income), higher housing prices reduce inequality (because home equity represents a very large share of the wealth of the middle class).

---

35. The BoE estimates that QE lifted GDP by about 2.5–3 percent relative to doing nothing (see Joyce, Tong, and Woods 2011).

As far as the impact on savers, pension funds, and insurers, large interest rate cuts, not asset purchases, drove most of the decline in interest rates. The negative impact of QE on long-term rates has to be compared with the positive impact on riskier assets. Whether the net impact is positive or negative is an empirical issue driven mostly by regulatory constraints and asset allocation decisions. For example, reputational concerns may have led pension funds to refrain from increasing their asset allocation to equities, depriving them of higher returns. The counterfactual is unclear. No policy action would have led to a deeper recession and a larger decline in long-term rates as a result of the collapse of nominal growth.

Financial repression (i.e., policies that use legislation or strong moral suasion keep interest rates abnormally low) did not cause the decline in interest rates experienced since the crisis. Historically, it has been used to facilitate the financing of government deficits. Examples of financial repression include requirements that domestic financial institutions hold a certain amount of domestic government bonds. Monetary policy is not financial repression. It has not kept rates *abnormally* low. Equilibrium real interest rates are determined by the marginal cost of capital and, based on the equilibrium real interest rate, central banks set interest rates at levels that deliver price stability and sustainable growth.

Every policy is bound to have some redistributional effects in the near term. In the case of monetary policy, assuming that easing will be followed by tightening, the redistributional impact should be largely neutral, as the effects generated during the easing should be unwound to a large extent during the tightening—although the asymmetric nature of easing and tightening cycles implies that this offset may not be perfect. The increase in inequality that monetary policy may create is not a reason not to ease monetary policy. It is a reason to address it with compensatory policies elsewhere.

Monetary Policy Worked—But It Can Do Better

Monetary policy has worked. It has affected asset prices and financial conditions in the expected direction, it has contributed to restoring growth and inflation, even if not fully, and it has not created major side effects. The worries expressed as some monetary policy actions were put in place—such as excessive inflation, asset bubbles, or runaway fiscal deficits—did not materialize, but the existence of these worries led central banks to use policy less aggressively than they should have, especially as far as the speed of deployment. As a result, almost a decade after the beginning of the crisis, economic slack remains in some countries, and inflation and inflation expectations remain low and below target levels. It is a fragile state of affairs for facing the next recession.

Many lessons have been learned since the crisis. Several economic and policy concepts that appeared sacrosanct are now being questioned. Monetary policy will never be the same. Central banks will have to take on more risk. The next chapter discusses the lessons learned and identifies changes that would improve the effectiveness of monetary policy and economic policy in general.

5

Have We Learned Anything? Crafting a Monetary Policy for All Seasons

> Consider the statement, "It is raining." That statement is true or false
> depending on whether it is, in fact, raining. Now consider the statement,
> "This is a revolutionary moment." That statement is reflexive,
> and its truth value depends on the impact it makes.
>
> —George Soros[1]

Monetary policy entered 2007 ready to fight inflation and cautioning about financial bubbles. A decade later it discovered that lifting inflation is difficult, that the travails of the BoJ over the last 20 years were not caused by a lack of understanding of economics. The monetary policy apparatus was ready to deal with excessive risk taking, not with a prolonged period of risk aversion and deleveraging. Its fair-weather framework was designed for shocks that did not shake the economy much.

What is needed is an all-weather monetary policy framework that can handle big shocks—a monetary policy for all seasons.

There is no room for complacency. Changes are needed because without them, trust in the ability of policymakers to respond to shocks will diminish—and without that trust, economic recoveries will be weaker, as households and businesses internalize that diminished ability of policymakers to react. The key reason why monetary policy may have been more effective during the Great Moderation is that, as economies went into recession, economic agents "knew" that interest rate cuts would restore the economy to the steady state. The interest rate–sensitive sectors of the economy—investment and housing—therefore responded to the decline in interest rates, assumed that demand would materialize, and pushed the economy back to trend.

---

1. George Soros, "Soros: General Theory of Reflexivity," *Financial Times*, October 26, 2009, www.ft.com/cms/s/2/0ca06172-bfe9-11de-aed2-00144feab49a.html#axzz4I0ciYklo (accessed on March 30, 2017).

If that trust in the future fails, the present will fail as well. A vision of a gloomier future will lead to a weaker present and make the gloomier future a reality.[2] When economies suffer large shocks, reflexivity becomes a critical driver of the recovery. The principle of reflexivity implies that economic agents always have a partial and imperfect view of the world and that these imperfect views can influence outcomes, by leading to actions that seem individually optimal but are socially inefficient. If everyone believes that monetary policy will be ineffective, their belief will end up becoming reality, and growth and inflation will fail to increase.[3] As George Soros explains, a revolution is only a revolution if everybody believes it is. If markets and economic agents do not believe that governments and central bankers are ready to do whatever it takes, to take enough risk to solve the problems, they will remain risk averse and the economic outlook will be riskier. It is the paradox of risk.

Nothing in life is certain. The future is stochastic, large shocks can happen, the Great Moderation may never return, short-term interest rates could be at zero for decades to come. Monetary policy may never again be boring.

Fortunately, the last decade has provided a real-life experiment, much richer than anything that could have been designed in a laboratory or in the minds of PhD economists. Previous chapters describe the multiple and multidimensional actions undertaken by central banks, their impact, and side effects. This chapter draws lessons and provides suggestions for crafting a monetary policy for all seasons.

A critical step in building such a monetary policy is to eliminate the concept of "unconventional" policies. Policies operate along different channels to affect long-term rates, asset prices, and risk aversion. Central banks always operate by changing the size and composition of their balance sheets. Changing short-term interest rates is just a subset of this framework. Calling some policies "unconventional" introduces an unnecessary stigma that dents their effectiveness and leads to less policy easing than is necessary.

This point cannot be emphasized enough. To be effective, central banks must counteract the widespread moral judgment that low rates are bad because they hurt savers. Savers do not have the economic moral high ground. At times more saving is needed, at times more borrowing is needed; interest rates must be adjusted accordingly. Central banks must be prepared to use all their tools at all times. They should explain in detail to

---

2. Kozlowski, Veldkamp, and Venkateswaran (2015) argue that when economies suffer a shock never seen before (and no one therefore knows the true underlying distribution of shocks), a transitory shock can have very persistent effects.

3. See Soros (1987) on the development of reflexivity applied to economics and finance.

the public that there is no difference between "conventional" and "unconventional" policies, that all are legal and within their mandates. They should strengthen the institutional settings to be able to operate free from political interference.

The experience since 2007 suggests that changes are required to the four main elements of central banking articulated in chapter 3: goals, tools, strategies, and communication. In addition, the realization that monetary policy may have to modulate risk aversion has implications for institutional design.

Goals: A Program of Opportunistic Reflation

Central bankers choose 2 percent as the inflation targets mostly by accident. The consensus was heavily determined by the size of the shocks of the Great Moderation. As the consensus moved away from pure price stability (zero inflation) to building some buffer against deflation, the debate shifted toward the cost-benefit analysis of positive inflation. How much inflation was too much?

The costs included (1) the confusion inflation creates between nominal and real variables, (2) the "shoe-leather effect" (the cost in time and effort of holding less cash and having to go the bank), and (3) the "menu effect" (the cost of having to change prices more often). The main benefits included (1) the "grease effect" (providing more room for real wages to adjust when there is downside nominal rigidity), (2) the reduction in the probability of deflation, and (3) the creation of more room to cut real interest rates to cushion a recession.

The view in the late 1990s, when this debate took place, was that, taking as a reference the shocks experienced in the postwar period, the zero-bound constraint would be hit only very rarely and that most of the problems would be avoided at rates of inflation as low as 2 percent.[4] Most of these results assumed not only small shocks but also positive equilibrium real interest rates—in the 1.5–4.5 percent range (Haldane 1997, Viñals 2001). Viñals (2001) uses simulation exercises to argue that the probability of hitting the zero bound was below 5 percent for the United States and below 1 percent for the euro area for equilibrium real rates as low as 1.5 percent and inflation rates as low as 1 percent.

Similar exercises were the basis for establishing 2 percent inflation targets. The evidence was not conclusive, though. Based on empirical evidence, Charles Wyplosz (2001) argued that inflation of 0–2 percent in the

---

4. See, for example, Fuhrer and Madigan (1997), Orphanides and Wieland (1998), and Reifschneider and Williams (1999) for the United States and Viñals (2001) for the euro area.

euro area would raise the NAIRU by about 2–4 percentage points, because it would reduce the grease effect of inflation on the price and wage process.[5] He argued that an inflation rate of 4 percent would greatly eliminate this effect. In hindsight he was right.

Fast forward to today, and it seems clear that if 2 percent was the right number during the Great Moderation, it has to be too low today. History has shown that the size of the shocks to consider must be higher, and the equilibrium real interest rate possibly lower, which makes the zero-bound constraint more structural (see, for example, Chung et al. 2011). The precrisis expectation was that with 2 percent inflation the US economy would spend just 5 percent of the time at the EZLB. In fact, it has been closer to 25 percent of the time since inflation stabilized around 2 percent in the early 1990s. Model simulations suggest that with an inflation target of 2 percent and neutral real interest rates of 1 percent, the economy could be at the EZLB close to 40 percent of the time (Kiley and Roberts 2017).

A higher inflation target allows for a bigger decline in real interest rates during a recession. If the EZLB is binding, and inflation is at target before a recession starts, the real interest rate could be cut to at most –2 percent (0 nominal minus 2 percent inflation) assuming that inflation does not fall during the recession, not a very realistic assumption. A more realistic estimate would be that the floor for real interest rates is closer to –1 percent, the level of short-term real interest rates in the developed world today. English, López-Salido, and Tetlow (2013) simulate the impact for the United States of a credible increase in the inflation target to 3 percent while at the EZLB. The results show a materially faster decline in unemployment, thanks to the decline in real interest rates generated by the higher inflation target.

With this in mind, Blanchard, Dell'Ariccia, and Mauro (2010); Ball (2014); and Ball et al. (2016) argue in favor of a higher inflation target, of up to 4 percent, in order to create enough room for real interest rates to be cut and cushion the negative impact of shocks. If inflation is at 2 percent or lower when the next recession hits, there will probably not be enough room to cut real interest rates as much as needed. Haldane compares the statistical probability of recession over the next 10 years versus the market-priced probability that short-term interest rates will have reached at least 3 percent, the lower bound of the average size of rate cuts in easing cycles.[6] He concludes that over the next 10 years, the probability of a recession is

---

5. The proponents of the grease effect argue that for various reasons (including efficiency wages, fairness, nominal downward rigidity, and information costs), a moderate level of inflation provides some "grease" to the price- and wage-setting process. Such a source of real wage flexibility durably reduces the natural, or long-run, rate of unemployment.

6. Andrew Haldane, "Stuck," speech at the Open University, London, June 30, 2015.

twice as large as the probability of interest rates reaching 3 percent. Paul De Grauwe and Yuemei Ji (2016) show that with inflation targets below 3 percent, the distribution of output gaps is negative. Because monetary policy cannot respond enough to shocks, the economy spends more time below than above potential. Michael Kiley and John Roberts (2017) show that with an inflation target of 2 percent and neutral interest rates below 2 percent, economic growth would be about 1 percent below potential on average. A few regional Fed presidents, including Eric Rosengren[7] and John Williams (2016), have made similar points about the need for a higher inflation target, at least in theory.

The average rate-cutting cycle has been about 400–500 basis points. It is very likely that central banks will reach the EZLB again in the next easing cycle, possibly very quickly. Then what? David Reifschneider (2016) simulates the impact of a recession in the United States in which the unemployment rate increases from 5 percent to 10 percent. Assuming short-term rates at 3 percent and long-term rates at 4 percent when the recession hits, he argues that in a best-case scenario a combination of rate cuts to zero, large asset purchases, and aggressive threshold-based forward guidance might be enough to cushion the recession. However, it is a best-case scenario. It seems unlikely that interest rates will be as high as he assumes by the time the next recession hits, and the evidence shows that balance sheet policies are rarely used to the extent necessary.

A higher inflation target is needed to provide more room to cut real interest rates. Targeting higher inflation would also provide the added benefit of giving the central bank more leeway to deviate from the target temporarily—for example, choosing to return to the target in a more gradual way in order to address financial stability issues—with a much smaller risk of falling into deflation if policy remained too tight for too long.

If a Higher Inflation Target Is the Obvious Thing to Do, Why Isn't It Happening?

Beyond political pressures, the main economic argument against a higher inflation target is inertia. All changes imply costs, and the cost of shifting to a higher inflation target is seen as high and unpredictable. Ben Bernanke argues that inflation volatility would increase and inflation expectations become more unstable.[8] English, López-Salido, and Tetlow (2013) argue

---

7. Sam Fleming, "Inflation Goal May Be Too Low, Says Rosengren," *Financial Times*, April 20, 2015, www.ft.com/content/6e9815ae-e776-11e4-8e3f-00144feab7de (accessed on March 30, 2017).

8. Ben S. Bernanke, "The Economic Outlook and Monetary Policy," speech at the Federal Reserve Bank of Kansas City's Annual Economic Symposium, Jackson Hole, WY, August 27, 2010.

that if the increase in the inflation target is not credible, economic performance will worsen, because economic agents may react to the expected increase in inflation by reducing their real income expectations and curtailing spending. Others argue that higher inflation might lead to higher volatility and dispersion of individual prices. However, some recent research, such as the paper by Emi Nakamura et al. (2016), shows that price dispersion did not increase during the higher inflation of the 1970s and that this cost may therefore have been exaggerated.

One of the main fears about increasing inflation targets is that it could lead to "accelerated" and more volatile inflation: If the central bank raises the target once, what prevents markets from assuming that it may do so again?

The experiences of two central banks should allay this concern. The first is the Reserve Bank of New Zealand, a pioneer in inflation targeting. Since its establishment, in 1990, it has gradually increased its inflation target from the initial 0–2 percent to 0–3 percent (in 1996) to the current 1–3 percent (in 2002), with no credibility cost (Reserve Bank of New Zealand 2002).

The second is the BoJ. It was initially very reluctant to move from the zero inflation target directly to a 2 percent inflation target, because it worried about inflation expectations becoming unhinged after such a long period of deflation. As a result, it moved in small steps, first targeting 1 percent inflation, then 2 percent inflation. The outcome was a very gradual upward shift in inflation expectations that has, for now, underperformed the target.

At the end of the day, the stability of inflation expectations will depend on the credibility of the actions implemented to achieve them, regardless of the level. In the current environment, the main problem would not be excessive inflation but rather lack of credibility regarding the desire to hit the new target.

A change to a higher inflation target requires a shift in the policy stance, as the BoJ experience has shown, and likely an explicit coordination of monetary and fiscal policy to achieve it. Right now it would require a new round of policy easing (or a longer period of policy on hold), which policymakers seem loath to consider. In fact, it seems that the strong desire to exit from the EZLB as soon as possible rather than the desire to reach the policy goals and maximize economic welfare has driven the monetary policy setting.

This strong desire to exit the EZLB can be seen in the reluctance to even consider a transitory period of above-target inflation. Despite the fact that both inflation and inflation expectations are below target, the Fed and the ECB have adopted a policy stance that reverts inflation to the target only from below, thus refusing to achieve a faster economic recovery that would be compatible with price stability. The BoE has been more tolerant of transitory overshoots in inflation, but until the Brexit shock, it also refused to contemplate a policy stance that would entail some temporary overshooting of the inflation target. Its stance changed, however, with the easing package of August 2016, which assumes an explicit and persistent overshooting of the inflation target (the BoE easing strategy following the Brexit referendum is discussed in the next chapter).

This reluctance to adopt a policy that generates a period of above-target inflation is suboptimal. Reluctant to take some risks, central banks are making the recovery riskier—the paradox of risk. If this reluctance generates an anchoring of inflation expectations at a lower level or a reduction in the credibility of the inflation target, it will also reduce the flexibility of monetary policy to react to shocks.

Ironically, the very central banks that refuse to temporarily overshoot the inflation target seem to agree that doing so would be a good idea. Janet Yellen shows simulations comparing the interest rate path compatible with the FOMC projections and the interest rate of "optimal control"—the policy that would maximize the welfare of the economy in terms of the combination of inflation, unemployment, and growth.[9] They show that, as of January 2012, the optimal control path involved raising rates about a year later than the FOMC January 2012 *Summary of Economic Projections* suggested and pursuing a path of inflation that pushed core personal consumption expenditure inflation a bit above 2 percent for a few years to then converge to 2 percent by 2018, generating a faster decline in unemployment. English, López-Salido, and Tetlow (2013) update this exercise with data up to September 2013. They find a similar pattern, with the optimal policy implying a later liftoff than suggested by the FOMC dots and inflation overshooting the target for a couple of years to then converge to 2 percent from above.

The concept of overshooting is simple. If monetary policy is not (or cannot be) eased enough, it should compensate by delaying the tightening once the economy recovers, even if doing so implies transitorily higher inflation. Kiley and Roberts (2017) call the idea that policy must be more accommodative than in normal times in order to make up for the inability to ease enough in bad times "risk adjustment." One could take this a step farther and commit to track the "shadow interest rate" (the rate that would have existed had the EZLB not been binding). In some sense, shadow interest rate tracking implies calculating the "deficit" of forgone rate cuts

---

9. Janet Yellen, Revolution and Evolution in Central Bank Communications, speech at the Haas School of Business, University of California, Berkeley, November 13, 2012, www.federalreserve.gov/newsevents/speech/yellen20121113a.htm.

and not raising rates until the deficit has been erased. Charles Evans et al. (2015) use this concept to argue that policymakers should remove accommodation only once inflation has overshot its objective—only then can central bankers safely declare mission accomplished.

In the event, even if the Fed never projected an overshooting of inflation, it significantly delayed the beginning of the tightening cycle; by early 2017 interest rates were below what would be recommended by the optimal control rule. Whether this strategy will lead to an eventual overshooting of inflation, time will tell.

The better anchoring of inflation expectations in the United Kingdom than in the United States or the euro area is likely related to the fact that the BoE allowed a temporary overshooting of its inflation target during 2010–12, as shown in the previous chapter. If it works, why not do it?

Adding a Dual Mandate to Protect against Hysteresis

The reluctance to increase the inflation target—or at least aim for a period of above-target inflation that compensates the long period of below-target inflation—is even more suboptimal for economies suffering from hysteresis effects. DeLong and Summers (2012); Blanchard, Cerutti, and Summers (2015); and Fatás and Summers (2015) argue that a prolonged period of weak growth dents potential growth and that a transitory recession can therefore have a permanent negative impact on growth. According to this view, monetary policy can affect potential growth. By running the economy "hot" during periods of insufficient demand, especially insufficient investment, it can help prevent a deterioration of potential growth. Demand would create its own supply. Fed chair Yellen has argued that addressing this concern should be a major avenue of economic research.[10]

An additional factor to consider is the flatness of the Phillips curve. The Phillips curve relates the evolution of inflation to the evolution of the labor market and inflation expectations. In principle, a stronger labor market or an increase in inflation expectations should increase the probability that inflation increases later on. This relationship has changed over the decades. Blanchard (2016), IMF (2016a) and Miles et al. (2017) present evidence that the Phillips curve has become flatter in most advanced economies—that is, the response of inflation to changes in the unemployment rate has declined—and more responsive to inflation expectations. Blanchard (2016) shows that the variance of the error term in the Philips curve is very large

---

10. Janet L. Yellen, "Macroeconomic Research After the Crisis," speech at conference on the "Elusive 'Great' Recovery: Causes and Implications for Future Business Cycle Dynamics," 60th annual economic conference sponsored by the Federal Reserve Bank of Boston, October 14, 2016.

and similar in magnitude to the level of inflation—meaning that the ability of the Phillips curve to forecast inflation is very weak. In addition, inflation expectations have become more adaptive—they have become more dependent on past inflation. A long period of very low inflation could thus push inflation expectations lower and (because the impact of the labor market on inflation has declined) anchor inflation at a lower level. These results imply that a period of economic expansion that leads to inflation above target does not require a period of recession to stabilize inflation at target, all it needs is for the economy to return to the steady state. This finding reinforces the desirability of aiming for a period of above-target inflation to compensate for the recent period of below-target inflation.

The combination of very flat Phillips curves and likely hysteresis in the labor market implies that the "divine coincidence"—the fact that, assuming no real wage rigidities, output reaches its potential level once inflation is stabilized (Blanchard and Galí 2005)—no longer holds. The divine coincidence was one of the bases for adopting single price-stability mandates, as stabilizing inflation delivers maximum growth. If it fails, then it will be optimal for monetary policy to have a dual mandate that seeks both price stability and maximum employment on an equal basis.

If the divine coincidence no longer holds and fluctuations in unemployment have small effects on wage and price inflation, then monetary policy that focuses only on inflation risks tolerating excessive weakness in unemployment and growth. In this environment the failure of monetary policy to react strongly enough to a large increase in unemployment (or a deep recession) because it observes that inflation is not reacting as much as expected would risk leaving the economy at a permanently higher level of unemployment. Interestingly, when, in the mid-1990s, the Fed was debating whether to set a target for inflation, Janet Yellen, then a member of the Federal Reserve Board of Governors, opposed it, because of the potentially negative impact on employment (Mallaby 2016).

The dual mandate explains one of the main differences in the policy actions of the Fed versus the ECB. Because inflation did not initially react much to the sharp increase in unemployment, the ECB interpreted most of the decline as an increase in the NAIRU (wrongly, in hindsight) and did not feel the need to ease aggressively to minimize the increase in unemployment. In contrast, the Fed had the obligation to meet the employment part of its mandate and eased policy more aggressively, even if it also (wrongly in hindsight) interpreted part of the increase in unemployment as an increase in the NAIRU. A dual mandate reduces the scope for errors.

The adoption of a dual mandate would facilitate the reaction to a large shock, as it would allow the central bank to adopt a more balanced approach and take more time to move inflation toward its target. The change in the BoE's remit in 2013 provided the BoE with maximum flexibility to react to a shock. The BoE made use of this flexibility in its reaction to the Brexit shock by adopting a policy stance that projects persistent overshooting of inflation, as discussed in the next chapter.

A dual mandate would also facilitate communication with the public at times of sharp recessions. A central bank talking only about inflation while the unemployment rate skyrockets risks losing political support and compromising its independence. Central banks are political institutions and must continuously earn their independence. The BoE's introduction of the unemployment threshold in 2013 was driven, in part, by its desire to reinforce the democratic legitimacy of the inflation-targeting regime.[11] At times of financial crisis, when central banks have to engage in financial rescues (which are usually unpopular), inserting the real economy into the conversation will strengthen the independence of the central bank.

At the same time, with a dual mandate it is important that it remain clear that when unemployment is near the NAIRU, the binding constraint is price stability; the unemployment level is just an intermediate target. A dual mandate should be interpreted as maximum employment subject to price stability.

Starting a Process of Opportunistic Reflation

How do central banks get from here to there? They should start a process of "opportunistic reflation," mirroring the process of opportunistic disinflation that led to the convergence toward 2 percent inflation rates since the 1980s (Orphanides and Wilcox 2002). The BoJ has shown the way. As it felt more confident that inflation was picking up, it moved the inflation target in small steps, from zero to 1 percent and then 2 percent. The BoJ is already engaging in opportunistic reflation. If it can be done from 0 to 2 percent inflation, it can be done from 2 to 4 percent inflation. The other central banks should do the same. As inflation approaches 2 percent, they should aim for a temporary overshooting of inflation to first consolidate the current target and then settle on a higher one. This may involve taking advantage of exogenous inflationary shocks to achieve the increase in inflation, possibly over a few business cycles, while aggressively resisting disinflationary forces. Such a move is not as heretical as some might think. Kiley and Roberts (2017) argue in favor of a policy rule that targets inflation at 3 percent when interest rates are positive, so that inflation can average 2 percent over the medium term (under the assumption that monetary

---

11. See Spencer Dale, "Inflation Targeting and the Monetary Policy Committee's Forward Guidance," speech at the International Journal of Central Banking Annual Conference, Warsaw, September 6, 2013.

policy will not be able to avoid a decline of inflation toward 1 percent during recessions, because the low neutral interest rate will preclude the central bank from easing policy enough).

The recent underperformance of inflation despite the large increase in central banks' balance sheets should create a more benign environment for a gradual transition toward a higher inflation target. Introducing regular reviews of the policy framework—as Canada does—would help overcome the inertia inherent to this process. Recent experience suggests that an inflation target of at least 3 percent, preferably 4 percent, would be advisable.

Tools: Be Ready to Use All the Tools at All Times

Even if central banks were to decide to increase their inflation targets, the probability of reaching the EZLB in the next recession remains high, as the target would change only over time. Therefore, central banks should be ready to use their full arsenal of tools, including cutting interest rates to the EZLB, buying assets in large amounts, and actively deploying forward guidance. If needed, they should use balance sheet policies at all times, not just when interest rates are zero. Once central banks recognize that financial frictions are a feature of financial markets, relying only on short-term interest rates will likely be suboptimal.

The size and composition of the balance sheet provides central banks with a finer degree of precision than the short-term interest rate. The interest rate on excess reserves (IOER) allows central banks to run monetary policy with a larger balance sheet. A financial system with excess reserves is likely to be more stable. It is true that introducing multiple tools could generate some additional uncertainty about specific asset prices, but it is a cost worth assuming in exchange for the greater ability to manage the economic cycle. Some central banks have decided to hold the assets purchased to maturity, others have decided to delay the sales of bonds at least until short-term interest rates have reached a positive level.

Active use of the balance sheet allows central banks to fine-tune their management of the yield curve and address specific risk premia in more direct ways, depending on the needs of the economy. Doing so is especially useful in an environment of large and persistent changes to financial regulation that may alter the demand for different assets and the ability of the financial sector to arbitrage and intermediate them. Of course, active use of the balance sheet must be symmetric. At times of excessive risk taking in certain segments of the markets, the central bank should be willing to use its balance sheet and lending policies to modulate excesses—by, for example, changing margin calls or shifting schedules of asset sales. If, say, the housing market is looking particularly frothy because of speculative demand, the central bank could sell mortgage assets to cool it down while keeping the main interest rate unchanged.

In addition to being willing to actively use their balance sheets, central banks should be open-minded regarding the range of assets they are willing to purchase. One reason some central banks may have eased less than optimally in the last few years is that they were reaching the limits of their purchases in the asset class they were purchasing and reluctant to move into other asset classes, a point made forcefully by Ball et al. (2016). The Fed, for example, was very mindful of market-functioning constraints when designing the flow rate of purchases in QE3.

These restrictions applied especially to the ECB and the BoJ. The ECB set up several rules—including purchases based on the ECB's capital key instead of market weights, and limits on purchases as a percent of issue and issuer—that constrained the availability of bonds for purchase. These rules were driven mostly by political concerns, at the expense of economic effectiveness. They created very severe dislocations in the market for German bunds during 2016–17, with the private sector competing with the ECB for ownership of scarce bunds. The size of this dislocation can be seen by the opening up of a wide spread between the two-year Eonia (money market) rate and the two-year bund rate, which reached record levels in early 2017 (figure 5.1). In fact, while Eonia rates were increasing, reflecting the improving performance of the euro area economy and the shift in stance of ECB policy, bund yields were declining. As a result, they fell to record negative levels, denting the profitability of financial institutions—and, along the way, providing an important subsidy to the German budget (because the lower rates reduced the interest rate cost of German government borrowing).

The BoJ's limits to purchases were not self-imposed but driven by the sheer size of its program. At the pace of purchases of ¥80 trillion a year and given the expected issuance of government bonds, the BoJ could reach the limits of possible purchases some time in 2018, under the assumption that banks, pension funds, and insurance companies will want to hold minimum amounts of government bonds. Holdings of Japanese government bonds by the banking sector are projected to fall to 5 percent of total assets by 2018, for example, when the BoJ would be holding more than half of all Japanese government bonds (Arslanalp and Botman 2015).

One obvious alternative is to expand the menu of eligible assets for purchase. The ECB has been very active in a variety of asset markets, including corporate bonds and asset-backed commercial paper. The BoJ has also ventured into private sector assets, including ETFs and REITS, but even there it is approaching capacity limits (e.g., its holdings of ETFs are approaching 50 percent of total ETF assets). This limit is not binding, as

Figure 5.1 Two-year bund yields and Eonia rates, 2012–17

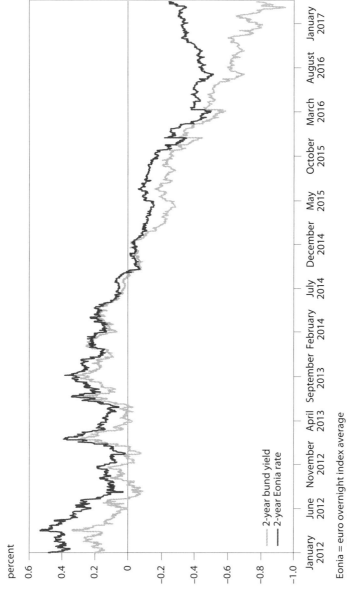

percent

Eonia = euro overnight index average
Source: Bloomberg.

the supply of ETFs grows endogenously with demand. The binding limit would be the share of all stocks owned by the BoJ, which is still very low, at about 2 percent.

The BoE and the Fed limited their QE purchases to sovereign bonds (BoE) and government-guaranteed bonds, such as agency bonds (the Fed), although the BoE expanded into corporate bonds in the post-Brexit easing package. The lesson is that central banks should be able to buy all kinds of assets in a nondisruptive way. The Fed is severely handicapped, in comparison with the other main central banks, by its inability to buy private assets. The US market is the deepest and most liquid, yet the Fed cannot participate in it to ease policy. The Fed should be allowed to buy corporate bonds or equities.

Balance sheet policies seek to generate portfolio rebalancing. They want to increase the total purchases of risky assets of the economy to increase asset prices and reduce risk premia. Buying bonds is a way to do so in an indirect and, by definition, uncertain way. In some instances, it can backfire: The more bonds the central bank wants to buy, the more bonds the private sector wants to buy, creating at times severe dislocations. Buying equities, indices, or REITs would be a way to rebalance directly and more effectively.

Buying private assets would offer several advantages. First, it would reach sectors of the economy that are at a disadvantage when the banking sector is weak, such as small and medium-size enterprises (SMEs), by having central banks purchase the asset-backed securities of SME loans, for example. Second, it would probably reduce the amount of assets that need to be purchased to achieve the desired change in financial conditions, because it directly reduces risk premia and would not depend on the portfolio-rebalancing effect. Third, it would palliate the problem of the shortage of risk-free assets that large-scale purchases of bonds generates, which can create a self-fulfilling prophecy of ever lower interest rates.[12] A case in point is the acute shortage of German bunds generated by the ECB's purchases during 2016–17. The sharp decline in interest rates created a perverse dynamic for the European banking sector, as markets became gloomier about the sector's profitability (lower interest rates compress interest rate margins) and therefore reduced the valuation of European bank shares. For most of 2015–17, the relative performance of European bank shares just mimicked the evolution of German bund yields (figure 5.2). The ECB would have been more effective buying fewer German bunds and buying equities via ETFs,

---

12. Caballero and Fahri (2017) describe the related phenomenon of the "safety trap," where a shortage of risk-free assets depresses asset prices. They argue that the safety trap can be alleviated by increasing the relative supply of risk-free assets, either via issuance of government bonds or purchases of risky assets.

Figure 5.2   Performance of European bank shares and German 10-year rates, 2015–17

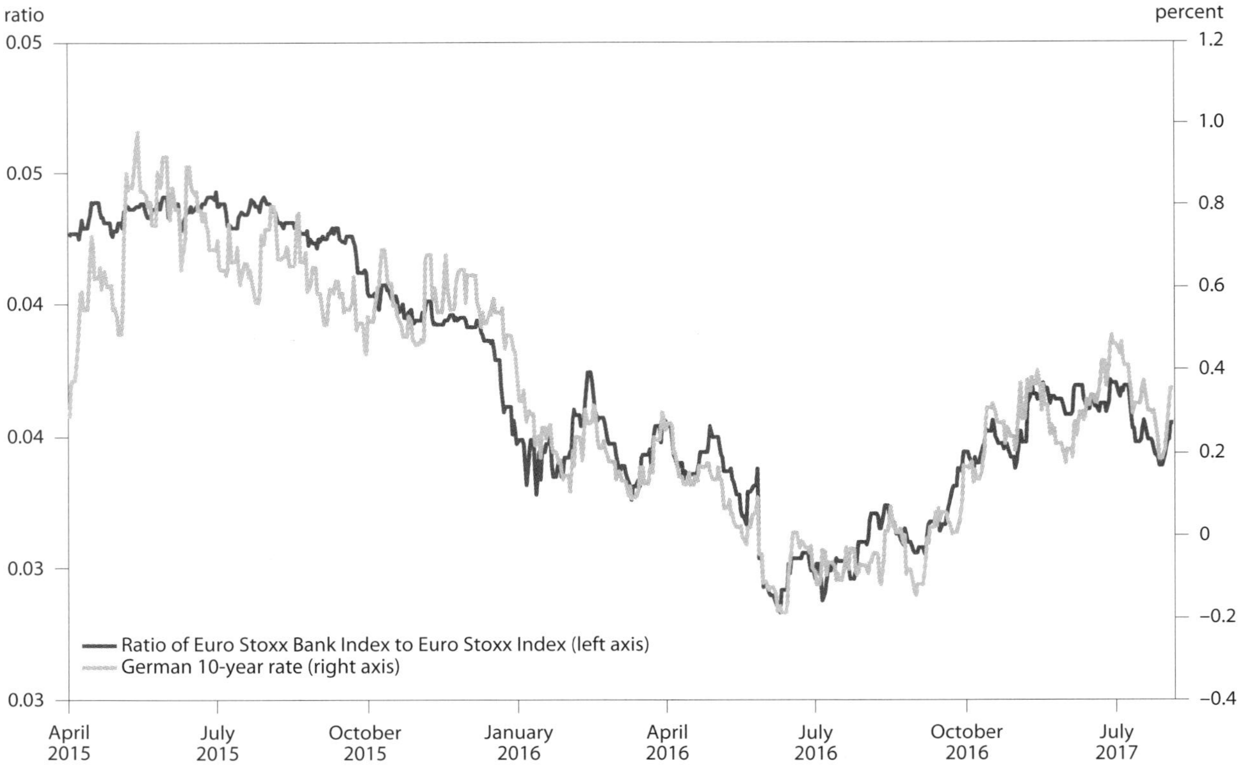

ratio

0.05	
0.05	
0.04	
0.04	
0.03	
0.03	

percent
1.2
1.0
0.8
0.6
0.4
0.2
0
-0.2
-0.4

April 2015   July 2015   October 2015   January 2016   April 2016   July 2016   October 2016   July 2017

—— Ratio of Euro Stoxx Bank Index to Euro Stoxx Index (left axis)
—— German 10-year rate (right axis)

Source: Data from Bloomberg.

which would have contributed more to lowering the elevated equity risk premium in the euro area. Fourth, buying private assets would reduce the incentive for corporate buybacks and the associated increase in corporate debt.[13]

This listing of advantages is not blind to the potential distortions that asset purchases introduce in markets, especially regarding eligibility constraints (e.g., the spreads on corporate bonds eligible for ECB purchases are narrower than the spreads on bonds that are not eligible, regardless of the intrinsic risk of the issuers). Overall, however, the weight of the evidence is in favor of purchases of private assets.

Widening the range of assets would also apply to lending operations. Central banks should be ready to lend against any collateral, properly priced and discounted. Bagehot's principle (lend against "good" collateral) should be updated. With the prevalence of market financing, central banks should be ready to accept all types of collateral. The definition of "good" collateral is, after all, arbitrary, as it is a function of the evolution of the economy. It is also endogenous, as it depends, to a large extent, on the actions of the central bank. The key issue is the pricing of that collateral. At the right price, all collateral is good, in the sense that the central bank is not expected ex ante to incur a loss. During times of stress, the solvency of firms could depend on judgments about the creditworthiness of assets; the central bank should therefore be very careful not to trigger a self-fulfilling crisis by not accepting certain types of collateral.

Establishing a Target Zone for Yields When the Assets Run Out

What if the central bank starts running out of assets to buy? A critical limit to the extent of asset purchases is the potential distortions to market functioning. It is possible that certain market participants would want to hold a minimum amount of certain classes of assets, such as government bonds, for regulatory reasons or because they do not want to face the possibility of principal losses. It is also possible that the extent of the easing program is such that the central bank ends up being the main owner of an asset class. For example, as part of its QQE program, the BoJ owns more than half of the ETFs on the Nikkei 225 and is one of the top five owners of almost half of the stocks on the Nikkei 225. This high level of ownership is not a problem in itself, as the BoJ does not own the shares directly but rather via its ETF holdings. It could increase the volatility of stocks with low free float (shares available for trading), however, and raise governance

---

13. A potential disadvantage is that equities are infinite-duration assets, and therefore at some point they would have to be sold. But this problem is not necessarily bigger than having to sell bonds—the key is to do it at the right time and in a gradual and transparent fashion.

questions if it were to continue for an extended period and the BoJ were to become majority shareholder.

The possibility of running out of assets to buy is a strong argument in favor of being as aggressive as needed when an asset purchase program starts. The BoJ has been buying equities for a few years, but always in token quantities and with a clear focus on not interfering with the price-formation mechanism. Limiting the quantities is understandable—the BoJ would not want to be accused of manipulating the stock market—but at the same time, the purpose of the purchases has to be to reduce the equity risk premium. If the quantity purchased is too small, the central bank could end up in a situation in which it already owns a large amount of assets but the impact has been minimal.

When the central bank starts running out of space to buy assets, an alternative would be to shift back from quantity targets to price targets. For example, in the case of government bonds, the central bank could adopt a strategy of target zones for the yield curve. It would have to be willing to buy all the bonds necessary to achieve the desired yield curve, but if the target is properly chosen, it may not have to buy many bonds. In an environment in which market participants become ever more reluctant to sell their government bonds and long-term yields have probably declined too much, the central bank could maintain the target zone with little intervention. The target zone would allow some price discovery to take place around point estimates of the neutral yield curve and avoid some of the rigidities of a yield target while keeping rates low enough.[14] As the economy improves, these target zones could be widened—and eventually eliminated.

The issuance of Eurobonds would allow the ECB to apply this system of target zones for the euro area yield curve. In an environment of acute scarcity of risk-free assets, which may be a key factor behind the decline in neutral interest rates, the issuance of Eurobonds would also contribute to increasing neutral interest rates in the euro area—yet another manifestation of the paradox of risk. Skeptics oppose Eurobonds because they see them as increasing the risk for core countries, ignoring the fact that the issuance of Eurobonds, by allowing better sharing of risks and increasing the supply of risk-free assets, would reduce the risk for the euro area as a whole and for each of its members (see Ubide 2015b).

A target zone for yields would complete the toolkit of central banks at the zero lower bound. When yields are high and central bank holdings are

---

14. Imakubo, Kojima, and Nakajima (2015) provide a thorough discussion of the concept of the neutral yield curve, and the extension of the concept of the neutral interest rate to the shape of the yield curve.

low, central banks would purchase assets. When yields are already very low and central bank asset holdings high, they should set target yield zones.

Raising Capital to Protect the Central Bank from Potential Losses

Central banks should try to minimize macroeconomic risks, not the risks to their balance sheet. But central banks do not operate in a political vacuum, and potential central bank losses can have political implications. The story of the crisis shows that reluctance to incur eventual losses from asset purchases and foreign exchange intervention deterred central banks from being as aggressive as they should have been. Therefore, for central banks to be able to use their complete set of tools they need to strengthen their loss-absorption capacity.

Potential losses can look big, but they need to be looked at in context. For example, Seth Carpenter et al. (2013) show that a 100 basis point increase in long-term rates would lead to mark-to-market losses for the Fed of about $300 billion, which is higher than its current loss-absorption capacity (about $230 billion). In addition, an increase in the interest paid on reserves would reduce its profits from normal central bank operations to the point that the Fed could incur operational losses. These potential operational losses need to be set against profits, however, which generated more than $400 billion in remittances to the Treasury during 2009–15, an amount several times greater than the precrisis level. In fact, under all their scenarios, even some that generate years of negative remittances, Carpenter et al. project cumulative remittances for 2009–25 of $800–$1,000 billion. The profit and loss assessment has to be made over the cycle—and over the cycle central banks are profitable most of the time.

In the case of the ECB, the distribution of potential losses became a thorny issue during the debate on the design of the QE program. The ECB operates under a risk-sharing framework for monetary policy operations. However, it adopted a special framework for QE in which most of the losses, if they were to occur, would remain with the national central banks (see Ubide 2015a). The issue is political, not economic, as valuation changes would become relevant only if the ECB were to sell the bonds (because they are valued at amortized cost and thus not subject to marking-to-market) or a country were to default. The BoE adopted a more explicit policy of full coverage for any potential losses by requesting an indemnity from the Treasury for each portion of its asset purchases.

Focusing on central banks' capital, and their profit and losses, is to a very large extent irrelevant. Central banks are not commercial banks. Their goal is to maximize national welfare, not their profits. Central banks can always create money to earn seigniorage and pay their bills, and they cannot be declared bankrupt by a court. They do not need capital to cover startup costs or buttress their credibility to borrow in markets (unless they have to borrow in foreign exchange). In abstract, central banks do not need capital to operate.

If central bank profits are irrelevant, why the worry? Empirical evidence, mostly on less developed countries, shows a negative correlation between inflation performance and the financial strength of central banks. However, causation and the exact nature of the relationship have remained vague (see Stella 1997, Ize 2005, Stella and Lönnberg 2008, and Schobert 2008).

In its simplest form, a central bank earns a return on its monetary policy operations, its assets, and its issuance of base money (banknotes and reserves) and incurs operational costs. In principle, it steadily generates profits as long as people are willing to hold its liabilities at no interest and base money grows at least as quickly as operating expenses. A temporary shock that creates enough losses to deplete the central bank's capital would thus always be reversed in the medium run, except (a) when the economy falls into a persistent deflationary trap and the growth rate of banknotes falls below the growth rate of operating costs and (b) when the growth rate of the demand for banknotes falls short of nominal interest rates (Bindseil, Manzanares, and Weller 2004).

But even a negative long-term profitability outlook should not necessarily lead to failure to conduct monetary policy in an effective way.[15] For that failure to happen, a relationship between central bank capital and other institutional factors, such as credibility or independence, is needed. From a conceptual standpoint, a better concept than capital for assessing the soundness of a central bank would be net worth (or financial strength). Net worth takes into account the central bank's "franchise value" (its monopoly over the issuance of money and the right to impose reserve requirements on commercial banks) and its off-balance sheet obligations (such as the potential need to bail out banks during crises or defend an exchange rate regime). Net worth depends on the functions for which the central bank has independent responsibility, and it varies over time. Therefore, the optimal size of a central bank's capital varies across countries. It depends on the bank's risk exposure (including currency, interest rate, and credit risks); profit-sharing and accounting arrangements; institutional strength; and crisis management responsibilities. The higher the risk exposure and crisis management responsibilities and the weaker the institutional strength and profit-sharing arrangements, the greater the capital buffers the central bank should build during good times.

---

15. For example, the Central Bank of Chile incurred significant losses during the 1990s from sterilization and bank recapitalization activities. It recorded negative net worth as late as 1997.

Central banks can be run with persistently negative capital, but doing so could create perverse incentives over time. A loss-making central bank may attempt to restore profitability by easing monetary policy in order to accelerate the demand for banknotes—which could be incompatible with its price-stability objective (Stella and Lönnberg 2008 define this problem as "policy insolvency"). For its part, the government may be tempted to put conditions on the recapitalization that could jeopardize the credibility and independence of monetary policy, leading to fiscal dominance.

Thus a condition for a credible central bank is to have positive net worth (its future stream of profits), regardless of whether current profits and capital are positive. Recapitalization arrangements must focus on the rapid rebuilding of equity. Most modern central bank laws require that in case of negative capital, the government issue to the central bank interest-bearing securities at market rates to restore capital levels and provide a level of core earnings that covers operating expenses, thus reducing the scope for further operational losses. A fully automated and fully credible rule of recapitalization by the government of the central bank in case of losses can be regarded as a substitute for positive capital.

Because such rules are difficult to implement in practice, however, positive capital levels remain a key tool to ensure that independent central bankers always concentrate on achieving their mandate.

This link between net worth and credibility is even more critical when central banks have to deploy tools that are highly dependent on the ability to do whatever it takes for as long as it takes, such as QE or foreign exchange intervention. If market participants doubt the resolve of the central bank because of its reluctance to incur losses (as happened recently in the case of the Swiss National Bank and its exchange rate floor), the policy may fail.

Therefore, a critical condition for the ability to use balance sheet tools effectively is a higher level of capital and loss-absorption abilities. For example, central banks should build reserves during good times to be able to deploy them in bad times, as the ECB has done. The government's commitment to recapitalize the central bank in case of losses could become part of an agreement to be ratified every, say, three years. Such a scheme would increase the democratic oversight of balance sheet operations, which are, de facto, quasi-fiscal activities but are needed to maximize economic welfare.

Strategies: Adopt Cyclically Adjusted Forward Guidance

The successes and failures of forward guidance in the last several years have raised three main issues: Should forward guidance be explicit or implicit, should it focus on the baseline forecast or on alternative scenarios, and should it be adjusted depending on the cyclical position of the economy?

The debate on the specific form of forward guidance is as long as the debate on inflation targeting. No two central banks have adopted a similar strategy.

Explicit or Implicit Guidance?

A few central banks have used explicit forward guidance. The Czech National Bank, the Bank of Israel, the Reserve Bank of New Zealand (RBNZ), the Norges Bank, and the Sveriges Riksbank all publish a path of interest rates. In 2012 the Federal Reserve started to publish a path for its policy rate, in the form of the dot plot, collecting individual FOMC participants' judgments of the appropriate level of the policy rate over three calendar years and the longer run. The BoE uses forward guidance implicitly, by publishing the path of market interest rates that underlies the inflation forecast. The ECB and the BoJ, still buying assets and at the zero lower bound, give calendar guidance on rates.

Explicit forward guidance outside the zero lower bound has had a mixed record. In general, markets have been reluctant to price the central bank path, especially beyond horizons of six months. Lars Svensson (2014) reviews the experience of the Sveriges Riksbank since 2007. He finds periods of success (2007–09) and periods of failure—for example, September 2011, when the Riksbank announced a policy rate path showing an increase of about 75 basis points over the next six quarters while market expectations before and after the announcement indicated a fall of about 75 basis points over the same period. Ex post the market expectations were right, and the Riksbank lowered the policy rate by 100 basis points over the next six quarters (Svensson 2015). The experience of Norges and RBNZ is similarly mixed, although there have not been long periods of explicit disagreement on the near-time direction of rates.

The experience of the FOMC with the dot plot is also mixed. During 2012 and 2013, market expectations were broadly aligned with the FOMC policy rate path. Sharp divergence appeared in 2014, with market expectations of policy rates falling increasingly below the FOMC dots. This divergence has remained ever since. Several reasons may explain this divergence. Chief among them is the fact that the market rate is a probability-weighted interest rate whereas the FOMC dots are an optimal policy path. The market shows the average across different scenarios, whereas the dots show what the Fed assesses to be the most likely path under its economic scenario.

The main difference between the Fed's experience and the experience of the other central banks is that market pricing has always been either in line with or below the FOMC dots, never above. The discrepancy has been

Figure 5.3   Probability distribution of US three-month interest rates in November 2015

a. Probability distribution of three-month interest rates

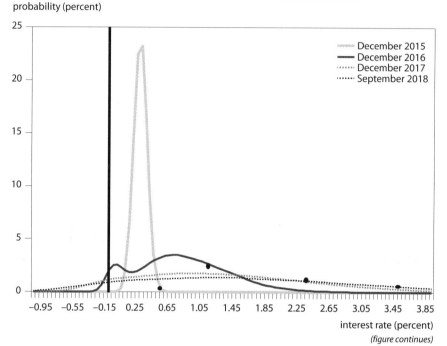

probability (percent)

interest rate (percent)

(figure continues)

one-sided—and at times extreme. In fact, not only do markets think (rationally) that the probability of a bad scenario is not zero, they also think that the single most likely outcome for interest rates is lower than the FOMC's.

Figure 5.3 illustrates this point by showing the probability distribution of three-month interest rates in the United States in early November 2015, just a few weeks after publication of the September 2015 dot plot. It shows that the market-assigned probability to the dot plot was very low. For example, the market suggested that there was close to a 90 percent probability that interest rates by December 2016 would be below the December 2016 dot. The range of probabilities for 2016–18 was very wide, but the mode (the peak probability) of the market distribution was always lower than the dots.

One possible explanation for this wide discrepancy is that the Fed was starting the tightening cycle after a long period of expansion and markets assumed a nonzero probability of a recession in the near term. Market pricing therefore reflected a probability-weighted path that included a nonzero probability of the Fed having to cut rates before having reached neutral levels. The market was pricing some probability of a policy mistake.

Figure 5.3   Probability distribution of US three-month interest rates in November 2015 *(continued)*

b. Cumulative probability distribution of three-month interest rates

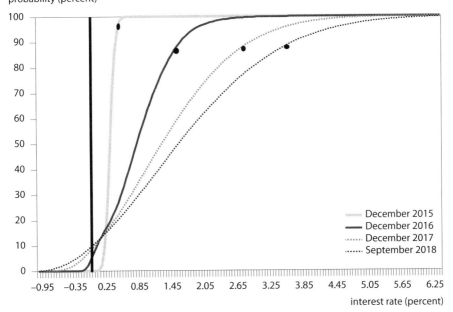

Note: The dots in the figures illustrate the location of the dots, for each dataset, from the September 2015 FOMC dot plot.

Source: Data from Bloomberg.

The BoE methodology—publish the inflation forecast under constant rates and under market rates and let markets make inferences—has its own problems. If the inflation forecast under market rates is at target, markets infer that the BoE is endorsing the market path. But, as BoE deputy governor Ben Broadbent stresses, this inference may not be correct.[16] To start, if risk premia vary over time, it may not be easy to extract the path of expected interest rate moves from market pricing. In addition, several interest rate paths may lead to a similar inflation forecast, especially in situations in which inflation and the output gap are of the same sign. There are trade-offs in terms of timing and speed of interest rate moves that cannot be explained by an inflation forecast. The decision of when to start selling assets, for example, could introduce a kink in the interest rate path that cannot be inferred from the inflation forecast. A similar consid-

16. Ben Broadbent, "The MPC's Forecasts and the Yield Curve: Predictions versus Promises," speech at Reuters, Canary Wharf Midlands, London, November 18, 2015.

eration could apply to the exchange rate and how tolerant the central bank may be about rapid moves in it resulting from interest rate changes.

The experiences of the Fed and the BoE show that there is no perfect method for delivering forward guidance on interest rates. Central banks have made very large growth and inflation forecasting mistakes in recent years, which have cast doubt on their credibility. Precision is dangerous when the variables to be forecast are uncertain and subject to shocks.

Therefore, a better strategy is to focus forward guidance on describing the central bank's reaction function and its deep parameters (e.g., the desirable tradeoff between inflation and slack)—in other words, to communicate how the central bank would react to different scenarios. Doing so would allow central banks to deemphasize their published macro forecast as "illustrative"—an example of an outlook that the central bank sees as plausible and "likes" because it achieves the mandate objectives in a balanced manner—rather than as the best possible forecast of the economy at that time.

The Fed is close in spirit to this concept, as the forecasts it publishes in the dot plot for growth, inflation, and unemployment are conducted under optimal policies (and thus it is a forecast that the Fed "likes") and Fed officials have discussed extensively the use of policy rules as informal ways of understanding their thinking. However, the dot plot is also prone to creating confusion, for two main reasons. First, because the dots are anonymous, it is impossible to link changes in them to changes in the growth and inflation forecast—and thereby infer the true reaction function of FOMC members. An improvement would be to identify each dot with its growth and inflation forecast on a historical basis (e.g., once a year for the previous year), so that analysts can better identify the reaction function.

Second, the dot plot forces the Fed to communicate in a time dimension—"three rate hikes this year"—leading markets to believe that this optimal path is the most likely outcome. However, markets do not believe this optimal path is likely to happen—and they have been right. In December 2015, for example, the Fed's path was suggesting four rate hikes in 2016; it ended up delivering only one. No wonder a survey of Fed communications gave the Fed a median grade of B−, highlighting the flip-flopping nature of this dimension of its discourse.[17] Partly because of these problems, in mid-2016 St. Louis Federal Reserve Bank president James Bullard stopped submitting his rate forecast, arguing that the economy shifts among different regimes and that the accuracy of any rate forecast will therefore be very low and add more confusion than clarity.

---

17. Peter Olson and David Wessel, "Improving the Fed's Dots," Up Front (blog), December 13, 2016, www.brookings.edu/blog/up-front/2016/12/13/improving-the-feds-dots (accessed on March 30, 2017).

This suggested emphasis on communicating the reaction function would also imply stressing possible alternative paths for growth and inflation and the policy responses that these alternative paths would require. The Norges Bank and Sveriges Riksbank have adopted this strategy, always showing alternative interest rate paths together with the baseline case. The BoE has started a similar, more narrative, approach in its *Inflation Report*, explaining the main assumptions underlying the forecast. Providing alternative rate paths is a way to educate markets on the likely reaction of the central bank to changes in the macroeconomic outlook and better approximate the concept that forward guidance is a conditional forecast rather than a promise.

Using Cyclically Adjusted Forward Guidance to Manage Leverage

The degree of explicitness and the focus on baseline or alternative scenarios are not static. Forward guidance should be cyclically adjusted, and vary depending on the cyclical position and the degree of risk aversion of the economy. Thought about this way, forward guidance would be the way monetary policy addresses financial stability and an integral part of the macroprudential toolkit.

A useful way to think about the relationship between forward guidance and financial stability is in terms of stabilizing the macroeconomic value at risk (VaR). VaR is a risk management tool widely used by financial institutions. It measures the expected loss of a portfolio as a function of portfolio size and the volatility of its assets relative to the capital available. The larger the portfolio size and the greater the volatility of its assets, the higher the expected loss. VaR is therefore a function of leverage (defined as portfolio size relative to capital) and uncertainty (for which volatility is a proxy). Financial institutions typically aim for a stable VaR, which makes leverage procyclical. During good times uncertainty is lower; for a given level of capital, portfolio size can be increased. During bad times higher uncertainty or portfolio losses that reduce capital require a reduction in portfolio size.[18]

This framework can be applied to the macroeconomic outlook. Assuming the economy wants to preserve a constant macroeconomic VaR, less uncertainty would make room for more leverage and vice versa.

A major source of macroeconomic uncertainty is the path of interest rates. If a central bank communicates a high degree of certainty about the expected path of interest rates, the economy will likely respond by

---

18. See the discussion about the interlink between leverage and uncertainty in crises in Ubide (2008) and Adrian, Colla, and Shin (2012).

increasing leverage—as happened when the Fed adopted the "measured pace" language in 2004–07. The economy became confident that there would be no interest rate surprises, and leverage rose. When interest rates are within normal ranges, the level of leverage is thus not a function of the level of interest rates but of the degree of certainty about the path of rates.

Leverage is a slow-moving variable, but uncertainty is not. Leverage should therefore be the purview of macroprudential supervisory and regulatory policies, and uncertainty should be the focus of monetary policy. For a given level of leverage, when uncertainty is within "normal" levels, monetary policy should focus on stabilizing inflation and maximizing GDP growth. When uncertainty becomes abnormal, either too high or too low, monetary policy should focus on restoring it to more normal values.

Uncertainty can be too low. The best indicator of financial stability is not past stability but moderate volatility in the recent past. In his 2015 book *Foolproof: Why Safety Can Be Dangerous and How Danger Makes Us Safe*, Greg Ip provides vivid examples from economics and finance as well as aviation and sports, making a strong case that too much safety can be dangerous and that some danger makes us safe. Forward guidance should aim at stabilizing uncertainty and risk premia within normal levels—not too low, not too high. This concern about stabilizing uncertainty around normal levels also applies to international capital flows. Hélène Rey (2014) documents the negative comovement between capital flows and credit growth on the one hand, and measures of uncertainty, such as the VIX, on the other. Abnormally low uncertainty leads to large capital inflows and rapid credit growth and vice versa.

How should the cyclical adjustment of forward guidance operate? Let's start from a recession. Especially if it is driven by financial crisis, recession leads to elevated levels of risk aversion and uncertainty, which can become very elevated if monetary policy is constrained by the EZLB and there are doubts about the ability of policies to restore growth.[19] In fact, a major drawback of the dynamic stochastic general equilibrium (DSGE) models used for policy analysis is that they assume that agents "know" that the economy will recover to the steady state after the shock. This assumption may be fair for a small shock, but it is not reasonable for a large, systemic shock with policies constrained by the EZLB.

Therefore, during crises and deep recessions, monetary policy should focus on reducing uncertainty, lowering risk aversion (the insurance channel of monetary policy), communicating a change in the reaction function that overcomes the restriction of the EZLB, and increasing confidence in a

---

19. According to the finance literature, time-varying risk premia are the main drivers of asset price changes (see, e.g., Cochrane 2012).

rebound to the steady state. In the context of the macro VaR, by reducing uncertainty, monetary policy can preclude an excessive reduction in leverage and contain its recessionary impact.[20] Narayana Kocherlakota and Jeremy Stein argue along similar lines, using a mean-variance approach.[21] They suggest that policymakers should care not only about the level of inflation and unemployment but also about their variability. Doing so requires the central bank to be as precise and detailed as possible about the expected path of rates. Explicit calendar guidance becomes a useful complement to state-contingent guidance at the peak of the crisis, especially when the central bank has high confidence in the need to keep the strong easing stance for at least two years, the standard forecasting horizon of central banks.

This insurance channel of monetary policy suggests the design of balance sheet policies in an open-ended, state-contingent fashion, combined if needed with threshold-based forward guidance that "insures" the delivery of economic outcomes. Threshold-based forward guidance has an advantage over pure calendar guidance in that it is asymmetric: It promises to keep the easy policy stance during bad times, but if data provide sufficient surprise to the upside, it will breach the thresholds and the policy will end (see Boneva, Harrison, and Waldron 2015).

In fact, all of the most successful strategies during the crisis were open-ended and contingent on achieving economic objectives. Beyond the insurance motive, there is an additional logic to it. When a central bank starts an easing cycle from a sufficiently positive interest rate, markets immediately price the whole easing cycle, based on experience and a notion of the neutral rate. In principle, central banks could cut rates as much as needed, so cutting rates was akin to an open ended program.

With balance sheet policies, there is no such guidance. Markets do not have enough history to calibrate the amount of easing they should be pricing. If, however, QE is open-ended and based on credible forward guidance about economic outcomes, markets can use that guidance to price those outcomes. An additional advantage of an open-ended strategy is that if the central bank provides calendar guidance and then has to extend it, there is a risk of losing

20. Caballero and Simsek (2017) model a similar dynamic, in economies where the output and risk gaps are joint phenomena that feed into each other, and where policy needs to address both gaps. In their models, an increase in volatility depresses Sharpe ratios, lowering asset prices and growth. Policies that reduce volatility help increase Sharpe ratios and stabilize asset prices and growth.

21. Narayana Kocherlakota, "Discussion of 2014 USMPF Report," presentation at the US Monetary Policy Forum, University of Chicago Booth School of Business, New York, February 28, 2014; Jeremy Stein, "Incorporating Financial Stability Considerations into a Monetary Policy Framework," speech at International Research Forum on Monetary Policy, Washington, March 21, 2014.

credibility along the way, as the public may wonder if the policy is just ineffective rather than insufficient. Therefore, if political imperatives force the central bank to use calendar, rather than open-ended state-contingent, guidance, it should err on the side of too much, not too little.

As the crisis and recession subside and the economy recovers, forward guidance should become less explicit. Risk aversion and leverage probably stabilize around normal levels, and the central bank reaction function likely returns to its steady-state formulation. Guidance should therefore be based on the macroeconomic forecast, the expected pace of hikes, and the neutral rate. There is no longer a need to be as detailed as before, which provides the central bank with more flexibility to respond to unexpected shocks and avoid being boxed in by an explicit rate path that becomes, de facto, calendar guidance (as has happened to the Fed with the dot plot).

The mixed experience of the Norges Bank, RBNZ, and Riksbank would advise against providing the explicit interest rate path after liftoff. Because the noise-to-signal ratio in central banks' interest rate forecasts is high, more transparency is not necessarily welfare improving. If a central bank clearly communicates its economic outlook and reaction function, there is no need to also communicate the interest rate path that delivers that outlook; doing so is redundant, as one is a function of the other. Furthermore, central banks do not communicate only with financial markets—they also communicate with firms and households. What firms want to know in order to hire and invest—and what households need to know in order to make their consumption and saving decisions—is not the precise path of interest rates but that the central bank is ready to do what it takes to deliver strong growth and stable inflation and that average interest rates over the next few years will not be too high. The travails of the Fed with the dot plot show that communicating an explicit interest rate path can create a tremendous amount of noise, with very little benefit.

As the cycle matures and inflation is at or above target, the central bank will be facing the unpredictability of the next recession. It should communicate its growth and inflation forecast, its assessment of the amount of slack, and the balance of risks, but there is little information in the explicit path of interest rates, beyond signaling the best estimate of the neutral rate. Recessions are impossible to predict, and central banks do not have superior information in this regard. They should therefore probably reduce the amount of forward guidance.

In addition, at the top of the cycle, forward guidance should be reduced on financial stability grounds. When the economic cycle is advanced, there is a possibility that uncertainty could be reduced to abnormally low levels. Reduced uncertainty reduces margin calls and haircuts for levered investors and fosters an increase in maturity mismatches, either by shortening the terms of debt financing or extending the horizons of investment projects (see the discussion in Brunnermeier and Pedersen 2009).

For example, the VIX was at record lows in 2006 and 2007, indicating very low expected volatility of asset prices. At that time the "measured pace" guidance of the FOMC was contributing to a high level of certainty about the expected path of rates. Certainty about the expected path of rates is a major determinant of carry trades, much more important than the level of interest rates. In the macro VaR framework presented above, the lower the uncertainty, the higher the leverage possible for a given level of VaR risk. Lower uncertainty leads to higher leverage.[22] Therefore, when the cycle is more advanced, and asset valuations are typically richer, the excessive provision of monetary policy insurance can increase financial stability risks. Monetary policy should be wary of offering one-way bets. Systemic crises happen when paradigms are broken; monetary policy should avoid reinforcing paradigms.[23]

Forward guidance is essentially akin to selling an option to the markets, an economic put; it is critical that this option be properly priced. As the cycle matures, the price of the option should increase, and the amount of forward guidance should diminish.

In summary, forward guidance should focus on describing the reaction function of monetary policy and be cyclically adjusted, varying the degree of explicitness as a function of the cyclical position of the economy and of risk aversion.

Communication: Stop Calling It Unconventional

Central banks entered the crisis hoping to return soon to standard interest rate policies, but they are going to spend the best part of a decade at the EZLB, and the odds are very high that the next downturn will arrive while interest rates are still low. At the same time, trust in central banks has declined. The share of respondents in polls who evaluated the job of the Fed as good or excellent fell from 53 percent in 2003 to 38 percent in 2014.[24] Forecasting mistakes have been large at times, low interest rates and

---

22. This relationship between volatility and leverage is a simple way to describe the "volatility paradox" of Brunnermeier and Sannikov (2014).

23. The crisis saw the smashing of three paradigms essential for asset pricing: house prices cannot decline, securitized assets are informationally insensitive, and repo has no counterparty risk (Ubide 2009). A fourth paradigm—there is no risk of the euro area breaking up—was broken later.

24. Jon Hilsenrath, "Years of Fed Missteps Fueled Disillusion With the Economy and Washington," *Wall Street Journal*, August 26, 2016, www.wsj.com/articles/years-of-fed-miss teps-fueled-disillusion-with-the-economy-and-washington-1472136026 (accessed on March 30, 2017).

asset purchases have been politically controversial, and central banks have increased their reach and power. As a result, their activities have become more salient, and the potential for a political backlash has increased.

Central banks need to step up their outreach to regain the confidence of the people. They can take several steps to enhance their communication.

First, central banks should change the language they use to communicate their policies. They must stop using the word *unconventional* to describe asset purchases, negative interest rates, or forward guidance—all of which are part of the arsenal of tools that the central bank must have at its disposal. Similarly, they should stop talking about *exit*. They should talk about adding or reducing accommodation, which describes a continuous process, not exit, which describes a discrete process. Central banks should stop using negative narratives to describe their policies. Doing so creates confusion and negative sentiment and fuels political opposition to these policies.

Second, central banks, especially the ECB, must explicitly stress that their inflation targets are symmetric. The ECB's "close but below" formulation is a handicap in the face of the need to increase inflation and inflation expectations, because it creates confusion among politicians, policymakers, and market participants. This lack of precision in its mandate is a key reason why the ECB has been persistently behind the curve. What is "close but below"? 1.5 percent? 1.9 percent? The answer makes an important difference at the time of recommending policies that could be politically costly in some countries.

Third, it is important to better prepare the public so that central banks can handle large shocks. The Fed's statement of monetary policy provides a good benchmark with its "balanced" approach to achieving its mandate. This balanced approach is the narrative expression of the lambda (the ratio of the expected reduction of the inflation gap versus the output gap) in the inflation forecast targeting literature (see the discussion in Qvigstad 2006 and Svensson 2010). The lambda need not be constant, but it should change depending on the relative size of the inflation versus output gap. The central bank may at times prioritize the reduction of one of the gaps and communicate it clearly. This time-varying nature of lambda reinforces the recommendation made earlier about the adoption of dual mandates. Decisions about the tradeoff between growth and inflation should be made explicit in order to enhance the transparency and credibility of monetary policy.

Fourth, central banks should increase their efforts at educating the public about the way they reach monetary policy decisions—for example, by making available the model they use for simulations and policy preparations. Making the FRB/US model available has enhanced the public's understanding of the tradeoffs involved in different interest rate paths. Other central banks should follow the Fed's example.

Central bank speeches that explicitly discuss this tradeoff could complement this step. Members of monetary policy committees should articulate their views around this tradeoff, explaining their outlook and what it implies for the near-term path of interest rates. It is important for markets to learn about the diversity of views inside the central bank, but the diversity needs to be well articulated. There is an inherent conflict between transparency and efficiency in deliberations: Too much transparency when addressing complex policies can lead to public confusion and a deterioration of trust (Faust 2016). However, in the current context of increasing mistrust of central banks, the approach should be better, not less, communication. A well-informed community watching the central bank is the best way to ensure an efficient transmission of monetary policy actions to the real economy and to counteract the political criticism that central banks have become too discretionary, powerful, and unaccountable.

Fifth, central banks should explain to the public that they need the widest possible arsenal of tools. Financial crises typically require central banks to adopt policies that are not politically popular, such as bailouts that involve public funds, or asset purchases that lower interest rates for savers. Unfortunately, legislation adopted after the crisis, such as the Dodd-Frank Act in the United States, has restricted the ability of the central bank to manage crises, leaving the economy more vulnerable as a result.[25] Central banks should explain that the policies they adopt may look unfair but are designed to maximize economic welfare. They should actively counteract the criticism that QE increases inequality, hurts pensioners, or saves banks at the expense of workers. While chair of the Fed, Ben Bernanke went on 60 Minutes, a popular TV program, to explain Fed policies. Mark Carney, the governor of the BoE, has done similarly in the United Kingdom. Central bankers need to earn the trust of citizens. They should not shy away from communicating with the public at large in simple language.

Institutional Design: Financial Stability as Part of Central Banking, Not Monetary Policy

Perhaps the most important transformation of central banking since the crisis has been the focus on macroprudential policies. The debate on whether monetary policy should "lean against the wind" and preemptively tighten monetary policy to avoid financial excesses or "clean up" after the bust of a financial bubble has not been resolved. Who should take care of financial stability?

---

25. The Dodd-Frank Act included reforms designed to limit the discretion available to the Fed, the FDIC, and the Treasury to act without congressional approval, reducing their ability to act as a lender of last resort, guarantee liabilities, and safely unwind failing firms.

Conceptually, monetary policy should address the residual macro risks that regulation, micro, and macro prudential policies do not or cannot address (assuming that the cost-benefit ratio of addressing that residual policy risk is positive; otherwise, the central bank should try to convince other policymakers to address it). But defining these residual risks is challenging. Assessing asset mispricing is complex; there is no reason why central banks should be better able to price than markets. In addition, because innovation and financial development are an integral part of economic growth, Type II errors are easy to make in bubble spotting. Macro measures of leverage, such as the credit-to-GDP ratio, have given plenty of false signals, and monetary policy is difficult to calibrate for such a slow-moving variable.[26] Regulation and macroprudential policies, including horizontal assessments and stress tests, not monetary policy, should be used to control leverage.

Price stability may not be sufficient to guarantee financial stability. The financial cycle and the business cycle can become out of sync, especially during periods of persistent structural change, and risks can emerge in the periods of disconnect between the two cycles. In the run-up to the global financial crisis, for example, imbalances were building up in the housing and financial sectors while inflation was low and stable.

The mandate of monetary policy should be to deliver maximum growth subject to price stability. It should not include addressing potential instability in financial markets (beyond changing the nature of forward guidance as a function of the cycle, as discussing above). Financial stability should be the remit of macroprudential policy. Such policy is not a panacea that will forever prevent financial crises—and it can introduce unforeseen distortions—but it is superior to burdening monetary policy with an additional objective for which it does not have an effective instrument.

Monetary policy cannot, and should not, be used to deal with financial instability in asset markets, for several reasons. First, price-stability and financial-stability objectives can at times lead to contradictory policy needs, and monetary policy should not abandon its publicly stated priorities. It would be highly controversial, for example, to engineer a mini-recession to cool down asset markets while inflation was in line with price stability or to refrain from boosting economic activity as needed to achieve the inflation target in order to guard against perceived financial excesses. As the recent Swedish experience shows (see the discussion below), the latter strategy could seriously endanger the price-stability mandate of the central bank and dent its credibility.

---

26. Stein, "Incorporating Financial Stability Considerations into a Monetary Policy Framework."

Second, it is unclear whether monetary policy, through its interest rate policy instrument, can effectively influence and target asset market prices. Capital asset price models (CAPMs) assess prices as a function of the discounted stream of future earnings, using the interest rate as the discount factor. But the empirical relationship between interest rates and asset prices is weak and unstable and, as Greenspan's famous "irrational exuberance" speech showed, verbal interventions have very limited, if any, effectiveness.

Third, monetary policy simultaneously affects all sectors of the economy. It is therefore a very rough and ineffective tool for coping with specific imbalances in the financial sector.

Fourth, it is essentially impossible to define an operational interest rate rule to deal with financial instability, given the very vague, imprecise, and often contradictory evidence on the effects of interest on asset prices and of asset prices on economic activity.

Finally, by independently addressing financial stability concerns, macroprudential policy provides monetary policy with additional input for its decision and room for maneuver to better focus on ensuring price stability, thus enhancing the welfare of the economy.

Add Macroprudential Policy to Central Banking

Macroprudential policy uses regulatory measures to deal with systemic financial risk, which may originate from three sources: (1) macroeconomic shocks, which can make the financial sector vulnerable; (2) contagion, which may stem from the default of a few financial institutions as a result of growing interconnectedness in the system; and (3) the development of endogenous financial imbalances associated with credit booms, excessive leverage, and risk taking by financial institutions. A systemic approach is critical, because sound capital and liquidity at the level of individual institutions, as monitored by microsupervision, does not guarantee the stability of the system as a whole, as the crisis showed. Systemic risk arises from the intrinsic excess procyclicality of the financial system and the complex interconnections across institutions.

In this context macroprudential policy has two main objectives: to enhance the resilience of the whole system and to smooth the financial cycle. The first challenge for macroprudential policy is to identify the variables policy should aim to lean against, in order to reduce excess procyclicality and interconnectedness. Standard variables include equity, the interest rate, and housing and credit markets as integral components of the financial cycle. The most important driver of the financial cycle is credit flows into real estate. The correlation between mortgage credit flows and house prices is strongly self-reinforcing (Favara and Imbs 2015).

Having the tools to address the link between credit and real estate is therefore critical to the success of macroprudential policy. The instruments should span the domain of lenders and borrowers and include most of the microsupervision instruments related to capital and liquidity when applied to the system as a whole, beyond the specific characteristics of individual exposures. They also extend to other categories, such as limits to loan-to-value ratios in housing credit, countercyclical capital buffers, global leverage ratios, and haircuts and margin requirements in securities transactions and clearing activities.

Acting on the lending side involves imposing conditions on banks and other lending institutions that enhance the resilience of the financial institutions either in case of losses (capital-based instruments) or in funding crises (liquidity-based instruments). These conditions include capital buffers, sectoral risk weights, loan-to-deposit ratios, and loan-to-core funding ratios. The Basel Committee on Banking Supervision (BCBS 2010) suggests that a 1 percentage point increase in capital requirements reduces the likelihood of a systemic crisis by 20–50 percent. Acting on the borrower side involves imposing restrictions on borrowers that limit their risk taking and reduce their probability of default and loss given default. These restrictions include, among others, loan-to-value ratios, loan-to-income ratios, and debt service-to-income ratios.

Both sets of instruments are necessary. There are several potential problems with using only lending-side instruments to smooth the financial cycle. First, capital-based measures tend to focus on building resilience and are hence applied in a static way (with the exception, of course, of the countercyclical buffer). Second, even if applied in a more dynamic fashion, such measures have only indirect and limited effects on the costs of loans and thus on mortgage lending growth, limiting their effectiveness in environments of optimistic expectations of house price appreciation. Thierry Tressel and Yuanyan Zhang (2016) find that, for the euro area, capital-based measures are effective in slowing credit growth and house price appreciation, with the main channel of transmission the cost of loans and banks' interest rate margins.

Third, it is not clear that lending-side instruments have any effect during asset price downturns. They are essentially ways to force banks to adopt more conservative valuations of their balance sheets during boom times, something that markets could agree on. It is very difficult to make a convincing case in favor of a more aggressive valuation during downturns and to convince markets of it. There is therefore a certain degree of asymmetry in lending-side instruments that could be very difficult to overcome.

Borrower-side instruments are generally more effective in curtailing excessive credit growth via lower bank leverage and weaker asset growth during booms (see Cerutti, Claessens, and Laeven 2015). Whenever possible, these indicators should be constructed as ratios to income, not prices, in order to prevent undesirable procyclicality. As the recent experience in the United States and Spain shows, during housing booms loan-to-value ratios likely underestimate the true amount of leverage. These indicators should be time varying, in order to be effective and avoid procyclicality. An alternative to varying the ratios over time would be to conduct borrower stress tests that incorporate interest rates, housing price, employment uncertainty, and the speed of repayment.

Borrower-side instruments should be applied based on activity (lending) rather than institutional characteristics (bank versus nonbank), in order to minimize leakage. Institution-based application can lead to leakage via cross-border activities of branches and cross-sector activity of nonbank lending activities. These leakages are likely to be dynamic: Financial markets will evolve as new regulations and policies are put in place. Monitoring of coverage therefore has to be continuous.

A strong case can thus be made in favor of a solid macroprudential policy framework. But who should be in charge of macroprudential policy? Monetary policy and macroprudential policy are very closely related. Monetary policy action and its transmission to the real economy via the financial sector determine the impact of monetary policy. Markus Brunnermeier and Yuliy Sannikov (2014) argue that in a world with financial frictions, central banking should follow a "bottleneck approach," constantly trying to identify the sectors that impair the transmission mechanism. This approach leads to an integrated view of monetary and macroprudential policies, as causality runs both ways. Forward guidance can affect risk taking and leverage. At the same time, tighter macroprudential policies create downward pressure on inflation. Coordination between monetary and macroprudential policies should therefore be close.[27]

The institutional setting is critical in this regard. The lack of response by the Swedish Financial Stability Authority to the repeated calls by the Riksbank to tighten macroprudential settings in the Swedish housing market led to the Riksbank's decision to use the flexibility embedded in its inflation-targeting mandate to tighten policy with the near-term objective of preventing overheating of the housing market and reduce longer-term recession and disinflationary risks. The result was too low inflation, which led the Riksbank to change strategy and ease policy aggressively, despite a still overheated housing market.

---

27. See the discussion on the interaction between monetary and macroprudential policies in Borio and Drehmann (2009); Agur and Demertzis (2010); and Angelini, Neri, and Panetta (2011).

The lack of a proper institutional setting for macroprudential policies in the United States is a major risk factor for the US economy. The euro area setting is more solid but still suboptimal, as many macroprudential policies are decided at the national level while monetary policy is set at the euro area level. National macroprudential policies can have spillovers for the entire euro area. For example, a refusal by, say, Germany to tighten macroprudential policies in its housing market could lead the ECB to have to adopt a suboptimal policy for the euro area.

The Financial Policy Committee (FPC) is close to an optimal institutional setting. It is part of the BoE, independent of the Monetary Policy Committee (MPC) but with some shared membership. The close cooperation in the BoE between the MPC and FPC was displayed during the period after the Brexit referendum. The easing package delivered by the BoE had elements of both monetary and macroprudential policy (e.g., the decision to reduce the countercyclical capital buffer for banks). The risk of housing macroprudential policies in the central bank is that financial crises could hurt its credibility and contaminate the credibility of monetary policy. But the benefits of better coordination and flow of information surpass these potential costs.

In summary, financial stability should not be the mandate of monetary policy, but it should be part of central banking. Because of the endogeneity between the two policies, macroprudential policy should be independent of monetary policy, but the central bank should closely coordinate both.

A Game Plan for the Future

Expansions do not die of old age. But the odds of a recession increase as the business cycle progresses. As the output gap closes, the odds of overheating—be it in the real economy, via goods and services inflation, or in the financial sector, via emergence of asset mispricings and, eventually, bubbles—increase.

A standard recession requires at least a 300 basis point cut in real interest rates. Given the secular downward trend in equilibrium real interest rates, current market pricing of future nominal interest rates, and inflationary trends, the probability that major central banks will have that room to cut real interest rates when the next recession hits is low. The package of structural changes for central banks and their monetary policy framework outlined in this chapter is based on the experience since 2007 and the lessons learned from it. It includes a process of opportunistic reflation toward a higher inflation target and the adoption of dual mandates; a willingness to use the full arsenal of tools at all times, combined with higher capital to protect against losses and free central banks from political interference; cyclically adjusted forward guidance to better manage risk taking; more effective communication to eliminate the stigma of asset purchases and forward guidance; and better integration of macroprudential policies in the institutional setting of central banks.

Some of these changes may prove to be politically impossible or may not be ready in time for the next recession. But there should be no doubt that they are badly needed. Some central banks are already putting some of these suggestions in practice, as the next chapter shows.

6

Conclusion: The Future Is Not What It Used to Be

When the facts change, I change my mind. What do you do, Sir?

—John Maynard Keynes

Before the crisis, economists believed that fiscal policy should not be used for business cycle stabilization; that central banks should focus on containing inflation, which monetary policy could always increase; that structural reforms were the key to higher potential growth. Experts thought that Japan's problems reflected Japan's mistakes, that the West would do better. A decade later, central bankers are screaming for help from fiscal policy, interest rates are at historical lows while inflation fails to increase, and public investment is seen as the last resort for boosting dwindling productivity growth.

Paraphrasing Keynes, the facts have changed, it is therefore time to change our mind. Perhaps it was all obvious and we did not want to see it, we were all looking under the lamppost rather than looking for the keys. A very large negative demand shock combined with zero interest rates puts the economy in a liquidity trap. Paul Krugman has been making this case since 1998 (Krugman 1998b, 1). Rereading his 1998 piece should be mandatory. In it he writes: "I believe that actual business cycles aren't always real business cycles, that some (most) recessions happen because of a shortfall in aggregate demand. I and most others have tended to assume that such shortfalls can be cured simply by printing more money. Yet Japan now has near-zero short-term interest rates, and the Bank of Japan has lately been expanding its balance sheet at the rate of about 50% per annum—and the economy is still slumping. What's going on?"

The distance between the precrisis intellectual and political consensus (described in chapter 2) and the consensus that is emerging from this long decade of postcrisis management is significant. Joseph Overton, a political scientist, developed a concept (known as the Overton window of discourse) to describe this process of evolving consensus. In his view, political ideas move along a scale of less to more political acceptability, from unthinkable to radical, then acceptable, sensible, and popular, before finally becoming policy. When ideas enter the range from acceptable to popular (the Overton window) they have a chance of becoming policies. Intellectuals, pundits, and politicians engage in a tug of war to push their ideas inside the window.

Since 2007 the Overton window of economic discourse has shifted materially. In 2010 policymakers were talking about how to manage the exit from zero interest rates and asset purchases, the potential implications of higher long-term interest rates, and the need for fiscal austerity. In her 2016 Jackson Hole speech, Fed chair Janet Yellen made clear that QE and strong forward guidance will be part of the toolkit of the Fed in the next recession.[1] She called for more research on increasing the inflation target. And, joining central bankers around the world, she called for more active fiscal policy. Figure 6.1, which shows the skyrocketing number of stories in Bloomberg containing the words *fiscal stimulus* since mid-2016, may say it all.

Unless something changes soon, the next easing cycle will start from very low levels of interest rates. Monetary policy will have to use its full arsenal of policy tools, and fiscal policy may have to take a leading role. In fact, we are already seeing the future, and it is not what it used to be, as three examples—the BoE's easing package following the Brexit vote, the resetting of Abenomics, and the market reaction to Trump's victory—show. Each corresponds to a different situation. The BoE eased to offset a negative shock on an otherwise healthy economy with well-anchored inflation expectations. Japan eased to push inflation expectations higher at a time when the BoJ may be running out of assets to buy. The United States faced a potentially significant change in economic policies, including a large fiscal expansion, at a time when the economy was approaching full employment but expectations for inflation and potential growth were languishing.

The Brexit Easing

The BoE's easing package following the Brexit vote applied most of the lessons from the crisis and conformed to most of the suggestions made in chapter 5 (BoE 2016). To achieve maximum impact, the BoE presented a package consisting of rate cuts, purchases of public and private assets, liquidity assistance, forward guidance, and macroprudential easing. It

---

1. Janet L. Yellen, "The Federal Reserve's Monetary Policy Toolkit: Past, Present, and Future," speech at the Designing Resilient Monetary Policy Frameworks for the Future symposium, sponsored by the Federal Reserve Bank of Kansas City, Jackson Hole, WY, August 26, 2016.

Figure 6.1   Number of news stories in Bloomberg containing words *fiscal stimulus* or *monetary stimulus*, 2004–17

number of stories per month

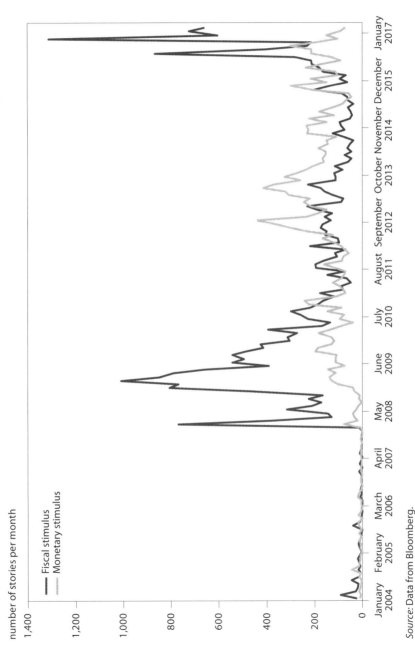

Source: Data from Bloomberg.

explained its decisions in detail not just to financial markets but also to households and companies.[2] It explicitly incorporated the potential impact of its decision on financial stability. And it explicitly designed the package to provide insurance on the economic outlook. Paraphrasing Andy Haldane, the BoE's chief economist, the BoE chose to run the risk of deploying a sledgehammer to crack the Brexit nut rather than taking a miniature rock hammer to tunnel its way out of prison.[3] The insurance channel of monetary policy was at play.

The BoE preemptively flushed the financial system with liquidity before the referendum. It could do so because the postcrisis liquidity facilities were already in place. Despite potential worries about the UK banking sector in case of Brexit, spreads in money markets remained stable. The BoE cut short-term rates and announced that it was likely to cut them further but explicitly stated that it would refrain from moving into negative territory. By doing so, it sought to avoid changing the market's reference point and triggering a race to pricing ever more negative rates, which could jeopardize the solvency of financial institutions. It launched the Term Funding Scheme, a package of long-term loans for banks, explicitly to mitigate the negative impact of lower rates on the financial sector. To increase the reduction in risk premia of private assets, it added corporate bonds to QE. To foster credit provision, it reduced the countercyclical capital buffer and excluded central bank reserves from the leverage ratio.

And, more importantly, it adopted a policy stance that projected an overshooting of the inflation target, thereby providing enough insurance to restore growth and keep inflation expectations well anchored. Because the economy was at full employment and inflation close to target, the BoE could not implement threshold-based forward guidance; it therefore could not implement QE in an open-ended manner. But it extended the initial duration of QE (six months versus the standard three months of previous QE programs) to compensate for it and announced its willingness to extend it as much as needed.

The easing package was very effective. By preemptively providing insurance, the BoE prevented financial sector instability and a potential increase in private savings that could have sunk the economy into a recession. The BoE understood well the paradox of risk. It took the right amount of risk and made the economy safer.

Ironically, the BoE has been the victim of its own success. Because it

2. Bank of England, "How Will Changes from the Bank of England Help You?" www.bankofengland.co.uk/publications/PublishingImages/crediteasing_large.jpg (accessed on April 4, 2017).

3. Andrew G. Haldane, "Whose Recovery?," speech at Port Talbot, Wales, June 30, 2016.

forecast a large downside risk, it adopted a very aggressive package. Because of the aggressive package, the downside risks have not materialized, and the BoE is being criticized for having made too gloomy a forecast. Of course, this criticism is mostly politically driven. It highlights how central banks have become an easy political target.

The Resetting of Abenomics

By mid-2016 it became clear that the BoJ was facing the limits of portfolio rebalancing. As its purchases of government bonds reached the limits of what the market was able to manage and as the cut to negative interest rates had broken the reference point for the bond market and opened the door to very negative bond yields, it became clear that the hoarding of safe assets at the long end of the yield curve was putting excessive downward pressure on long-term interest rates, flattening the curve to levels that jeopardized the long-run business model of the financial sector.

A rethink of the policy mix was in order—with *mix* the key word. Fiscal policy took the lead, with monetary policy playing a supporting role, focusing mostly on additional credit easing. In a first step, on July 29, 2016, the BoJ increased its purchases of equities and provided dollar liquidity to banks, so that they could continue to buy foreign assets. This dollar liquidity provision was possible in part because of the existence of the foreign exchange swaps among the main central banks—another important improvement in the monetary policy framework that emerged as a result of the crisis. A few days before the BoJ meeting, the Cabinet Office announced the size of a large, multiyear fiscal package. Its announcement allowed the BoJ to incorporate the fiscal stimulus into its forecast and to present its package as a coordinated action. The result was a soft version of helicopter money—a fiscal expansion supported by monetary policy.

The second step was the change in the BoJ monetary policy framework, in September 2016. This new framework had two parts: (1) a shift from quantity targeting back to interest rate targeting (called yield curve control), with an explicit targeting of both the overnight and the 10-year rate, and (2) a commitment to temporarily overshoot the inflation target. The commitment to overshoot the inflation target made the policy easing "permanent," creating a modern version of helicopter money—a fiscal expansion financed by a permanent monetary stimulus. "Permanent" is always relative. The way the fiscal expansion is financed is irrelevant. What matters is the commitment of the central bank not to reverse its monetary easing in the foreseeable future.

The new monetary policy framework of targeting the shape of the yield curve has worked well so far. The yield curve steepened as desired, alleviating pressure on the profitability of financial institutions (figure 6.2). In

Figure 6.2 Yield curve for Japanese government bonds, before and after the introduction of yield curve control

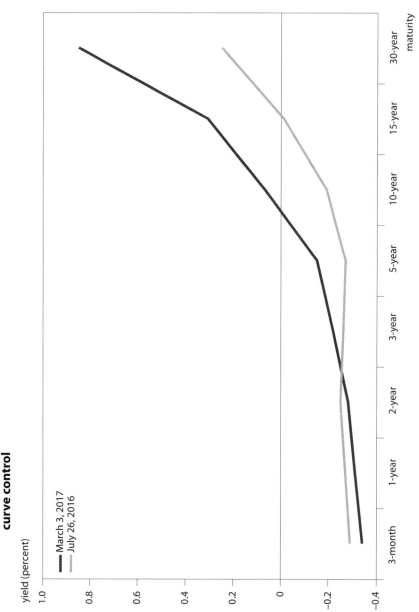

yield (percent)

—— March 3, 2017
····· July 26, 2016

3-month   1-year   2-year   3-year   5-year   10-year   15-year   30-year

maturity

Source: Bloomberg.

Table 6.1   Impact of 2016 US presidential election on asset prices

| | Basis points | | | | | Percent | |
Term	10-year nominal rate	10-year real rate	10-year inflation	2017 hikes	2017–18 hikes	DXY	SPX
1 day	20.2	9.0	11.2	4.5	13.5	0.7	1.1
1 week	36.4	24.3	12.1	12.0	34.5	2.4	1.9
1 month	55.2	28.7	26.6	18.5	43.0	3.3	5.0
3 months	48.2	23.5	24.7	23.0	46.5	2.5	7.2

Note: DXY is the US dollar index. SPX is the S&P 500 Index.

Source: Data from Bloomberg.

addition, the BoJ managed to keep the 10-year rate well anchored around the 0 percent target, even during the rapid increase in global rates in late 2016 that pushed US 10-year yields almost 100 basis points higher, without having to increase its purchases of Japanese government bonds. With inflation expectations increasing, the stability of 10-year nominal rates allowed Japanese long-term real rates to decline.

The Trump Surprise

The election of Donald Trump as president of the United States provides a perfect experiment to assess the impact of a change in the policy mix. The expectations under a Hillary Clinton presidency were of some more active use of fiscal policy, albeit very limited. As a result, long-term interest rates and inflation expectations, although they had rebounded from the post-Brexit lows, had remained low until election day.

The surprise victory of Donald Trump led to a sharp upward revision of the expectations for fiscal stimulus. Nominal long-term interest rates moved higher, with the impact distributed evenly between real interest rates and inflation breakevens (table 6.1). The shift reflected the expected increase in deficits, which increase real rates, and the reduction in the downside risks to inflation. Monetary policy was not going to be the only game in town. In fact, markets increased the pricing of rate hikes by almost 50 basis points over two years. The dollar appreciated, reflecting this new policy mix conducive to higher interest rates. The S&P Index rallied to new highs. Animal spirits had been unleashed.

The verdict was clear: More fiscal policy stimulus was welcome. However, even this expectation of fiscal stimulus was not enough for markets to price a return to precrisis normalcy. By early 2017 most interest rates remained near historical lows. US 10-year interest rates, though higher, were around 2.5 percent—still far from the precrisis range of 4–5 percent. Ten-year inflation breakevens, while higher, were still at about 2 percent, well below the precrisis range of 2.5 percent. There seems to have been some persistent damage to inflation expectations from the crisis. Market proxies for neutral interest rates, such as the 10-year rate 10-year forward, were at 2.95 percent, near historical lows. The term premium on 10-year interest was still about zero.

Fiscal Policy in the Lead

It would seem obvious that fiscal policy should always cooperate with monetary policy. A key reason why it is not obvious is that decades of economic research were based on a concept of optimal policy design for the stabilization of the business cycle that did not include fiscal policy. Welfare functions were defined and optimized as a function of interest rates; fiscal policy was thought of only as an instrument with which to correct distortions and imperfections of the steady state (see, e.g., the seminal work of Rotemberg and Woodford 1998). Combined with the assumption of full credibility of monetary policy, this framework made monetary policy the residual claimant of policy, the only game in town.

The last few years have shown that the days when the central bank announced its intentions—for example, a new inflation target—and markets fully and immediately believed them are over. Central banks are no longer fully credible, especially when rates are very low. At the EZLB fiscal policy must complement monetary policy, to take advantage of the higher multiplier of fiscal policy when interest rates are very low. In fact, it should go beyond that: At the EZLB, fiscal policy must be the leading policy. Governments must show the money.

At very low interest rates, a well-designed fiscal stimulus focused on measures that enhance potential growth would reduce the debt-to-GDP ratio. If it focuses on income support policies, as in the discussion in Japan on equal pay for equal jobs, it contributes to wage growth and can raise inflation expectations, and it reduces inequality. In addition, it lifts the neutral equilibrium interest rate, amplifying the expansionary impact of monetary policy (see Summers and DeLong 2014 and Ubide 2016). The government is better equipped than some parts of the private sector, such as households, to take on risk.

As interest rates reach very low levels, it is possible that the net impact of the income and substitution effect of even lower interest rates on consumption and saving decisions is no longer positive for consumption.[4]

---

4. The substitution effect implies that as interest rates decline, saving becomes relatively less attractive and households increase consumption. The income effect implies that as interest rates decline, the income from saving declines and consumers reduce their consumption.

If savers target a minimum amount of return on their savings—and do not feel confident to move into stocks because they cannot handle the risk of suffering principal losses—then, as interest rates decline to very low levels, they may just increase their saving to keep their interest income stable.

A new generation of models—known as heterogeneous agent new Keynesian models (HANKs)—put the emphasis on this potential prevalence of the income effect, driven by liquidity constraints and disparities in wealth holdings, among other factors. In these models the positive impact on demand from low interest rates must come from higher employment and wage growth; if the corporate sector is risk averse, the contribution of fiscal policy is required (see Kaplan, Moll, and Violante 2017). The question remains mostly an empirical one, to which it is too early to have a firm answer. It is a question that deserves further study.

At the EZLB the fiscal stimulus should last multiple years. The objective has to be to convince economic actors that there will be enough support for demand for an extended time so that they do not reduce their estimates of potential growth and depress consumption and investment today. Olivier Blanchard, Guido Lorenzoni, and Jean-Paul L'Huillier (2017) make a convincing case that pessimism about future potential growth has reduced growth by 0.5–1 percent a year since 2012. This negative effect could have been avoided by a multiyear public investment program that boosted potential growth—or at least offset the pessimism induced by the crisis. But a large public investment program will raise interest rates, critics will say. Yes, that is precisely the desired outcome. A combination of higher growth and higher interest rates is certainly preferable to the current combination of weak growth and low interest rates.

What if the economy fails to take off even with monetary and fiscal policy coordination and a commitment to higher inflation? Taken to the extreme, the central bank should try to minimize the debt overhang effect of fiscal policy on the economy. The debt overhang occurs because, fearful that higher taxes will be needed in the future to pay the government debt, economic agents invest less and save more today.

One way to solve this problem is to make the government debt "disappear" from a debt service standpoint. Central banks currently hold government bonds. Some plan to sell them, others plan to hold them to maturity. While they are on the balance sheet of the central bank, they are costless to the government, as the interest rate paid on them is earned by the central bank (net of the IOER) and returned to the government via remittances. Therefore one solution would be to announce that the central bank's holdings of bonds will always be rolled off as they mature.

A more permanent solution, which would generate a one-time reduction in the expected debt service flow, would be to swap the central bank bond holdings for very long-maturity zero-coupon government bonds. Such a move would make the debt service on those bond holdings "disappear" for a few generations, reducing to a very large extent the debt overhang effect. The central bank would see its income reduced, but that income would be compensated for, in part, by the increase in seigniorage revenues from stronger economic activity. This concept of a debt swap to make the debt "disappear" is similar to the debt relief package being offered to Greece (which includes, among other measures, an extension of maturities and payment grace periods) in the context of the 2017 program negotiations.[5]

It's All about Risk Management

All of these options entail risks. Markets could react badly to explicit monetary and fiscal policy coordination and volatility could increase. Inflation may indeed accelerate too much. Public investment may fail to increase potential growth. Politicians may want to interfere with central banks. Economic policymaking is always an exercise in decision making under uncertainty; there is always a tradeoff between risk and reward. It may not be a coincidence that Robert Rubin, the former Wall Street trader and US Treasury secretary, writes in his memoirs that his guiding principle is that "nothing in life is certain, and that consequently, all decisions are about probabilities" (Rubin 2004, x). The answer to the risk/reward tradeoff is not to avoid taking risks, but to take the right amount of risk.

Economic policymaking is an exercise in risk management. The main difference between a policymaker and a portfolio manager is the outcome of their analysis. Both have to assess the economic situation. The policymaker needs to decide what actions to take to change the outlook, taking into account the potential reaction of markets. The portfolio manager needs to decide what actions to take to profit from what he or she thinks the outlook will look like, taking into account the potential policy changes. Both cases involve uncertainty—about the analysis, about the impact of policies, about the behavior of markets. In both cases taking on the right amount of risk is key to success.

In order to manage risks, policymakers must recognize that they face the same behavioral biases that portfolio managers face when taking investment decisions. Such biases are pervasive. Policymakers suffered from the anchoring effect (overweighting the initial pieces of information) when they shifted toward fiscal austerity based mostly on the Greek case. They suffered from the endowment effect (aversion to change by overvaluing what one

---

5. Jeromin Zettelmeyer, "The Eurogroup on Greece: Debt Relief with a Fiscal Straitjacket," PIIE RealTime Economic Issues Watch blog, June 20, 2017.

owns) and loss aversion (holding on to losing positions for too long because of aversion to realizing the loss) when they stuck with the wrong policies for too long (e.g., the ECB's initial opposition to QE, the generalized reluctance by governments to engage in fiscal expansion, central banks' refusal to increase inflation targets). They suffered from overconfidence, by taking the stability of inflation expectations for granted. These biases cannot be eliminated, but recognizing them helps reduce their impact. Understanding better the consequences of not acting is as important as being mindful of the consequences of acting. As traders know well, improving processes—by, for example, conducting regular reviews of the inflation target that force an evaluation of the status quo, reduce the risk of inertia, and weaken the endowment effect—can help overcome some of these biases.

Central bankers are humans, who make many mistakes. They have been overconfident in their ability to restore growth and inflation. Taking on risk involves making mistakes and adopting decisions that may not be shared by all and that may generate winners and losers. But central banks are not the enemy. Governments and politicians have left them alone to fight the crisis and then put them under undue political pressure that has made them, at times, too risk averse. Given the environment, central banks have done a very good job.

All of the main central banks face a very difficult environment; they need all the support we can provide. The Fed is under political attack, it cannot buy private assets in case of need, and it has been deprived of some powerful crisis management tools. The BoE is under political attack from pro-Brexit politicians and is facing the large unknown of the impact of Brexit on the economic outlook. The ECB is under political attack in Germany and cannot rely on a fiscal authority to provide policy stimulus and support at short notice. Given Japan's demographic profile and its massive debt burden, the BoJ is engaged in what could probably be the last chance to restore price stability in Japan.

Central banks would not hesitate to trigger a recession to cool down an inflationary threat. They should show the same decisiveness in boosting a languishing economy and lifting dangerously low inflation. If monetary policy wants to be as effective as it should be, it should be firmly symmetric, politically savvy, and willing to take on all the necessary risks.

Appendices

Appendix A   Selected Policy Announcements by Major Central Banks

Table A.1   Important announcements by the Federal Reserve, 2008–15

Date	Program	Asset purchases/lending news	Interest rates/guidance news
November 25, 2008	QE1	Large-scale asset purchases (LSAPs) announced: Fed will purchase $100 billion in government-sponsored enterprise (GSE) debt and $500 billion in mortgage-backed securities.	
December 1, 2008	QE1	First suggestion via Federal Open Market Committee (FOMC) member public comments of extending quantitative easing (QE) to Treasuries.	
December 16, 2008	QE1	First suggestion by FOMC of extending QE to Treasuries.	Fed cuts fed funds rate from 1 percent to 0–0.25 percent; expects low rates "for some time."
January 28, 2009	QE1	Fed stands ready to expand QE and buy Treasuries.	
March 18, 2009	QE1	LSAPs expanded: Fed will purchase $300 billion in long-term Treasuries and an additional $750 in mortgage-backed securities and $100 billion in GSE debt.	Fed expects low rates for "an extended period."
August 12, 2009	QE1	LSAPs slowed: All purchases will finish by end of October, not mid-September.	
September 23, 2009	QE1	LSAPs slowed: Purchases of agency debt and mortgage-backed securities will finish by end of first quarter 2010.	
November 4, 2009	QE1	LSAPs downsized: Agency debt purchases will finish at $175 billion.	
August 10, 2010	QE1	Balance sheet maintained: Fed will reinvest principal payments from LSAPs in Treasuries.	
August 27, 2010	QE2	Fed chair Ben Bernanke suggests role for additional QE "should further action prove necessary."	
September 21, 2010	QE2	FOMC emphasizes low inflation, which is "likely to remain subdued for some time before rising to levels the Committee considers consistent with its mandate."	

(table continues)

Table A.1 Important announcements by the Federal Reserve, 2008–15 *(continued)*

Date	Program	Asset purchases/lending news	Interest rates/guidance news
October 12, 2010	QE2	FOMC members'"sense [is that additional] accommodation may be appropriate before long."	
October 15, 2010	QE2	Bernanke reiterates that Fed stands ready to further ease policy.	
November 3, 2010	QE2	QE2 announced: Fed will purchase $600 billion in Treasuries.	
June 22, 2011	QE2	QE2 finishes: Treasury purchases will wrap up at end of month, as scheduled; principal payments will continue to be reinvested.	
September 21, 2011	Maturity Extension Program	Maturity Extension Program (Operation Twist) announced: Fed will purchase $400 billion of Treasuries with remaining maturities of three years or less; mortgage-backed securities and agency debt principal payments will no longer be reinvested in Treasuries but instead in mortgage-backed securities.	
June 20, 2012	Maturity Extension Program	Maturity Extension Program extended: Fed will continue to purchase long-term securities and sell short-term securities through end of 2012. Purchases/sales will continue at current pace of about $45 billion a month.	
August 22, 2012	QE3	FOMC members "judged that additional monetary accommodation would likely be warranted fairly soon."	
September 13, 2012	QE3	QE3 announced: Fed will purchase $40 billion a month of mortgage-backed securities as long as "the outlook for the labor market does not improve substantially... in the context of price stability."	Fed expects low rates "at least through mid-2015."

Date	Program	Description
December 12, 2012	QE3	QE3 expanded: Fed will continue to purchase $45 billion of long-term Treasuries a month but will no longer sterilize purchases through sale of short-term Treasuries.	Fed expects low rates to be appropriate while unemployment is above 6.5 percent and inflation forecast is below 2.5 percent.
May 22, 2013	QE3	"If we see continued improvement, and we have confidence that that is going to be sustained, in the next few meetings we could take a step down in our pace of purchases."	
June 19, 2013	QE3	"Taper shock," as Bernanke says Fed could begin to reduce its $85 billion a month of bond purchases by end of year if economy continues to improve.	
September 18, 2013	QE3	"The Committee will…continue its purchases of Treasury and agency mortgage-backed securities and employ its other policy tools as appropriate, until the outlook for the labor market has improved substantially in a context of price stability."	Fed repeats that exceptionally low fed funds rate will continue "at least as long as" unemployment remains above 6.5 percent, inflation forecast one to two years out is below 2.5 percent, and longer-term expectations are "well anchored."
December 18, 2013	QE3	Tapering begins, reducing speed of asset purchases: Beginning in January, asset purchases will slow by $10 billion a month, split evenly between mortgage-backed securities and Treasuries.	
March 19, 2014	QE3		Fed ends use of thresholds, stating that "with the unemployment rate nearing 6.5 percent, the Committee has updated its forward guidance." Fed repeats that exceptionally low fed funds rate will continue, "especially" if projected inflation continues to run below target and longer-term expectations remain "well anchored."

(table continues)

Table A.1 Important announcements by the Federal Reserve, 2008–15 (continued)

Date	Program	Asset purchases/lending news	Interest rates/guidance news
April 30, 2014	QE3	Asset purchases slowed: "FOMC members noted that there had been little change in the economic outlook since the March meeting." Beginning in May Fed will add holdings of agency mortgage-backed securities at pace of $20 billion (rather than $25 billion) a month and add to its holdings of longer-term Treasury securities at pace of $25 billion (rather than $30 billion) a month.	
June 18, 2014	QE3	Asset purchases slowed. FOMC saw "sufficient underlying strength" in labor market conditions and return of inflation toward longer-term 2 percent objective and agreed on further reduction in pace of asset purchases. Beginning in July Fed will purchase mortgage-backed securities at pace of $15 billion (rather than $20 billion) a month and purchase Treasuries at $20 billion (rather than $25 billion) a month.	Fed reiterates that it would "likely be appropriate to maintain the current target range for the federal funds rate for a considerable time after the asset purchase program ends," especially if inflation stays below target.
July 30, 2014	QE3	Asset purchases slowed: Beginning in August Fed will purchase mortgage-backed securities at pace of $10 billion (rather than $15 billion) a month and purchase Treasuries at pace of $15 billion (rather than $20 billion) a month.	
September 17, 2014	QE3	Asset purchase slowed: Beginning in October Fed will purchase mortgage-backed securities at pace of $5 billion (rather than $10 billion) a month and purchase Treasuries at pace of $10 billion (rather than $15 billion) a month.	
October 29, 2014	QE3 ends	FOMC concludes asset purchases, citing "substantial improvement in the outlook for the labor market since the inception of its current asset purchase program."	Fed reaffirms previous forward guidance that current 0–0.25 percent target rate remains appropriate (rates on hold for a considerable time after Q3 ends).
December 16, 2015	Tightening begins		FOMC hikes rates 25 basis points.

Source: Federal Reserve.

Table A.2   Important announcements by the European Central Bank, 2008–16

Date	Program	Asset purchases/lending news	Interest rates/guidance news
March 28, 2008	Long-term refinancing operation (LTRO)	ECB announces six-month LTROs.	
July 3, 2008	Rate hike		ECB increases rates by 0.25 percent.
October 15, 2008	Fixed-rate full-allotment (FRFA) procedure	All refinancing operations conducted with fixed-rate tenders and full allotment; list of assets eligible as collateral in credit operations with ECB expanded to include lower-rated (with exception of asset-backed securities) and non-euro-denominated assets.	
May 7, 2009	Covered bond purchase program (CBPP)/LTRO	CBPP announced, LTRO expanded: ECB will purchase €60 billion in euro-denominated covered bonds; 12-month LTROs announced.	ECB lowers main refinancing rate by 0.25 percent to 1 percent and rate on marginal lending facility by 0.5 percent to 1.75 percent.
May 10, 2010	Securities Markets Program (SMP)	ECB will conduct interventions in euro area public and private debt securities markets; purchases will be sterilized.	
June 30, 2010	CBPP	CBPP purchases finished on schedule; bonds purchased will be held through maturity.	
April 7, 2011	Rate hike		ECB raises main refinancing rate for first time since 2008, by 0.25 percent to 1.25 percent.
July 7, 2011	Rate hike		ECB raises main refinancing rate by 0.25 percent to 1.5 percent.
October 6, 2011	CBPP2	CBPP2 announced: ECB will purchase €40 billion in euro-denominated covered bonds.	

(table continues)

Table A.2   Important announcements by the European Central Bank, 2008–16 (*continued*)

Date	Program	Asset purchases/lending news	Interest rates/guidance news
December 8, 2011	LTRO	LTRO expanded: 36-month LTROs announced; eligible collateral expanded.	ECB lowers main refinancing rate by 0.25 percent to 1 percent and rate on marginal lending facility by 0.25 percent to 1.75 percent.
July 5, 2012			ECB lowers main refinancing rate by 0.25 percent to 0.75 percent, a record low.
July 26, 2012		ECB president Mario Draghi gives "whatever it takes" speech.	
August 2, 2012	Outright monetary transactions (OMT)	Draghi indicates that ECB will expand sovereign debt purchases, proclaims that "the euro is irreversible."	
September 6, 2012	OMT	Countries that apply to European Stabilization Mechanism for aid and abide by its terms and conditions will be eligible to have their debt purchased by ECB in unlimited amounts on secondary market.	
May 2, 2013	Rate cut		ECB lowers main refinancing rate by 0.25 percent to record low of 0.5 percent.
July 4, 2013			ECB "expects the key ECB interest rates to remain at present or lower levels for an extended period of time."
November 7, 2013	Rate cut		ECB lowers main refinancing rate by 0.25 percent to record low of 0.25 percent.
February 13, 2014	Forward guidance		ECB "firmly reiterates its forward guidance: rates at present or lower levels for an extended period of time."

Date	Event	Description
June 5, 2014	Rate cut	ECB lowers main refinancing rate by 0.1 percent to 0.15 percent, interest rate on marginal lending facility by 35–40 basis points; deposit facility rate becomes negative (lowered by 0.1 percent to –0.10 percent.)
June 5, 2014	Targeted longer-term refinancing operations (TLTROs)	Initial announcement of TLTROs maturing in September 2018: "The TLTROs are designed to enhance the functioning of the monetary policy transmission mechanism by supporting bank lending to the real economy."
August 22, 2014	Jackson Hole speech	Draghi hints at QE and other unconventional measures, stating that the ECB will do more to halt falling inflation. "The Governing Council will acknowledge these developments and within its mandate will use all the available instruments needed to ensure price stability over the medium term."
September 4, 2014	Rate cut	ECB lowers main refinancing rate by 0.1 percent to 0.05 percent, interest rate on marginal lending facility by 0.1 percent to 0.3 percent, and deposit facility rate by 0.1 percent to 0.20 percent.
September 18, 2014	TLTRO	ECB allots €82.6 billion to 255 counterparties in first of eight TLTROs to be conducted between September 2014 and June 2016. "Will have a sizeable impact on the ECB's balance sheet."

(table continues)

Table A.2   Important announcements by the European Central Bank, 2008–16 *(continued)*

Date	Program	Asset purchases/lending news	Interest rates/guidance news
January 22, 2015	QE	ECB announces expanded asset purchase program that includes bonds issued by euro area central governments, agencies, and European institutions. Combined monthly asset purchases of €60 billion, carried out until at least September 2016.	
June 18, 2015	OMT	European Court of Justice finds that program falls within scope of ECB's mandate and includes sufficient safeguards to avoid monetary financing.	
December 3, 2015	QE/rate cut	ECB expands asset purchases to March 2017 and announces reinvestment of maturing bonds.	ECB lowers deposit rate to –0.3 percent
March 10, 2016	QE/rate cut	ECB increases monthly asset purchases from €60 billion to €80 billion and adds nonfinancial corporate bonds.	ECB lowers main refinancing rate to 0 and deposit rate to –0.4 percent. Rates "at present or lower levels for an extended period of time, and well past the horizon of our net asset purchases."
December 8, 2016	QE	ECB purchases extended from April to December 2017 at €60 billion a month. Purchases below deposit rate allowed, maturity range extended to 30 years.	

Source: European Central Bank.

Table A.3   Important announcements by the Bank of England, 2009–16

Date	Program	Asset purchases/lending news	Interest rates/guidance news
January 19, 2009	Asset purchase facility (APF)	APF established: BoE will purchase up to £50 billion of "high-quality private sector assets" financed by Treasury issuance.	
February 11, 2009	APF	BoE views slight downside risk to meeting inflation target, reiterates APF as potential policy instrument.	
March 5, 2009	APF	QE announced: BoE will purchase up to £75 billion in assets, now financed by reserve issuance; medium- and long-term gilts will constitute "majority" of new purchases.	BoE cuts policy rate from 1 percent to 0.5 percent; ECB cuts policy rate from 2 percent to 1.5 percent.
May 7, 2009	APF	QE expanded: BoE will purchase up to £125 billion in assets.	
August 6, 2009	APF	QE expanded: BoE will purchase up to £175 billion in assets. To accommodate increased size, it will expand purchases of gilts with remaining maturity of three years or more.	
November 5, 2009	APF	QE expanded: BoE will purchase up to £200 billion in assets.	
February 4, 2010	APF	QE maintained: BoE maintains stock of asset purchases financed by issuance of reserves at £200 billion; new purchases of private assets will be financed by Treasury issuance.	
October 6, 2011	APF	QE expanded: BoE will purchase up to £275 billion in assets financed by reserve issuance; ceiling on private assets held remains £50 billion.	

(table continues)

Table A.3 Important announcements by the Bank of England, 2009–16 *(continued)*

Date	Program	Asset purchases/lending news	Interest rates/guidance news
November 29, 2011	APF	Maximum private asset purchases reduced: HM Treasury lowers ceiling on APF private asset holdings from £50 billion to £10 billion.	
February 9, 2012	APF	QE expanded: BoE will purchase up to £325 billion in assets.	
July 5, 2012	APF	QE expanded: BoE will purchase up to £375 billion in assets.	
August 7, 2012	APF	Forward guidance provided: While unemployment rate remains above 7 percent, Monetary Policy Committee (MPC) stands ready to undertake further asset purchases until unemployment threshold reached; MPC intends not to reduce stock of asset purchases financed by issuance of central bank reserves. Consistent with that policy, it intends to reinvest cash flows associated with all maturing gilts held in APF.	MPC intends not to raise Bank Rate from current level of 0.5 percent until Labour Force Survey measure of unemployment falls to 7 percent.
August 7, 2013	Forward guidance		MPC maintains previous forward guidance on 7 percent unemployment rate threshold, subject to following conditions: consumer price index forecast does not exceed 2.5 percent, medium-term inflation expectations are sufficiently well anchored, and financial stability is not impaired.

| February 12, 2014 | Forward guidance | | "Despite the sharp fall in unemployment, there remains scope to absorb spare capacity further before raising the Bank Rate. When the Bank Rate does begin to rise, the appropriate path…is expected to be gradual. Even when the economy has returned to normal levels of capacity and inflation is close to target, the appropriate level of Bank Rate is likely to be materially below the 5 percent level set on average prior to the financial crisis." |
| August 4, 2016 | "Brexit easing" | BoE will purchase UK government bonds (£60 billion over six months) and UK corporate bonds (£10 billion over six months). New term funding scheme launched. | Bank Rate cut to 0.25 percent. |

Source: Bank of England.

Table A.4 Important announcements by the Bank of Japan, 2008–16

Date	Program	Asset purchases/lending news	Interest rates/guidance news
December 2, 2008	SFSOs (special funds–supplying operations)	Through end of April, BoJ will lend unlimited amount to banks at uncollateralized overnight call rate, collateralized by corporate debt.	
December 19, 2008	Outright purchases of Japanese government bonds and corporate finance instruments (CFI)	Outright purchases expanded: BoJ increases monthly purchases of Japanese government bonds (last increased in October 2002) from ¥1.2 trillion to ¥1.4 trillion; will also look into purchasing commercial paper.	BoJ lowers target for uncollateralized overnight call rate from 0.3 percent to 0.1 percent.
January 22, 2009	Outright CFI purchases	Outright purchases expanded: BoJ will purchase up to ¥3 trillion in commercial paper and asset-backed commercial paper and is investigating outright purchases of corporate bonds.	
February 19, 2009	Outright CFI purchases	Outright purchases expanded: BoJ will extend commercial paper purchases and SFSOs through end of September (previously end of March) and purchase up to ¥1 trillion in corporate bonds.	
March 18, 2009	Outright Japanese government bond purchases	Outright purchases expanded: BoJ increases monthly purchases of Japanese government bonds from ¥1.4 trillion to ¥1.8 trillion.	
July 15, 2009	Outright CFI purchases and SFSOs	Programs extended: BoJ extends SFSOs and outright purchases of corporate paper and bonds through end of year.	

October 30, 2009	Outright CFI purchases and SFSOs	Outright purchases of CFIs will expire at end of 2009 as expected, but SFSOs will be extended through first quarter of 2010. Ample liquidity provision past then will occur through funds-supplying operations against pooled collateral, which will accept a wider range of collateral.
December 1, 2009	Fixed-rate operations (FROs)	Facility announced: BoJ will offer ¥10 trillion in three-month loans against full menu of eligible collateral at uncollateralized overnight call rate.
March 17, 2010	FROs	Facility expanded: BoJ expands size of the FROs to ¥20 trillion.
May 21, 2010	Growth-supporting funding facility (GSFF)	BoJ will offer ¥3 trillion in one-year loans to private financial institutions with project proposals for "strengthening the foundations for economic growth."
August 30, 2010	FROs	Facility expanded: BoJ adds ¥10 trillion in six-month loans to FROs.
October 5, 2010	Comprehensive monetary easing (CME)	Asset purchase program (APP) established: BoJ will purchase ¥5 trillion in assets (¥3.5 trillion in Japanese government bonds and Treasury discount bills, ¥1 trillion in commercial paper and corporate bonds, and ¥0.5 trillion in ETFs and J-REITs). BoJ sets target for uncollateralized overnight call rate at about 0–0.1 percent. BoJ will "maintain virtually zero interest rates until it judges that price stability is in sight."

(table continues)

Table A.4 Important announcements by the Bank of Japan, 2008–16 *(continued)*

Date	Program	Asset purchases/lending news	Interest rates/guidance news
March 14, 2011	CME	APP expanded: BoJ will purchase additional ¥5 trillion in assets (¥0.5 trillion in Japanese government bonds, ¥1 trillion in Treasury discount bills, ¥1.5 trillion in commercial paper, ¥1.5 trillion in corporate bonds, ¥0.45 trillion in ETFs, and ¥0.05 trillion in J-REITs).	
June 14, 2011	GSFF	GSFF expanded: BoJ makes available another ¥0.5 trillion in loans to private financial institutions for purpose of investing in equity and extending asset-based loans.	
August 4, 2011	CME	BoJ will purchase ¥2 trillion in Japanese government bonds, ¥1.5 trillion in Treasury discount bills, ¥0.1 trillion in commercial paper, ¥0.9 trillion in corporate bonds, ¥0.5 trillion in ETFs, and ¥0.01 trillion in J-REITs; expands six-month collateralized loans through FROs by ¥5 trillion.	
October 27, 2011	CME	APP expanded: BoJ will purchase additional ¥5 trillion in Japanese government bonds.	
February 14, 2012	CME	APP expanded: BoJ will purchase additional ¥10 trillion in Japanese government bonds.	BoJ will "maintain virtually zero interest rates until it judges that its 1 percent inflation goal is in sight."
March 13, 2012	GSFF	GSFF expanded: BoJ makes available another ¥2 trillion in loans to private financial institutions, including ¥1 trillion in US dollar–denominated loans and ¥0.5 trillion in smaller-size (¥1 million–¥10 million) loans.	

Date	Type	Description
April 27, 2012	CME	APP expanded/FROs reduced: BoJ will purchase additional ¥10 trillion in Japanese government bonds, ¥0.2 trillion in ETFs, and ¥0.01 in J-REITs, and reduce availability of six-month FRO loans by ¥5 trillion.
July 12, 2012	CME	APP expanded/FROs reduced: BoJ will purchase additional ¥5 trillion in Treasury discount bills and reduce availability of FRO loans by ¥5 trillion.
September 19, 2012	CME	APP expanded: BoJ will purchase additional ¥5 trillion in Japanese government bonds and ¥5 trillion in Treasury discount bills.
October 30, 2012	CME/stimulating bank lending facility (SBLF)	APP expanded/SBLF announced: BoJ will purchase additional ¥5 trillion in Japanese government bonds, ¥5 trillion in Treasury discount bills, ¥0.1 trillion in commercial paper, ¥0.3 trillion in corporate bonds, ¥0.5 trillion in ETFs, and ¥0.01 trillion in J-REITs. Through SBLF it will fund up to 100 percent of depository institutions' net increase in lending to nonfinancial sector.
December 20, 2012	CME	BoJ will purchase additional ¥5 trillion in Japanese government bonds and ¥5 trillion in Treasury discount bills.
January 22, 2013	CME	BoJ will "maintain virtually zero interest rates until it judges that its 2 percent inflation goal is in sight."

(table continues)

Table A.4 Important announcements by the Bank of Japan, 2008–16 (continued)

Date	Program	Asset purchases/lending news	Interest rates/guidance news
April 4, 2013	Quantitative and qualitative monetary easing (QQE)	BoJ establishes price-stability target of 2 percent, adopts "monetary base control," and increases purchases of Japanese government bonds and extends their maturity (¥50 trillion annual increase in amount outstanding [¥7.5 trillion a month]; all maturities, including 40-year bonds, eligible). BoJ will expand monetary base at annual pace of about ¥60–¥70 trillion. Will purchase Japanese government bonds so that "amount outstanding will increase at an annual pace of about ¥50 trillion." Will purchase ETFs and J-REITs so that "amounts outstanding will increase at an annual pace of about ¥1 trillion and about ¥30 billion, respectively." Will continue to purchase commercial paper and corporate bonds until amounts reach ¥2.2 trillion and ¥3.2 trillion, respectively.	
October 31, 2014	QQE/asset purchases	BoJ increases Japanese government bond purchases to "approximately ¥8–¥12 trillion per month in principle," up from ¥6–¥8 trillion.	
November 19, 2014	QQE/asset purchases	BoJ increases annual monetary base by ¥80 trillion. Will purchase Japanese government bonds "so that their amount outstanding will increase at an annual pace of about ¥80 trillion." Will purchase ETFs and J-REITs "so that their amounts outstanding will increase at an annual pace of about ¥3 trillion and about ¥90 billion, respectively." Purchases of commercial paper and corporate bonds remain unchanged.	

Date	Policy	Description
November 21, 2015	GSFF	BoJ increases capacity of GSFF from ¥1 trillion to ¥2 trillion and increases maximum amount outstanding of its fund provisioning as a whole from ¥7 trillion to ¥10 trillion.
December 18, 2015	QQE/asset purchases	BoJ extends average maturity of Japanese government bond purchases to 7–12 years. Expands ETF purchases by ¥300 billion, with purchases of JPX-Nikkei 400 Index, and increases limit on J-REIT purchases from 5 percent to 10 percent of issuance.
January 29, 2016	QQE with negative interest rate	BoJ increases annual purchases of ETFs to ¥2.2 trillion and of J-REITs to ¥90 billion. Deposit rate cut to −0.1 percent.
September 21, 2016	QQE with yield curve control and inflation overshooting	BoJ will purchase Japanese government bonds so that 10-year rates remain about zero. Will increase purchases of ETFs to ¥6 trillion a year. BoJ will continue to expand monetary base until inflation exceeds 2 percent and stays above target in stable manner.

Source: Bank of Japan.

Table A.5   Important announcements by the Swiss National Bank, 2008–15

Date	Program	Asset purchases/lending news	Interest rates/guidance news
December 11, 2008			SNB lowers target range for three-month Libor by 50 basis points to 0–1.0 percent. "It will implement further measures should the situation so require."
March 12, 2009			SNB decides to "forcefully relax monetary conditions." Lowers target range for three-month Libor by 25 basis points, narrowing it to 0–0.75 percent. SNB "will use all means at its disposal to gradually bring the Libor down to the lower end of the new target range," at about 0.25 percent.
September 15, 2011	Exchange rate peg	SNB "will enforce the minimum exchange rate of CHF1.20 per euro set on September 6 with the utmost determination. It is prepared to buy foreign currency in unlimited quantities [to stem the] massive overvaluation of the CHF."	
December 18, 2014	Introduction of negative rates		SNB "is imposing an interest rate of –0.25 percent on sight deposit account balances at the SNB, with the aim of taking the three-month Libor into negative territory." Expands target range for three-month Libor to between –0.75 and 0.25 percent.
January 15, 2015	Rate cut and unpegging of the Swiss franc to the euro	SNB discontinues minimum exchange rate of CHF2.1 per euro.	SNB lowers target range for three-month Libor further into negative territory to between –1.25 and –0.25 percent, from current range of –0.75 to 0.25 percent. Interest rate on sight deposit account balances lowered by 0.5 percent to –0.75 percent.

Source: Swiss National Bank.

Appendix B   Impact of Quantitative Easing Announcements on Asset Prices

Figure B.1   Impact of quantitative easing announcements by Federal Reserve, Bank of England, European Central Bank, and Bank of Japan on two-year rates

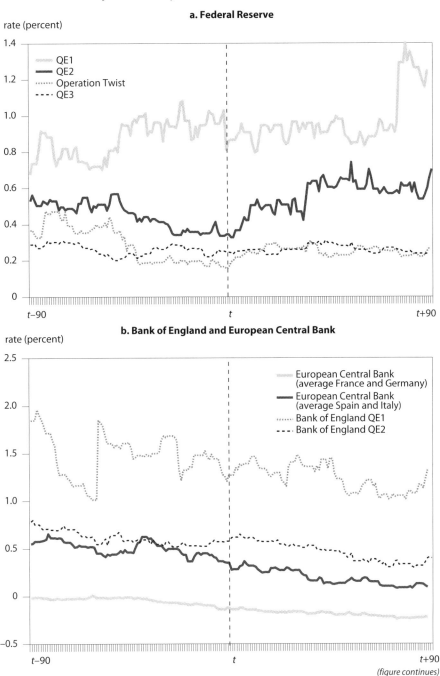

a. Federal Reserve

rate (percent)

QE1
QE2
Operation Twist
QE3

b. Bank of England and European Central Bank

rate (percent)

European Central Bank (average France and Germany)
European Central Bank (average Spain and Italy)
Bank of England QE1
Bank of England QE2

(figure continues)

**Figure B.1   Impact of quantitative easing announcements by Federal
Reserve, Bank of England, European Central Bank, and Bank
of Japan on two-year rates** *(continued)*

c. Bank of Japan

rate (percent)

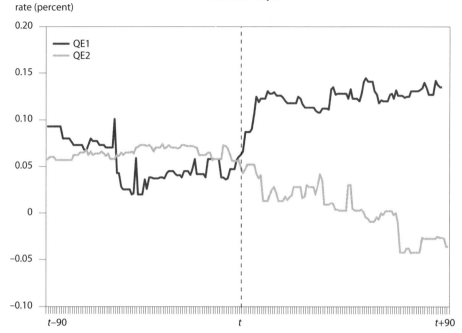

Source: Author's calculations.

Figure B.2 **Impact of quantitative easing announcements by Federal Reserve, Bank of England, European Central Bank, and Bank of Japan on 10-year nominal rates**

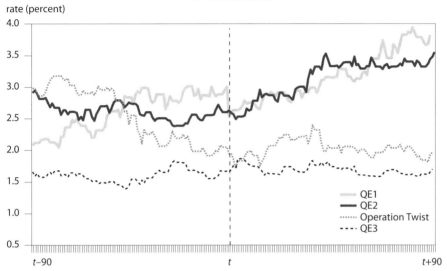

a. Federal Reserve

rate (percent)

Legend:
- QE1
- QE2
- Operation Twist
- QE3

t−90   *t*   *t*+90

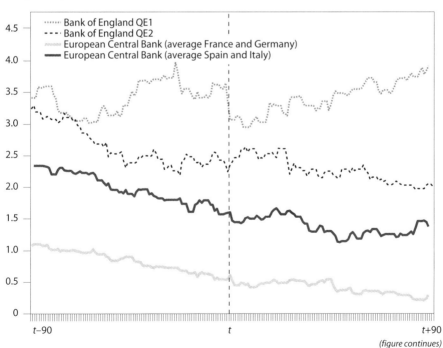

b. Bank of England and European Central Bank

rate (percent)

Legend:
- Bank of England QE1
- Bank of England QE2
- European Central Bank (average France and Germany)
- European Central Bank (average Spain and Italy)

t−90   *t*   *t*+90

(figure continues)

Figure B.2   Impact of quantitative easing announcements by Federal Reserve, Bank of England, European Central Bank, and Bank of Japan on 10-year nominal rates *(continued)*

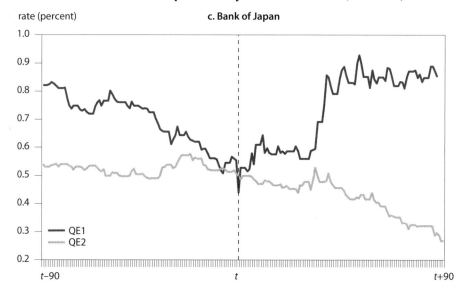

Source: Author's calculations.

Figure B.3   Impact of quantitative easing announcements by Federal Reserve, Bank of England, European Central Bank, and Bank of Japan on 10-year real rates

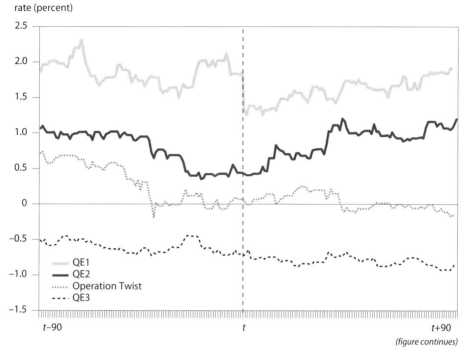

a. Federal Reserve

rate (percent)

QE1
QE2
Operation Twist
QE3

(figure continues)

Figure B.3   Impact of quantitative easing announcements by Federal Reserve, Bank of England, European Central Bank, and Bank of Japan on 10-year real rates *(continued)*

b. Bank of England and European Central Bank

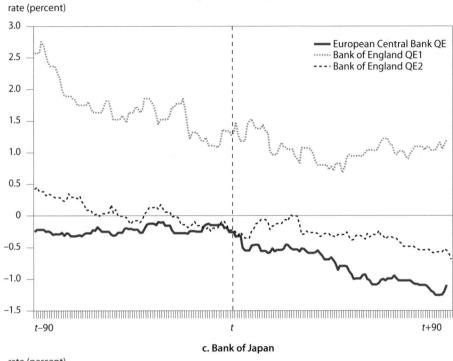

c. Bank of Japan

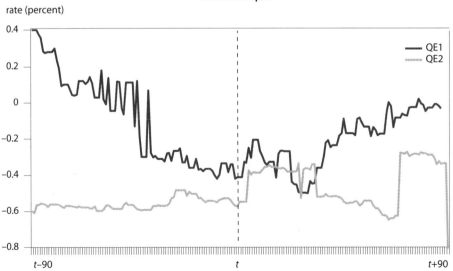

Source: Author's calculations.

Figure B.4   Impact of quantitative easing announcements by Federal Reserve, Bank of England, European Central Bank, and Bank of Japan on major stock indexes

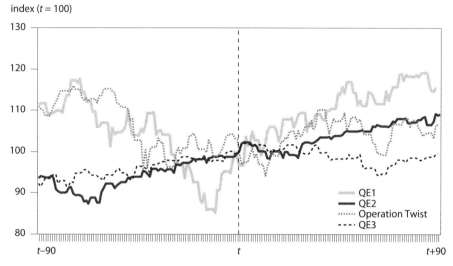

a. Federal Reserve

index (*t* = 100)

QE1
QE2
Operation Twist
QE3

t–90   *t*   *t*+90

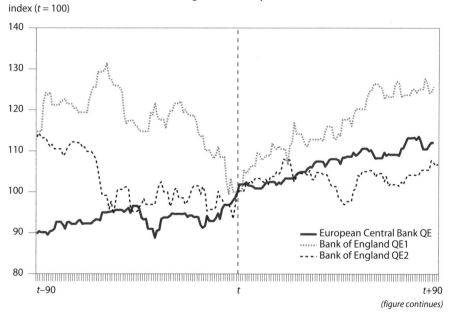

b. Bank of England and European Central Bank

index (*t* = 100)

European Central Bank QE
Bank of England QE1
Bank of England QE2

t–90   *t*   *t*+90

(figure continues)

Figure B.4   Impact of quantitative easing announcements by Federal Reserve, Bank of England, European Central Bank, and Bank of Japan on major stock indexes *(continued)*

c. Bank of Japan

index (*t* = 100)

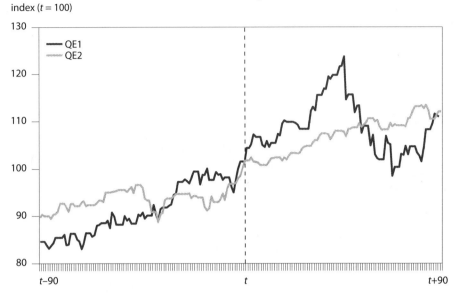

Source: Author's calculations.

Figure B.5   Impact of quantitative easing announcements by Federal Reserve, Bank of England, European Central Bank, and Bank of Japan on exchange rates

a. Federal Reserve

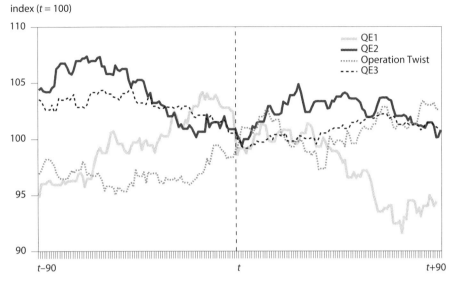

b. Bank of England and European Central Bank

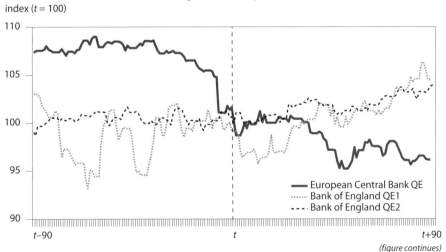

(figure continues)

**Figure B.5   Impact of quantitative easing announcements by Federal
Reserve, Bank of England, European Central Bank, and Bank
of Japan on exchange rates** *(continued)*

c. Bank of Japan

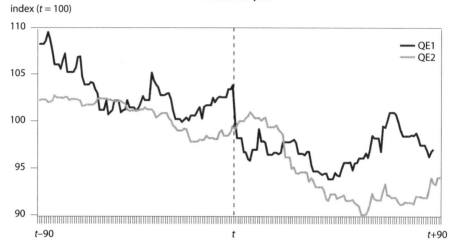

Source: Author's calculations.

Appendix C   Impact of Negative Rates on Asset Prices

Figure C.1   Impact of negative rates on two-year rates

interest rate (percent)

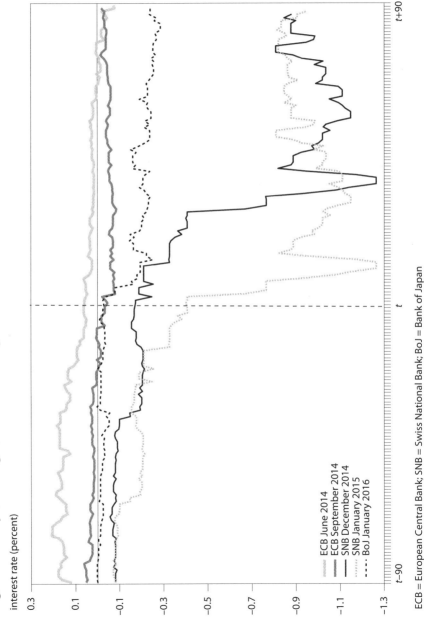

ECB = European Central Bank; SNB = Swiss National Bank; BoJ = Bank of Japan

Source: Author's calculations.

Figure C.2   Impact of negative rates on 10-year nominal rates

interest rate (percent)

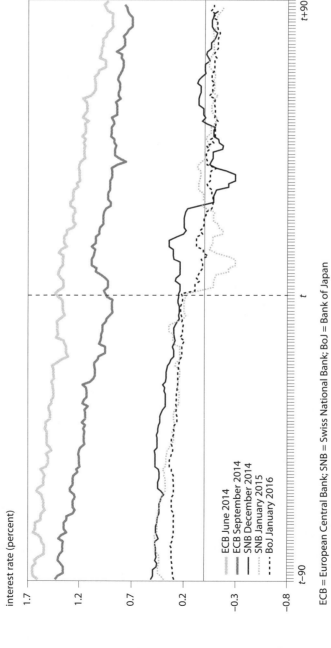

ECB = European Central Bank; SNB = Swiss National Bank; BoJ = Bank of Japan
Source: Author's calculations.

Figure C.3 Impact of negative rates on stock indexes

index (t = 100)

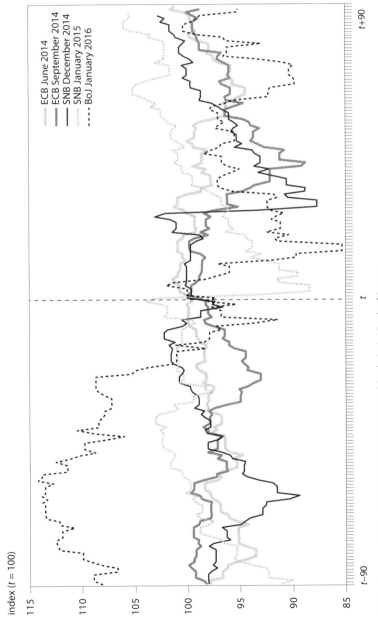

ECB = European Central Bank; SNB = Swiss National Bank; BoJ = Bank of Japan

Source: Author's calculations.

Figure C.4 Impact of negative rates on foreign exchange rates

index (*t* = 100)

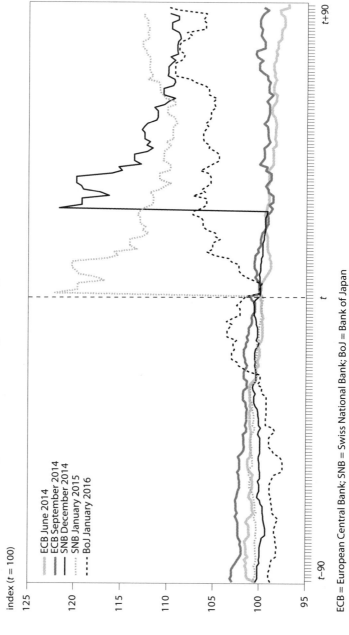

ECB = European Central Bank; SNB = Swiss National Bank; BoJ = Bank of Japan

Source: Author's calculations.

References

Acharya, Viral V., Tim Eisert, Christian Eufinger, and Christian Hirsch. 2015. *Whatever It Takes: The Real Effects of Unconventional Monetary Policy*. New York University. Available at http://pages.stern.nyu.edu/~sternfin/vacharya/public_html/pdfs/Acharya%20et%20al%20Whatever%20it%20takes.pdf.

Adrian, Tobias, Paolo Colla, and Hyun Song Shin. 2012. Which Financial Frictions? Parsing the Evidence from the Financial Crisis of 2007 to 2009. *NBER Macroeconomics Annual* 27: 159–214.

Adrian, Tobias, Richard K. Crump, and Emanuel Moench. 2013. Pricing the Term Structure with Linear Regressions. *Journal of Financial Economics* 110, no. 1 (October): 110–38.

Adrian, Tobias, Daniel Covitz, and Nellie Liang. 2014. *Financial Stability Monitoring*. Staff Report 601. New York: Federal Reserve Bank of New York.

Agur, Itai, and Maria Demertzis. 2010. *Monetary Policy and Excessive Bank Risk Taking*. DNB Working Paper 271. Amsterdam: Netherlands Central Bank.

Alesina, Alberto, and Roberto Perotti. 1997. Fiscal Adjustments in OECD Countries: Composition and Macroeconomic Effects. *IMF Economic Review* 44, no. 2 (June): 210–48.

Allen, Franklin, Charles Bean, and José De Gregorio. 2016. *Independent Review of BIS Research Final Report*. Basel: Bank for International Settlements.

Andrade, Philippe, Johannes Breckenfelder, Fiorella De Fiore, Peter Karadi, and Oreste Tristani. 2016. *The ECB's Asset Purchase Programme: An Early Assessment*. ECB Working Paper 1956. Frankfurt: European Central Bank.

Angelini, Paolo, Stefano Neri, and Fabio Panetta. 2011. *Monetary and Macroprudential Policies*. Temi di Discussione (Economic Working Paper) 801. Rome: Bank of Italy.

Armantier, Olivier, Giorgio Topa, Wilbert Van der Klaauw, and Basit Zafar. 2016. *An Overview of the Survey of Consumer Expectations*. Staff Report 791. New York: Federal Reserve Bank of New York.

Arslanalp, Serkan, and Dennis P. J. Botman. 2015. *Portfolio Rebalancing in Japan: Constraints and Implications for Quantitative Easing.* IMF Working Paper 15/186. Washington: International Monetary Fund.

Baily, Martin Neil, and Nicholas Montalbano. 2016. Why Is US Productivity Growth So Slow? Possible Explanations and Policy Responses. Paper presented at the joint Initiative on Business and Public Policy (*IBPP*)–Hutchins Center conference on the productivity slowdown, sponsored by the Brookings Institution, Washington, September 1.

Ball, Laurence. 2014. *The Case for a Long-Run Inflation Target of Four Percent.* IMF Working Paper 14/92. Washington: International Monetary Fund.

Ball, Laurence, Joseph Gagnon, Patrick Honohan, and Signe Krogstrup. 2016. *What Else Can Central Banks Do?* Geneva Reports on the World Economy. Geneva: International Center for Monetary and Banking Studies.

Bauer, Michael D., and Erin McCarthy. 2015. *Can We Rely on Market-Based Inflation Forecasts?* Economic Letter 2015-30. San Francisco: Federal Reserve Bank of San Francisco.

BCBS (Basel Committee on Banking Supervision). 2010. *An Assessment of the Long-Term Economic Impact of Stronger Capital and Liquidity Requirements.* August. Basel: Bank for International Settlements.

Bean, C. 1998. The New UK Monetary Arrangements: A View from the Literature. *Economic Journal* 108: 1795–809.

Bekaert, Geert, Marie Hoerova, and Marco Lo Duca. 2010. *Risk, Uncertainty and Monetary Policy.* NBER Working Paper 16397. Cambridge, MA: National Bureau of Economic Research.

Benhabib, Jess, Stephanie Schmitt-Grohé, and Martín Uribe. 2001. The Perils of Taylor Rules. *Journal of Economic Theory* 96, no. 1–2 (January): 40–69.

Berlin, Isaiah. 1953. *The Hedgehog and the Fox.* London: Weidenfeld and Nicolson.

Bernanke, Ben S. 2000. Japanese Monetary Policy: A Case of Self-Induced Paralysis? In *Japan's Financial Crisis and Its Parallels to US Experience, Special Report 13*, ed. Adam Posen and Ryoichi Mikitani. Washington: Institute for International Economics.

Bernanke, Ben S. 2015a. *The Courage to Act: A Memoir of a Crisis and Its Aftermath.* New York: W. W. Norton & Company.

Bernanke, Ben S. 2015b. Federal Reserve Policy in an International Context. Paper presented at the 16th Jacques Polak Annual Research Conference, hosted by the International Monetary Fund, Washington, November 5–6.

Bernanke, Ben S., and Mark Gertler. 1995. Inside the Black Box: The Credit Channel of Monetary Policy Transmission. *Journal of Economic Perspectives* 9, no. 4: 27–48.

Bernanke, Ben S., Vincent R. Reinhart, and Brian P. Sack. 2004. Monetary Policy Alternatives at the Zero Bound: An Empirical Assessment. *Brookings Papers on Economic Activity,* Economic Studies Program 35, no. 2: 1–100.

Bindseil, Ulrich, Andrés Manzanares, and Benedict Weller. 2004. *The Role of Central Bank Capital Revisited.* ECB Working Paper 392. Frankfurt: European Central Bank.

BIS (Bank for International Settlements). 2008. *Seventh Annual Report.* Basel.

Bivens, Josh. 2015. *Gauging the Impact of the Fed on Inequality during the Great Recession.* Hutchins Center on Monetary and Fiscal Policy Working Paper 12. Washington: Brookings Institution.

Blanchard, Olivier. 2016. *The US Phillips Curve: Back to the 60s?* PIIE Policy Brief 16-1. Washington: Peterson Institute for International Economics.

Blanchard, Olivier, and Jordi Galí. 2005. *Real Wage Rigidities and the New Keynesian Model*. NBER Working Paper 11806. Cambridge, MA: National Bureau of Economic Research.

Blanchard, Olivier J., Eugenio Cerutti, and Lawrence H. Summers. 2015. *Inflation and Activity—Two Explorations and Their Monetary Policy Implications*. Working Paper 070. Cambridge, MA: Harvard Kennedy School.

Blanchard, Olivier J., Giovanni Dell'Ariccia, and Paolo Mauro. 2010. *Rethinking Macroeconomic Policy*. IMF Staff Position Note 2010/03. Washington: International Monetary Fund.

Blanchard, Olivier, Guido Lorenzoni, and Jean-Paul L'Huillier. 2017. *Short-Run Effects of Lower Productivity Growth: A Twist on the Secular Stagnation Hypothesis*. NBER Working Paper 23160. Cambridge, MA: National Bureau of Economic Research.

Blyth, Mark. 2013. *Austerity: The History of a Dangerous Idea*. Oxford: Oxford University Press.

BoE (Bank of England). 2013. *Inflation Report* (August). Available at www.bankofengland.co.uk/publications/Documents/inflationreport/2013/ir13aug.pdf.

BoE (Bank of England). 2016. *Monetary Policy Summary* (August). London.

BoJ (Bank of Japan). 2015. Quantitative and Qualitative Monetary Easing: Assessment of Its Effects in the Two Years since Its Introduction. *Bank of Japan Review* 2015-E-3. Tokyo.

BoJ (Bank of Japan). 2016. *Comprehensive Assessment: Developments in Economic Activity and Prices as well as Policy Effects since the Introduction of Quantitative and Qualitative Monetary Easing (QQE)* (September 21). Tokyo.

BoJ (Bank of Japan). 2017. *Complementary Deposit Facility*. Tokyo. Available at www.boj.or.jp/en/mopo/measures/mkt_ope/oth_a/index.htm (accessed on March 27, 2017).

Boneva, Lena, Richard Harrison, and Matt Waldron. 2015. *Threshold-Based Forward Guidance: Hedging the Zero Bound*. Bank of England Working Paper 561. London: Bank of England.

Borio, Claudio. 2014. *Monetary Policy and Financial Stability: What Role in Prevention and Recovery?* BIS Working Paper 440. Basel: Bank for International Settlements.

Borio, Claudio, and Mathias Drehmann. 2009. Assessing the Risk of Banking Crises—Revisited. *BIS Quarterly Review* (March). Basel: Bank for International Settlements

Borio, Claudio, and Anna Zabai. 2016. *Unconventional Monetary Policies: A Re-appraisal*. BIS Working Paper 570. Basel: Bank for International Settlements.

Brunnermeier, Markus, and Yann Koby. 2017. The Reversal Interest Rate: The Effective Lower Bound of Monetary Policy. Princeton University.

Brunnermeier, Markus K., and Lasse Heje Pedersen. 2009. Market Liquidity and Funding Liquidity. *Review of Financial Studies* 22, no. 6: 2201–38.

Brunnermeier, Markus K., and Yuliy Sannikov. 2014. A Macroeconomic Model with a Financial Sector. *American Economic Review* 104, no. 2: 379–421.

Bullard, James. 2010. Quantitative Easing: Uncharted Waters for Monetary Policy. *The Regional Economist* (January). St. Louis: Federal Reserve Bank of St. Louis.

Caballero, Ricardo J. 2010. Macroeconomics after the Crisis: Time to Deal with the Pretense-of-Knowledge Syndrome. *Journal of Economic Perspectives* 24, no. 4 (Fall): 85–102.

Caballero, Ricardo J, and Emmanuel Farhi. 2017 (forthcoming). The Safety Trap. *Review of Economic Studies*. Available at https://scholar.harvard.edu/files/farhi/files/safety-trap011817_ef.pdf.

Caballero, Ricardo J., and Alp Simsek. 2017. *A Risk-centric Model of Demand Recessions and Macroprudential Policy*. NBER Working Paper 23614. Cambridge, MA: National Bureau of Economic Research. Available at www.nber.org/papers/w23614.

Campbell, Jeffrey R., Charles L. Evans, Jonas D. M. Fisher, and Alejandro Justiniano. 2012. Macroeconomic Effects of Federal Reserve Forward Guidance. *Brookings Papers on Economic Activity, Economic Studies Program* 44, no. 1: 1–79.

Carpenter, Seth, Jane E. Ihrig, Elizabeth C. Klee, Daniel W. Quinn, and Alexander H. Boote. 2013. *The Federal Reserve's Balance Sheet and Earnings: A Primer and Projection*. FEDS Working Paper 2013-01. Washington: Federal Reserve Board.

Cecchetti, Sara, Filippo Natoli, and Laura Sigalotti. 2015. *Tail Comovement in Option-implied Inflation Expectations as an Indicator of Anchoring*. Temi di Discussione (Working Paper) 1025 (July). Rome: Banca d'Italia.

Cerutti, Eugenio, Stijn Claessens, and Luc Laeven. 2015. *The Use and Effectiveness of Macroprudential Policies: New Evidence*. IMF Working Paper 15/61. Washington: International Monetary Fund.

Charbonneau, Karyne, and Lori Rennison. 2015. *Forward Guidance at the Effective Lower Bound: International Experience*. Bank of Canada Staff Discussion Paper 2015-15. Ottawa: Bank of Canada.

Christensen, Jens H. E., and Signe Krogstrup. 2016. *Transmission of Quantitative Easing: The Role of Central Bank Reserves*. Federal Reserve Bank of San Francisco Working Paper 2014-18. San Francisco: Federal Reserve Bank of San Francisco. Available at www.frbsf.org/economic-research/files/wp2014-18.pdf.

Christensen, Jens H. E., and Glenn D. Rudebusch. 2012. *The Response of Interest Rates to US and UK Quantitative Easing*. FRBSF Working Paper 2012-06. San Francisco: Federal Reserve Bank of San Francisco.

Chung, Hess, Jean-Philippe Laforte, David Reifschneider, and John C. Williams. 2011. *Have We Underestimated the Likelihood and Severity of Zero Lower Bound Events?* San Francisco: Federal Reserve Bank of San Francisco.

Cialdini, Robert. 2016. *Pre-Suasion: A Revolutionary Way to Influence and Persuade*. New York: Simon & Schuster.

Ciccarelli, Matteo, Angela Maddaloni, and José-Luis Peydró. 2010. *Trusting the Bankers: A New Look at the Credit Channel of Monetary Policie*s. ECB Working Paper 1228. Frankfurt: European Central Bank.

Cline, William R. 2015. *Estimates of Fundamental Equilibrium Exchange Rates, November 2015*. Policy Brief 15-20. Washington: Peterson Institute for International Economics.

Cochrane, John H. 2012. Continuous-Time Linear Models. *Foundations and Trends in Finance* 6, no. 3: 165–219.

Coibion, Olivier, Yuriy Gorodnichenko, Lorenz Kueng, and John Silvia. 2012. *Innocent Bystanders? Monetary Policy and Inequality in the US*. IMF Working Paper 12/199. Washington: International Monetary Fund.

Credit Suisse. 2016. *Japan Economic Adviser*. March 10. Washington.

Daly, Mary, Bart Hobijn, and Brian Lucking. 2012. *Why Has Wage Growth Stayed Strong?* FRBSF Economic Letter 2012-10. San Francisco: Federal Reserve Bank of San Francisco.

De Grauwe, Paul, and Yuemei Ji. 2016. *Inflation Targets and the Zero Lower Bound in a Behavioral Macroeconomic Model*. CEPR Discussion Paper 11320. Washington: Center for Economic and Policy Research.

De Grauwe, Paul, and Magdalena Polan. 2005. Is Inflation Always and Everywhere a Monetary Phenomenon? *Scandinavian Journal of Economics* 107, no. 2: 239–59.

Dell'Arricia, Giovanni, Luc Laeven, and Gustavo A. Suarez. 2016. Bank Leverage and Monetary Policy's Risk-Taking Channel: Evidence from the United States. *Journal of Finance* 72, no. 2: 613–54.

Del Negro, Marco, Domenico Giannone, Marc P. Giannoni, and Andrea Tambalotti. 2017. Safety, Liquidity, and the Natural Rate of Interest. Paper presented at the Brookings Papers on Economic Activity Conference, Washington, March 23.

DeLong, J. Bradford, and Lawrence H. Summers. 2012. Fiscal Policy in a Depressed Economy. *Brookings Papers on Economic Activity, Economic Studies Program* 44, no. 1 (Spring): 233–97.

De Rezende, Rafael B., David Kjellberg, and Oskar Tysklind. 2013. Effects of the Riksbank's Government Bond Purchases on Financial Prices. *Economic Commentaries*, October 16. Stockholm: Sveriges Riksbank.

Doepke, Matthias, Veronika Selezneva, and Martin Schneider. 2015. *Distributional Effects of Monetary Policy*. Hutchins Center on Monetary and Fiscal Policy Working Paper 14. Washington: Brookings Institution.

Duarte, Fernando, and Carlo Rosa. 2015. *The Equity Risk Premium: A Review of Models*. FRBNY Staff Report 714. New York: Federal Reserve Bank of New York.

ECB (European Central Bank). 2013a. *The ECB Survey of Professional Forecasters: 3rd Quarter of 2013*. Quarterly Report, July. Frankfurt.

ECB (European Central Bank). 2013b. *Monthly Bulletin*, July. Frankfurt.

ECB (European Central Bank). 2014. *Monthly Bulletin*, April. Frankfurt.

ECB (European Central Bank). 2016. *The ECB Survey of Professional Forecasters: 3rd Quarter of 2016*. Quarterly Report, July. Frankfurt.

Eggertsson, Gauti B., and Michael Woodford. 2003. The Zero Bound on Interest Rates and Optimal Monetary Policy. *Brookings Papers on Economic Activity*. Washington: Brookings Institution.

Engen, Eric M., Thomas Laubach, and David Reifschneider. 2015. *The Macroeconomic Effects of the Federal Reserve's Unconventional Monetary Policies*. FEDS Working Paper 2015-005. Washington: Federal Reserve Board.

English, William, David López-Salido, and Robert Tetlow. 2013. *The Federal Reserve's Framework for Monetary Policy: Recent Changes and New Questions*. FEDS Working Paper 2013-76. Washington: Federal Reserve Board.

Epley, Nicholas, and Thomas Gilovich. 2016. The Mechanics of Motivated Reasoning. *Journal of Economic Perspectives* 30, no. 3 (Summer): 133–40.

Evans, Charles, Jonas Fisher, Spencer Krane, and François Gourio. 2015. Risk Management for Monetary Policy Near the Zero Lower Bound. Paper presented at the Brookings Papers on Economic Activity Conference, Washington, March 19–20.

Fatás, Antonio, and Lawrence H. Summers. 2015. *The Permanent Effects of Fiscal Consolidations*. CEPR Discussion Paper DP10902. Washington: Center for Economic and Policy Research.

Faust, Jon. 2016. *Oh What a Tangled Web We Weave: Monetary Policy Transparency in Divisive Times.* Hutchins Center on Monetary and Fiscal Policy Working Paper 25. Washington: Brookings Institution.

Favara, Giovanni, and Jean M. Imbs. 2015. *Credit Supply and the Price of Housing.* CEPR Discussion Paper 8129. Washington: Center for Economic and Policy Research.

Fawcett, Nicholas, Lena Körber, Riccardo M Masolo, and Matt Waldron. 2015. *Evaluating UK Point and Density Forecasts from an Estimated DSGE Model: The Role of Off-Model Information over the Financial Crisis.* BoE Staff Working Paper 538. London: Bank of England.

Federal Reserve Board. 2007. *Meeting of the Federal Open Market Committee on September 18, 2007.* Washington.

Federal Reserve Board. 2012. *Statement on Longer-Run Goals and Monetary Policy Strategy* (January 24). Washington.

Federal Reserve Board. 2016a. *Statement on Longer-Run Goals and Monetary Policy Strategy* (January 26). Washington.

Federal Reserve Board. 2016b. *Supervisory Scenarios for Annual Stress Tests Required under the Dodd-Frank Act Stress Testing Rules and the Capital Plan Rule* (January 28). Washington.

Femia, Katherine, Steven Friedman, and Brian Sack. 2013. *The Effects of Policy Guidance on Perceptions of the Fed's Reaction Function.* FRBNY Staff Report 652. New York: Federal Reserve Bank of New York.

Filardo, Andrew, and Boris Hofmann. 2014. Forward Guidance at the Zero Lower Bound. *BIS Quarterly Review*, March. Basel: Bank for International Settlements.

Fischer, Stanley. 2016. Why Are Interest Rates So Low? Causes and Implications. Speech at the Economic Club of New York, October 17, New York, NY. Available at www.federalreserve.gov/newsevents/speech/fischer20161017a.htm.

Fratzscher, Marcel, Marco Lo Duca, and Roland Straub. 2014. ECB Unconventional Monetary Policy Actions: Market Impact, International Spillovers and Transmission Channels. Paper presented at the 15th Jacques Polak Annual Research Conference, hosted by the International Monetary Fund, Washington, November 13–14.

Friedman, Milton. 1963. *Inflation: Causes and Consequences.* New York: Asia Publishing House.

Friedman, Milton. 1965. A Program for Monetary Stability. In *Readings in Financial Institutions*, ed. Marshall D. Ketchum and Leon T. Kendall. Boston: Houghton Mifflin.

Friedman, M. 1969. The Optimum Quantity of Money. In *The Optimum Quantity of Money and Other Essays*, by in Milton Friedman. Chicago: Adline Publishing Company.

Fuhrer, Jeffrey C., and Brian F. Madigan. 1997. Monetary Policy When Interest Rates Are Bounded at Zero. *Review of Economics and Statistics* 79, no. 4: 573–85.

Gagnon, Etienne, Benjamin K. Johannsen, and J. David López-Salido. 2016. *Understanding the New Normal: The Role of Demographics.* FEDS Working Paper 2016-80. Washington: Federal Reserve Board.

Gagnon, Joseph E., Matthew Raskin, Julie Remache, and Brian P. Sack. 2011. Large-Scale Asset Purchases by the Federal Reserve: Did They Work? *FRBNY Economic Policy Review* (May): 41–59.

Gagnon, Joseph E., and Brian Sack. 2014. *Monetary Policy with Abundant Liquidity: A New Operating Framework for the Federal Reserve.* PIIE Policy Brief 14-4. Washington: Peterson Institute for International Economics.

Gardner, Dan, and Philip E. Tetlock. 2016. *Superforecasting: The Art and Science of Prediction*. New York: Broadway Books.

Geithner, Timothy. 2014. *Stress Test: Reflections on Financial Crises*. New York: Crown Publishers.

Gilchrist, Simon, David López-Salido, and Egon Zakrajsek. 2013. *Monetary Policy and Real Borrowing Costs at the Zero Lower Bound*. FEDS Working Paper 2014-03. Washington: Federal Reserve Board.

Glick, Reuven, and Sylvain Leduc. 2013. *Unconventional Monetary Policy and the Dollar*. FRBSF Economic Letter 2013-09. San Francisco: Federal Reserve Bank of San Francisco.

Goldman Sachs. 1997. New Tools for Forecasting Exchange Rates in Emerging Markets. *Economic Research*. New York.

Goodfriend, Mark. 2002. Interest on Reserves and Monetary Policy. *FRBNY Economic Policy Review* (May): 77–84.

Greenwood, Robin, and Samuel Hanson. 2013. Issuer Quality and the Credit Cycle. *Review of Financial Studies* 26, no. 6: 1483–525.

Greider, William. 1987. *Secrets of the Temple*. New York: Simon and Schuster.

Grisse, Christian, Signe Krogstrup, and Silvio Schumacher. 2017. *Lower Bound Beliefs and Long-Term Interest Rates*. IMF Working Paper 17/62. Washington: International Monetary Fund.

Gust, Christopher, Edward Herbst, David López-Salido, and Matthew Smith. 2017. The Empirical Implications of the Interest Rate Lower Bound. *American Economic Review* (forthcoming).

Haldane, Andrew G. 1997. Designing Inflation Targets. In *Monetary Policy and Inflation Targeting*, ed. Philip Lowe. Sydney: Reserve Bank of Australia.

Haldane, Andrew, Matt Roberts-Sklar, Tomasz Wieladek, and Chris Young. 2016. *QE: The Story So Far*. BoE Staff Working Paper 624. London: Bank of England.

Hall, Robert. 2013. The Routes into and out of the Zero Lower Bound. Paper presented at the Federal Reserve Bank of Kansas City Symposium, Jackson Hole, WY, August 23.

Hamilton, James D., Ethan S. Harris, Jan Hatzius, and Kenneth D. West. 2015. *The Equilibrium Real Funds Rate: Past, Present and Future*. NBER Working Paper 21476. Cambridge, MA: National Bureau of Economic Research.

Hancock, Diana, and Wayne Passmore. 2011. *Did the Federal Reserve's MBS Purchase Program Lower Mortgage Rates?* FEDS Working Paper 2011-01. Washington: Federal Reserve Board.

Hansen, Stephen, and Michael McMahon. 2016. *Shocking Language: Understanding the Macroeconomic Effects of Central Bank Communication*. CAMA Working Paper 4/2016. Canberra: Australian National University.

Hetzel, Robert. 2015. *Nominal GDP: Target or Benchmark?* Economic Brief 15-04. Richmond, VA: Federal Reserve Bank of Richmond.

Holston, Kathryn, Thomas Laubach, and John C. Williams. 2016. *Measuring the Natural Rate of Interest: International Trends and Determinants*. FRBSF Working Paper 2016-11. San Francisco: Federal Reserve Bank of San Francisco.

House, Christopher L., Christian Proebsting, and Linda Tesar. 2016. *Austerity in the Aftermath of the Great Recession*. NBER Working Paper 23147. Cambridge, MA: National Bureau of Economic Research.

Iida, Tomoyuki, Takeshi Kimura, and Nao Sudo. 2016. *Regulatory Reforms and the Dollar Funding of Global Banks: Evidence from the Impact of Monetary Policy Divergence*. Bank of Japan Working Paper 16-E-14. Tokyo: Bank of Japan.

Imakubo, Kei, Haruki Kojima, and Jouchi Nakajima. 2015. *The Natural Yield Curve: Its Concept and Measurement*. Bank of Japan Working Paper 15-E-5. Tokyo: Bank of Japan.

IMF (International Monetary Fund). 2011. *United States Spillover Report. 2011 Article IV Consultation*. IMF Country Report 11/203. Washington.

IMF (International Monetary Fund). 2013. *Unconventional Monetary Policies: Recent Experience and Prospects*. April. Washington.

IMF (International Monetary Fund). 2015a. Corporate Leverage in Emerging Markets—a Concern? In *Global Financial Stability Report: Vulnerabilities, Legacies, and Policy Challenges: Risks Rotating to Emerging Markets*. October. Washington.

IMF (International Monetary Fund). 2015b. Private Investment: What's the Holdup? In *World Economic Outlook: Uneven Growth. Short- and Long-Term Factors*. April. Washington.

IMF (International Monetary Fund). 2016a. Global Disinflation in an Era of Constrained Monetary Policy. In *World Economic Outlook: Subdued Demand. Symptoms and Remedies*. October. Washington.

IMF (International Monetary Fund). 2016b. *Japan: 2016 Article IV Consultation*. IMF Country Report 16/267. Washington.

IMF (International Monetary Fund). 2017. *Global Housing Watch*. Washington. Available at www.imf.org/external/research/housing (accessed on March 30, 2017).

Ip, Greg. 2015. *Foolproof: Why Safety Can Be Dangerous and How Danger Makes Us Safe*. Boston: Little, Brown and Company.

Ito, Takatoshi, and Frederic S. Mishkin. 2006. Two Decades of Japanese Monetary Policy and the Deflation Problem. In *Monetary Policy under Very Low Inflation in the Pacific Rim, NBER-EASE,* vol. 15, ed. Takatoshi Ito and Andrew K. Rose. Chicago: University of Chicago Press.

Ize, Alain. 2005. Capitalizing Central Banks: A Net Worth Approach. *IMF Economic Review* 52, no. 2: 289–310.

Jackson, Harriet. 2015. *The International Experience with Negative Interest Rates*. Staff Discussion Paper 2015-13. Ottawa: Bank of Canada.

Joyce, Michael, Matthew Tong, and Robert Woods. 2011. The United Kingdom's Quantitative Easing Policy: Design, Operation and Impact. *Bank of England Quarterly Bulletin* 51, no. 3: 200–12.

Joyce, Mike. 2013. The Bank of England's Unconventional Monetary Policies: Why, What and How. Paper presented at the European Central Bank Workshop on Non-standard Monetary Policy Measures, June 18.

Justiniano, Alejandro, and Giorgio E. Primiceri. 2010. Measuring the Equilibrium Real Interest Rate. *Economic Perspectives* 34, no. 1: 14–27.

Kahneman, Daniel. 2005. *Thinking, Fast and Slow*. New York: Farrar, Straus and Giroux.

Kamin, Steven, John Ammer, Michiel de Pooter, and Christopher Erceg. 2016. *International Spillovers of Monetary Policy*. IFDP Notes (February). Washington: Federal Reserve.

Kaplan, Greg, Benjamin Moll, and Giovanni L. Violante. 2017. *Monetary Policy According to HANK*. NBER Working Paper 21897. Cambridge, MA: National Bureau of Economic Research.

Kiley, Michael T. 2015. *What Can the Data Tell Us about the Equilibrium Real Interest Rate?* FEDS Working Paper 2015-077. Washington: Federal Reserve Board.

Kiley, Michael T., and John M. Roberts. 2017. Monetary Policy in a Low Interest Rate World. Paper presented at the Brookings Papers on Economic Activity Conference, Washington, March 23.

Kocherlakota, Narayana R. 2016. *Fragility of Purely Real Macroeconomic Models.* NBER Working Paper 21866. Cambridge, MA: National Bureau of Economic Research.

Kool, Clemens, and Daniel Thornton. 2012. *How Effective Is Central Bank Forward Guidance?* Working Paper 2012-063A. St. Louis: Federal Reserve Bank of St. Louis.

Kozlowski, Julian, Laura Veldkamp, and Venky Venkateswaran. 2015. *The Tail that Wags the Economy: Beliefs and Persistent Stagnation.* NBER Working Paper 21719. Cambridge, MA: National Bureau of Economic Research.

Krishnamurthy, Arvind, Stefan Nagel, and Annette Vissing-Jørgensen. 2014. ECB Policies Involving Government Bond Purchases: Impact and Channels. August 15. Available at faculty.haas.berkeley.edu/vissing/ECB%20paper.pdf.

Krishnamurthy, Arvind, and Annette Vissing-Jørgensen. 2011. The Effects of Quantitative Easing on Interest Rates. *Brookings Papers on Economic Activity, Economic Studies Program* 42, no. 2: 215–87.

Krugman, Paul. 1998a. It's Baaack: Japan's Slump and the Return of the Liquidity Trap. *Brookings Papers on Economic Activity, Economic Studies Program* 29, no. 2: 137–206.

Krugman, Paul. 1998b. *Japan's Trap.* Princeton, NJ: Princeton University. Available at www.princeton.edu/~pkrugman/japans_trap.pdf.

Krugman, Paul. 2000. Thinking about the Liquidity Trap. *Journal of the Japanese and International Economies* 14, no. 4: 221–37.

Kuhn, Thomas. 1962. *The Structure of Scientific Revolutions.* Chicago: University of Chicago Press.

Laubach, Thomas, and John C. Williams. 2003. Measuring the Natural Rate of Interest. *Review of Economics and Statistics* 85, no. 4: 1063–70.

Lo, Andrew W. 2017. *Adaptive Markets: Financial Evolution at the Speed of Thought.* Princeton, NJ: Princeton University Press.

López-Salido, David, Jeremy C. Stein, and Egon Zakrajsek. 2015. *Credit-Market Sentiment and the Business Cycle.* FEDS Working Paper 2015-028. Washington: Federal Reserve Board.

Łyziak, Tomasz, and Maritta Paloviita. 2016. *Anchoring of Inflation Expectations in the Euro Area: Recent Evidence Based on Survey Data.* ECB Working Paper 1945. Frankfurt: European Central Bank.

Mallaby, Sebastian. 2016. *The Man Who Knew: The Life and Times of Alan Greenspan.* New York: Penguin Press.

Mauro, Paolo, Rafael Romeu, Ariel Binder, and Asad Zaman. 2015. A Modern History of Fiscal Prudence and Profligacy. *Journal of Monetary Economics* 76, C: 55–70.

Michaelides, Alexander, and Athanasios Orphanides, eds. 2016. *The Cyprus Bail-in: Policy Lessons from the Cyprus Economic Crisis.* London: Imperial College Press.

Miles, David, Ugo Panizza, Ricardo Reis, and Ángel Ubide. 2017. *And Yet It Moves: Inflation and the Great Recession. Good Luck or Good Policies?* Geneva Reports on the World Economy. Geneva: International Center for Monetary and Banking Studies.

Modigliani, Franco, and Richard Sutch. 1966. Innovations in Interest Rate Policy. *American Economic Review* 56, no. 1/2: 178–97.

Monetary Policy Committee. 2009. *Minutes of the Monetary Policy Committee Meetings.* March 4 and 5. London: Bank of England.

Monetary Policy Committee. 2013. *Monetary Policy Trade-offs and Forward Guidance.* August. London: Bank of England.

Mussa, Michael. 2007. Global Economic Prospects 2007/2008: Moderately Slower Growth and Greater Uncertainty. Paper presented at the 12th semiannual meeting on Global Economic Prospects, Peterson Institute for International Economics, Washington, October 10.

Nakamura, Emi, Jon Steinsson, Patrick Sun, and Daniel Villar. 2016. *The Elusive Costs of Inflation: Price Dispersion during the U.S. Great Inflation.* NBER Working Paper 22505. Cambridge, MA: National Bureau of Economic Research.

Okina, Kunio, and Shigenori Shiratsuka. 2004. *Policy Duration Effect under Zero Interest Rates: An Application of Wavelet Analysis.* CESifo Working Paper 1138. Munich: CESifo Group Munich.

Orphanides, Athanasios, and Volker W. Wieland. 1998. *Price Stability and Monetary Policy Effectiveness When Nominal Interest Rates Are Bounded at Zero.* FEDS Working Paper 1998-35. Washington: Federal Reserve Board.

Orphanides, Athanasios, and David Wilcox. 2002. The Opportunistic Approach to Disinflation. *International Finance*, no. 5.

Orphanides, Athanasios, and John C. Williams. 2002. *Robust Monetary Policy Rules with Unknown Natural Rates.* FEDS Working Paper 2003-11. Washington: Federal Reserve Board.

Orphanides, Athanasios, and John C. Williams. 2006. Monetary Policy with Imperfect Knowledge. *Journal of the European Economic Association* 4, no. 2–3: 366–75.

Orphanides, Athanasios, and John C. Williams. 2007. Robust Monetary Policy with Imperfect Knowledge. *Journal of Monetary Economics* 54, no. 5: 1406–35.

Osborne, George. 2013. *Remit for the Monetary Policy Committee.* HM Treasury Letter, March 20. London: Bank of England.

Papaconstantinou, George. 2016. *Game Over: The Inside Story of the Greek Crisis.* Charleston, SC: CreateSpace Independent Publishing Platform.

Pescatori, Andrea, and Jarkko Turunen. 2015. *Lower for Longer: Neutral Rates in the United States.* Working Paper 15/135. Washington: International Monetary Fund.

Picault, Matthieu. 2015. The ECB Forward Guidance: Effects on Expected Interest Rates. October 30. Available at papers.ssrn.com/sol3/papers.cfm?abstract_id=2683281.

Qvigstad, Jan F. 2006. *When Does an Interest Rate Path "Look Good"? Criteria for an Appropriate Future Interest Rate Path.* Norges Bank Monetary Policy Working Paper 2006/05. Oslo: Norges Bank.

Rachel, Lukasz, and Thomas D. Smith. 2015. *Secular Drivers of the Global Real Interest Rate.* BoE Staff Working Paper 571. London: Bank of England.

Reifschneider, David. 2016. *Gauging the Ability of the FOMC to Respond to Future Recessions.* FEDS Working Paper 2016-068. Washington: Federal Reserve Board.

Reifschneider, David, and John C. Williams. 1999. Implications of the Zero Bound on Interest Rates for the Design of Monetary Policy Rules. Paper presented at the Computing in Economics and Finance conference, sponsored by the Society for Computational Economics.

Reifschneider, David, and John C. Williams. 2000. Three Lessons for Monetary Policy in a Low-Inflation Era. *Journal of Money, Credit and Banking* 32, no. 4: 936–66.

Reinhart, Vincent. 2004. Conducting Monetary Policy at Very Low Short-Term Interest Rates. Paper presented at the annual meeting of the American Economic Association, San Diego, January 3.

Reinhart, Carmen, and Kenneth Rogoff. 2009. *This Time Is Different*. Princeton: Princeton University Press.

Reis, Ricardo. 2016. *Can the Central Bank Alleviate Fiscal Burdens?* NBER Working Paper 23014. Cambridge, MA: National Bureau of Economic Research.

Reserve Bank of New Zealand. 2002. *Policy Targets Agreement for 2002*. Wellington.

Rey, Hélène. 2014. Capital Account Management. In *What Have We Learned? Macroeconomic Policy after the Crisis*, ed. George Akerlof, Olivier Blanchard, David Romer, and Joseph Stiglitz. Cambridge, MA: MIT Press.

Reza, Abeer, Eric Santor, and Lena Suchanek. 2015. *Quantitative Easing as a Policy Tool Under the Effective Lower Bound*. Bank of Canada Staff Discussion Paper 2015-14. Ottawa: Bank of Canada.

Robinson, Joan. 1966. *An Essay on Marxian Economics*. London: Palgrave Macmillan.

Rosa, Carlo, and Andrea Tambalotti. 2014. *How Unconventional Are Large-Scale Asset Purchases? The Impact of Monetary Policy on Asset Prices*. FRBNY Staff Report 560. New York: Federal Reserve Bank of New York.

Rose, Andrew K. 2017. Currency Wars? Unconventional Monetary Policy Does Not Stimulate Exports. January 3. Berkeley: University of California.

Rotemberg, Julio, and Michael Woodford. 1998. An Optimization-Based Econometric Framework for the Evaluation of Monetary Policy. *NBER Macroeconomics Annual* 12: 296–361.

Rubin, Robert. 2004. *In an Uncertain World: Tough Choices from Wall Street to Washington*. New York: Random House.

Rudebusch, Glenn D. 2009. *The Fed's Monetary Policy Response to the Current Crisis*. FRBSF Economic Letter 2009-17. San Francisco: Federal Reserve Bank of San Francisco.

Schobert, Franziska. 2008. Why Do Central Banks Make Losses? *Central Banking* 18, no. 3.

Shen, Pu. 2006. Liquidity Risk Premia and Breakeven Inflation Rates. *Economic Review, Federal Reserve Bank of Kansas City*, issue Q II: 29–54.

Soros, George. 1987. *The Alchemy of Finance*. Hoboken, NJ: Wiley.

Stella, Peter. 1997. *Do Central Banks Need Capital?* IMF Working Paper 97/83. Washington: International Monetary Fund.

Stella, Peter, and Åke Lönnberg 2008. *Issues in Central Bank Finance and Independence*. IMF Working Paper 08/37. Washington : International Monetary Fund.

Summers, Lawrence, and Bradford DeLong. 2014. *Fiscal Policy in a Depressed Economy*. Brookings Papers on Economic Activity (Spring). Washington: Brookings Institution.

Svensson, Lars. 2010. *Inflation Targeting*. NBER Working Paper 16654. Cambridge, MA: National Bureau of Economic Research.

Svensson, Lars E. O. 2014. Inflation Targeting and "Leaning against the Wind." *International Journal of Central Banking* 10, no. 2: 103–14.

Svensson, Lars E. O. 2015. *Forward Guidance*. CEPR Discussion Paper 10669. Washington: Center for Economic and Policy Research.

Swanson, Eric T., and John C. Williams. 2013. *Measuring the Effect of the Zero Lower Bound on Medium- and Longer-Term Interest Rates*. FRBSF Working Paper 2012-02. San Francisco: Federal Reserve Bank of San Francisco.

Taylor, John B. 1993. Discretion versus Policy Rules in Practice. *Carnegie-Rochester Conference Series on Public Policy* 39, no. 1: 195–214.

Taylor, John. 1999. A Historical Analysis of Monetary Policy Rules. In *Monetary Policy Rules*, ed. John Taylor. Chicago: University of Chicago Press.

Thorton, David. 2011. Monetary Policy at the Zero Bound. *Economic Synopses*. St. Louis: Federal Reserve Bank of St. Louis.

Tobin, James. 1969. Money and Income: Post Hoc Ergo Propter Hoc? *Quarterly Journal of Economics* 84, no. 2: 301–17.

Tobin, James, and William C. Brainard. 1962. *Financial Intermediaries and the Effectiveness of Monetary Controls*. Cowles Foundation Discussion Paper 159. New Haven, CT: Yale University.

Tressel, Thierry, and Yuanyan Sophia Zhang. 2016. *Effectiveness and Channels of Macroprudential Instruments*. Working Paper 16/4. Washington: International Monetary Fund.

Turner, Adair. 2015. The Case for Monetary Finance—An Essentially Political Issue. Paper presented at the 16th Jacques Polak Annual Research Conference, sponsored by the International Monetary Fund, Washington, November 5.

Ubide, Ángel. 2008. Anatomy of a Modern Credit Crisis. *Financial Stability Review* 14. Madrid: Bank of Spain.

Ubide, Ángel. 2009. Paradigm Lost. In *No Way Out: Persistent Government Interventions in the Great Contraction*, ed. Vincent Reinhart. Washington: American Enterprise Institute.

Ubide, Ángel. 2014. *Is the ECB Failing Its Price Stability Mandate?* PIIE Policy Brief 14-5. Washington: Peterson Institute for International Economics.

Ubide, Ángel. 2015a. *Sovereign Bond Purchases and Risk-Sharing Arrangements: Implications for Euro-Area Monetary Policy*. European Parliament Committee on Economic and Monetary Affairs. Brussels: European Parliament.

Ubide, Ángel. 2015b. *Stability Bonds for the Euro Area*. PIIE Policy Brief 15-19. Washington: Peterson Institute for International Economics.

Ubide, Ángel. 2016. The Case for an Active Fiscal Policy in the Developed World. *Business Economics* 51, no. 3: 158–60.

Ugai, Hiroshi. 2007. Effects of the Quantitative Easing Policy: A Survey of Empirical Analyses. *Monetary and Economic Studies* 25, no. 1: 1–48.

Vayanos, Dimitri, and Jean-Luc Vila. 2009. *A Preferred-Habitat Model of the Term Structure of Interest Rates*. NBER Working Paper 15487. Cambridge, MA: National Bureau of Economic Research.

Viñals, José. 2001. *Monetary Policy Issues in a Low Inflation Environment*. Bank of Spain Working Paper 0107. Madrid: Bank of Spain.

Weale, Martin, and Tomasz Wieladek. 2015. *What Are the Macroeconomic Effects of Asset Purchases?* CEPR Discussion Paper 10495. Washington: Center for Economic and Policy Research.

Wheelock, David C. 2002. Conducting Monetary Policy without Government Debt: The Fed's Early Years. *Federal Reserve Bank of St. Louis Review* 84, no. 3: 1–14.

Wicksell, Knut. 1936. *Interest and Prices.* London: Macmillan.

Williams, John C. 2016. Monetary Policy in a Low R-Star World. *FRBSF Economic Letter 2016-23.* San Francisco: Federal Reserve Bank of San Francisco.

Winters, Bill. 2012. Review of the Bank of England's Framework for Providing Liquidity to the Banking System. Paper presented to the Court of the Bank of England, October.

Woodford, Michael. 2003. *Interest and Prices: Foundations of a Theory of Monetary Policy.* Princeton, NJ: Princeton University Press.

Woodford, Michael. 2005. Central Bank Communication and Policy Effectiveness. *Proceedings of the Economic Policy Symposium held in Jackson Hole, WY,* 399–474.

Woodford, Michael. 2012. Methods of Monetary Policy Accommodation at the Interest Rate Lower Bound. Paper presented at the Changing Policy Landscape Symposium, sponsored by Federal Reserve Bank of Kansas City, Jackson Hole, WY, September 16.

Wu, Jing Cynthia, and Fan Dora Xia. 2016. Measuring the Macroeconomic Impact of Monetary Policy at the Zero Lower Bound. *Journal of Money, Credit and Banking* 48, no. 2–3: 254–91.

Wyplosz, Charles. 2001. *Do We Know How Low Inflation Should Be?* CEPR Discussion Paper 2722. Washington: Center for Economic and Policy Research.

Yamaguchi, Katsunari. 2013. Estimating Time-Varying Equity Risk Premium: The Japanese Stock Market 1980–2012. Paper presented to the Northfield Asia Research Seminar, Hong Kong, November 19.

Index

bonds
    cumulative flows, 176, 177*f*
    decline in income stream, 179–80
    with negative yields, market value, 2*f*
borrower-side instruments, 220–21
Brazil, 124
Brexit referendum, 115, 222, 226–29
Bridgewater, 38
Broadbent, Ben, 143, 209
Brunnermeier, Markus, 221
Bullard, James, 210
bund yields, two-year, 199*f*
Bundesbank, 181
    in 2007–08, 110
Burns, Arthur, 10

calendar guidance, by Fed, 84
Campbell, Jeffrey R., 114
Canada
    housing prices, 172
    unweighted average yield, 131
capital asset price models (CAPMs), 219
capital flows, redirection into emerging
    markets, 122
capital, raising to protect central banks
    from loss, 204–06
Carney, Mark, 111, 217
Carpenter, Seth, 204
causality, 7
central banks, 4, 6
    actions during crisis, 52–69
    asset purchase limits, 202–04
    balance sheets, 16
        and inflation, 163
    blame, 9–10
    capital, 204–05
    communication, 16, 214, 215–17
        of policy, 87–88
    conservative policies, 89
    and deflation risk, 24
    dual mandates, 15–16
        for protecting against hysteresis,
        194–96
    financial stability committees, 167
    focus on forward guidance, 210
    foreign exchange swaps, 79–81
    goals, 44–48, 189–97
    government bonds held by, 233
    independence and credibility, 10

independence to reduce inflation, 21
institutional design, 217–22
interest rates, 48
    cuts in recession, 143
    forecasts, noise-to-signal ratio, 214
    low, 188
    negative, 2008–16, 73*f*
    short-term reference, 70
on lenders of last resort, 69
liquidity from, 30
macroprudential policy, 219–22
net worth, 205
opportunistic reflation, 15, 196–97
policy framework components, 43–44
and price level-targeting framework, 157
public education efforts, 216–17
raising capital to protect from losses,
    204–06
recapitalization arrangements, 206
reduced confidence, 8
reference point change by, 117
selected policy announcements, 239–56*t*
tools, 197–206
transparency in, 87
Cerutti, Eugenio, 194
change, costs of, 191
Chung, Hess, 100
Cialdini, Robert, *Pre-suasion: A Revolutionary
    Way to Influence and Persuade*, 7
Clinton, Hillary, 231
commercial real estate prices, 171
    vs. residential, 183
commodity prices, 145
    decline, 156
competitiveness, European obsession with,
    26–28
Complementary Deposit Facility, 72
Comprehensive Monetary Easing (CME)
    program, of Bank of Japan, 63
Congressional Budget Office, 137
consensus model of thought, 19
convergence, 27
core inflation, 144, 158
corporate bonds
    Federal Reserve and, 200
    yields for euro-denominated, 171
corporations
    cost of borrowing in, 97*f*
    leverage increase, 171

Other Publications from the
PETERSON INSTITUTE FOR INTERNATIONAL ECONOMICS

WORKING PAPERS

POLICY ANALYSES IN INTERNATIONAL ECONOMICS SERIES

* = out of print

BOOKS IN PROGRESS

Implications of Sustained Low Productivity Growth in Advanced Countries
Jeromin Zettelmeyer and Adam S. Posen, eds.
Sustaining Economic Growth in Asia
Jérémie Cohen-Setton, Thomas Helbling, and Adam S. Posen, editors